BUSINESS & COMPANY LAW FOR IRISH STUDENTS

BUSINESS & COMPANY LAW FOR IRISH STUDENTS

EAVAN MURPHY

GILL & MACMILLAN

Gill & Macmillan Ltd
Hume Avenue
Park West
Dublin 12
with associated companies throughout the world
www.gillmacmillan.ie

© 2004 Eavan Murphy

ISBN-13: 978 07171 3705 3

Index compiled by Julitta Clancy
Print origination in Ireland by
Carrigboy Typesetting Services, Co. Cork

*The paper used in this book is made from the wood pulp of
managed forests. For every tree felled, at least one tree
is planted, thereby renewing natural resources.*

A catalogue record is available for this book from the
British Library.

'Table A, Companies Act, 1963' is reproduced with
permission of the Controller, Stationery Office.

In memory of my Dad, Seamus Murphy

CONTENTS

TABLE OF CASES

TABLE OF STATUTES

TABLE OF STATUTORY INSTRUMENTS, RULES AND ORDERS

TABLE OF EUROPEAN LEGISLATION

TABLE OF ARTICLES OF THE CONSTITUTION

INTRODUCTION

This text covers the core issues in business law and company law which provide the legal framework within which Irish businesses operate. Although Irish businesses both large and small come into contact with a myriad of legal issues, these mainly fall into the categories of contract law and company law.

The first two chapters deal with how the Irish legal system operates and introduce such concepts as legal precedent and the operation of the courts, which will be useful in later chapters. Chapters 3 to 6 explain the law of contract, focusing on common examples of buying and selling goods for illustration. Once students have grasped the basics of contract law, Chapters 7 and 8 will make sense, as they deal with general contract law as applied to the specific situations of the sale of goods and employment law.

The second half of the text deals with Irish company law. This area of law has undergone great change in the past ten years, with the introduction of three major pieces of company legislation, most recently in 2003. This legislation, particularly the Company Law Enforcement Act 2001, has led to major changes in the way in which Irish companies do business.

Business & Company Law for Irish Students will be of use to people studying business and company law as part of a non-law qualification, such as in business, accountancy or marketing. Third-level students and those undertaking professional exams will all find it useful. The clear language, explanatory diagrams and chapter summaries make the text easy to read and use.

Some Points on Studying Law and Answering Exam Questions

Although you are not going to be a lawyer, you will need a knowledge of the law as it applies to business and corporate situations. Your legal knowledge should enhance your practical knowledge of other aspects of your study and work. In addition, it is also very important to be aware of the law so you know when to get legal advice.

Students often find it difficult to retain the level of detail covered in some of the topics in this text. With this in mind, each chapter starts with a brief summary, to put it into context. Within each chapter, topics are presented in a clear and concise manner, with the main headings highlighted. The best approach to learning a volume of unfamilar material is to start by simply reading through part of or a whole chapter. Then break the information down according to the headings, and try to grasp the main points, perhaps making a note of them. Over a few study periods, fill in more details on your notes. You should then have a handy summary set of notes on each topic, which you can review in spare moments as well as in the time you actually set aside for studying.

With examinations, the best advice is to be as prepared as possible. The following suggestions may serve as a good guide for answering exam questions.

(1) Read the question—take your time and read all the parts. If it is a problem question, read through it a number of times, if necessary, to assess the importance of the facts.

(2) Question the question—ask yourself what the question is getting at. With problem questions, try and identify the number of points in each question and their relative importance.

(3) Plan your answer—decide on how you are going to approach your answers. In a problem question, you should deal with each issue separately, preferably in a separate paragraph.

(4) Write your answer—remember to begin and end your answer. You should begin by identifying the legal issue in the question, perhaps defining the main issue to be discussed. Stick to one point per paragraph, and present your information as clearly as possible. If a question asks you something specific, such as 'Is this an enforceable contract?' remember to answer it, either at the start or the end of your answer. Similarly, if you are asked to 'Advise Nick', summarise your advice at the start or the end of your answer.

Section A

An Introduction to Law and the Irish Legal System

CHAPTER 1

The Nature of Irish Law

Summary of chapter

This first chapter introduces a number of characteristics of the Irish legal system that form the basis of the following chapters and is an examinable topic in its own right. This chapter covers the major categories of law, the structure of the courts and some alternatives to the court system.

A. Definitions

The Meaning of Law

The word 'law' is difficult to define because it can have many meanings, depending on whether it applies to the laws of physics, the law of nature, religious law or the laws of the GAA.

However, when discussing the law of a country, 'law' is usually defined as a system of legal principles, rules and procedures. Each of these terms has a different meaning. The system of legal principles is the basic policy underlying a piece of law, for example, the policy of protecting the consumer in the Sale of Goods and Supply of Services Act 1980. The rules of law are how the pieces of law are actually stated in practice, for example, the sections of the Sale of Goods and Supply of Services Act 1980. The procedures of law are the practical details of the law and its enforcement, such as providing for remedies, fines, etc. A decision of a judge in an employment court case is another example of a piece of law and is a mixture of the ruling or result in the case, the procedures that apply to the case and the underlying principle in the case.

Categories of Law

The major distinction in categories of law is between criminal and civil law. Each type is then subdivided into a number of other categories. Examples of criminal law are murder, manslaughter and insider dealing. Examples of civil law are contract, tort, employment and consumer law. Most of this text is concerned with civil law.

B. Criminal versus Civil Law

Criminal Law

Criminal law has four hallmarks that identify it. If an issue does not have all four essential elements, it is not a crime and, therefore, must be civil law.

The hallmarks of a crime are deliberate intention, threat to society, prosecution by the State and punishment.

1. Deliberate Intention

A criminal must intend to commit a criminal offence. However, this may be assumed by the courts in some circumstances, as, for example, when a person has driven home after drinking eight pints. Although that person may not have actually intended to injure anyone, he or she will be deemed to have the necessary intention because he or she took the risk of injury.

2. Threat to Society

A crime is said to threaten the fabric of society. It is behaviour that is considered socially unacceptable. (The concept of the threat to society leads to the third and fourth elements of the definition of a crime.)

3. Prosecution by the State

A criminal prosecution is brought by the State because the State believes that it should decide when to litigate over socially unacceptable behaviour. Criminal cases are brought by the Director of Public Prosecutions (DPP) on behalf of the State.

4. Punishment

A criminal wrong will be punished by a fine or imprisonment or both. The concept of punishment is limited to criminal law.

The words 'prosecution', 'guilt' and 'punishment' all indicate criminal cases, which are dealt with in the criminal courts. The burden of proof in a criminal case is on the State to prove that the defendant is guilty 'beyond a reasonable doubt'. This basically means that there can be no other convincing reason in the case, other than the guilt of the accused.

Civil Law

By contrast, in a civil case, these four features will not be present. The intention of the defendant is irrelevant; in some civil cases, the defendant's action was intended, and in others, it was not. There is no threat to society in a civil case, and as a result, the State does not get involved in the case. It is a private issue between the parties. Finally, if a person is shown to be in breach of a civil law, he or she will not be punished. Instead, the person will usually have to pay compensation and may also be subject to other legal remedies.

The burden of proof in a civil case is to prove the matter 'on the balance of probabilities'. This is a lower standard than in a criminal case and requires the case as explained in court to be more likely than not to be true.

However, sometimes one incident will give rise to two cases, a criminal and a civil case. An obvious example of this is a traffic accident. If a pedestrian is knocked down by a motorist, the Director of Public Prosecutions may decide to prosecute the driver for dangerous driving. This will give the injured person moral satisfaction but will not usually provide any money to compensate for injuries. Thus the injured person might bring a civil action against the driver, seeking compensation. The two cases will be dealt with at different times in different courts with different procedures and burdens of proof. Another example of one incident giving rise to two proceedings is an accident in the workplace. In that case the State may seek to punish the employer, and the injured employee may seek compensation.

Citation of a Case

The citation of a case is the way it is reported. The citation will tell you whether it is a criminal or a civil case. It will also tell you the names of the parties, the year and, in the case of this book, if it is an Irish case. In this book, the word 'Ire' is used to show that a case is an Irish decision.

> *Director of Public Prosecutions v Murphy* (2000) Ire
> This is a criminal case, as it is being prosecuted by the Director of Public Prosecutions on behalf of the state.

> *Holden v Murphy* (2004) Ire
> This is a civil case, as it is a private issue between individual parties.

Note: For most exam purposes, it is not necessary to remember the years of cases. They are given in this book for information only. If you are unable to remember the name of a case, try to remember one of the parties' names or to describe it in some way, e.g. 'the case about the flick knife'.

C. The Courts

The Structure of the Courts

Having dealt with the two major types of law, it is appropriate to look at the structure of the courts at this point, because the courts are organised into civil and criminal divisions. However, for exam purposes, the civil courts are more important, and their structure is summarised in Figure 1.1.

Article 34 of the Constitution of 1937 provides that justice shall be administered in courts established by law and, except in limited cases, shall be administered in public. It also states that the courts shall comprise courts of first instance (where a case starts off) and a court of final appeal.

Figure 1.1 The Structure of the Courts

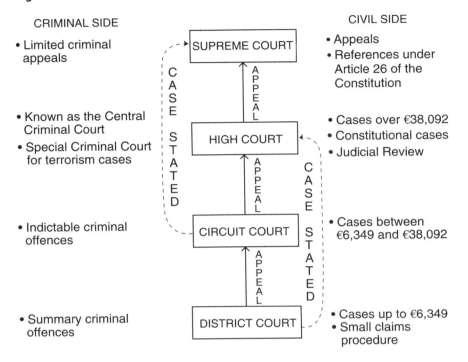

CRIMINAL SIDE

- Limited criminal appeals

- Known as the Central Criminal Court
- Special Criminal Court for terrorism cases

- Indictable criminal offences

- Summary criminal offences

CIVIL SIDE

- Appeals
- References under Article 26 of the Constitution

- Cases over €38,092
- Constitutional cases
- Judicial Review

- Cases between €6,349 and €38,092

- Cases up to €6,349
- Small claims procedure

A court's jurisdiction consists of the types of cases with which it can deal. Each court has set monetary limits and subject matters that set the boundaries of its jurisdiciton. This is referred to as a court's 'original jurisdiction', i.e. the type of case that can originate, or start off, in that court (as opposed to its appellate jurisdiction, which consists of the types of cases with which it can deal on appeal).

1. District Court

The present District Court was established by section 5 of the Courts Act 1961. Under Article 34 of the Constitution of 1937, it has 'local and limited jurisdiction', where 'local' refers to the geographical area with which that court can deal, and 'limited' refers to the subjects and the monetary limits. The Court has fifty District Justices and is presided over by a president.

Civil Cases: Since the Courts (Establishment and Constitution) Act 1991, the District Court can deal with:

- general claims for damages up to €6,349 in cases of contract, tort and ejectment of a tenant for nonpayment of rent, where rent is not more then €6,349 per annum;

- grants of and objections to liquor and dance licences;
- family law;
- miscellaneous subjects.

There is also a small claims procedure in the District Court since the passing of the District Court (Small Claims Procedure) Rules 1991. The procedure applies to consumer contracts worth up to €1,270.

Criminal Cases: The District Court can hear summary offences, i.e. minor cases heard without a jury. These cases are punishable by up to six months' incarceration and/or a fine. It also hears indictable offences, i.e. more serious offences that could be tried in front of a jury when defendants waive their right to trial by jury. Most criminal cases are handled in the District Court.

2. Circuit Court

The Circuit Court was established by section 4 of the Courts Act 1961. Again, it has local and limited jurisdiction under the Constitution. The Circuit Court has twenty-eight judges, including the president.

Civil Cases: The Circuit Court can deal with:

- general cases with the same subject matter as the High Court. Since the Courts (Establishment and Consitution) Act 1991, it can only award up to €38,092. (However, if both parties consent, the Circuit Court can have *unlimited* monetary jurisdiction. The advantage of this procedure is that the costs will be lower than in the High Court.);
- exclusive landlord and tenant jurisdiction;
- the 'family court' for nonadversarial procedures;
- granting of new liquor licences;
- miscellaneous cases dealing with equity and land.

Criminal Cases: The Circuit Court deals with more serious criminal cases, i.e. indictable offences that are tried by a jury. The judge can impose penalties as specified by the various acts applicable or based on similar past cases.

3. High Court

The High Court was established by the Courts (Establishment and Constitution) Act 1961. It is the only court specifically mentioned in the Constitution of 1937. Article 34.3 states that the High Court shall have 'full original jurisdiction'. This means that, in theory, the High Court can deal with any case that is in the jurisdiction of lower courts. The High Court has twenty-eight judges, including the president. Since the Courts Acts 1988, juries are rare in civil cases. In practice, the High Court deals with the following types of cases.

Civil Cases: The High Court deals with:

- cases over €38,092;
- cases questioning the validity of any law or legislation in relation to the Constitution (except references under Article 26);
- cases under the Companies Acts 1963 to 2003;
- cases under the Bankruptcy Act 1988;
- the judicial review of the decisions of lower courts or tribunals.

'Judicial review' means the High Court reviews the proceedings and operation of another body to decide if they were run fairly and in accordance with the principles of the Constitution and of natural justice.

Criminal Cases: The criminal side of the High Court is known as the Central Criminal Court. It is used for serious crimes, e.g. murder, rape, treason, and uses a jury. Trials are usually conducted by a single judge and a jury of twelve people, but two or more judges may be directed to hear a particular trial. A majority verdict of the jury is required.

There is also the Special Criminal Court. The Offences against the State Act 1939 provided for the establishment of the Special Criminal Court, which was created in 1972. This Court is used when the ordinary criminal courts are deemed to be inadequate to protect the administration of justice and peace. It is used mainly for terrorism cases. There are three judges and no jury in the Special Criminal Court.

The Court of Criminal Appeal consists of a judge of the Supreme Court and two judges of the High Court. It deals with appeals by persons convicted on indictment in the Circuit or Central Criminal Court, in certain circumstances. The decision of the Court of Criminal Appeal is final in most circumstances.

4. The Supreme Court

The Supreme Court was also established by the Courts Act 1961. The Supreme Court is mentioned in the Constitution insofar as it refers to a 'Court of Final Appeal'. The Supreme Court is comprised of the Chief Justice and seven judges. Since the Courts and Court Officers Act 1995, the Supreme Court may sit in two or three divisions at the same or different times. Its jurisdiction is to hear appeals from lower courts. The Supreme Court deals with criminal appeals only in limited cases. The Supreme Court has two additional functions.

- Under Article 12 of the Constitution, the Supreme Court may remove the President from his or her position due to the permanent incapacity of the President. This function has never been exercised.
- Under Article 26 of the Constitution, the President may refer a bill to the Supreme Court prior to signing it into law. The purpose of such a referral is to test whether the bill is repugnant to the Constitution. Once a bill has

been approved by the Supreme Court, it will then be signed into law by the President, and it cannot be rechallenged at a later date. Part V of the Planning and Development Bill 1999, which required house builders to reserve up to twenty per cent of their land for affordable housing, was challenged in 2001. It was held to be constitutional by the Supreme Court.

Appeals

1. Types of Appeals

There are two types of appeals in the Irish courts: an appeal de novo, which literally means a new appeal and is a complete rehearing of a case, as if for the first time; and an appeal on a point of law, which is a more limited type of appeal, in which the facts of the case are accepted from the original hearing, and only a point of law is being challenged. This type of appeal is based on the original transcript of the evidence in the case.

2. Appellate Jurisdiction

The appellate jurisdiction of the courts in civil cases is divided among the various courts' jurisdictions.

The District Court hears appeals from decisions of lower statutory bodies and officers, such as the issuing of a prohibition notice by a health and safety inspector.

The Circuit Court can conduct an appeal de novo from the District Court and other bodies such as the Employment Appeals Tribunal.

The High Court can conduct an appeal de novo from the Circuit Court and other bodies such as the Controller of Patents. The High Court can also hear appeals on a point of law from the District Court. This procedure is called a 'case stated'. The District Court Justice makes a written request to a higher court, questioning whether his or her legal determination in the case was correct. In this procedure, both parties agree on the facts of a case, and the District Court Justice writes up the case in the first person, basically asking the higher court 'was I correct in law?'. The High Court then reviews the decision, and answers either yes or no, which is the decision in the appeal. The Supreme Court can also hear appeals from the Circuit Court by way of case stated.

D. Alternatives to the Courts System

Article 34 of the Constitution states that justice is to be administered by the Courts. However, Article 37 then provides for 'the exercise of limited functions and powers of a judicial nature, in matters other than criminal matters, by any person or body of persons duly authorised by law . . . , notwithstanding that such person or such body of persons is not a judge or a court . . . under this Constitution'. This means, in effect, that judicial-type decisions may be made outside of the courts. This allows for the establishment of quasi-judical tribunals and the operation of arbitration, which are collectively known as 'alternative methods of dispute resolution'.

Quasi-Judicial Tribunals

Quasi-judicial tribunals are special miniature 'courts', established to deal with routine issues of law in a particular area. Examples are the Employment Appeals Tribunal and An Bord Pleanála. Quasi-judical tribunals have become popular in the last thirty years, due to the numerous advantages that they have over courts when it comes to solving disputes.

1. Specialist

Tribunals generally use specialists to decide cases. For example, the Employment Appeals Tribunal has a legally qualified chairperson and a staff nominated by employers' organisations and the Irish Congress of Trade Unions.

2. Informal

The tribunal procedure is informal. A tribunal takes place in ordinary rooms without the formalities and gowns of a court case. As such, it is less intimidating and less adversarial.

3. Expense

Tribunals are cheaper than litigation. The expense of legal representation is not necessary, and although parties may have legal representation, they will not receive costs to cover this.

4. Flexibility

Tribunals are flexible in their sitting times. As such, going to a tribunal is usually quicker than going to court. Also, tribunal procedures are simpler, making the process quicker.

5. Workload

The number of cases heard before tribunals greatly reduces the courts' workloads. Cases before a tribunal are often routine and can be dealt with very quickly, so a tribunal can get through a large caseload.

6. Speed

The decisions of tribunals are given quickly and are not usually written. (This may be seen as disadvantageous.)

Relationship with the Courts: The decision of a tribunal can be appealed to the courts. Such an appeal is usually on a point of law only. The High Court can carry out a judical review of a tribunal's decision. The courts also interpret the legislation that creates and empowers tribunals, so they have a supervisory role.

Investigative Tribunals

There are also investigative tribunals, which are not court-type bodies exercising quasi-judical power but are one-off public investigations into an issue of national importance. An investigative tribunal is simply a fact-finding inquiry into an issue. It has no powers to make a legally binding decision. Examples of this type of tribunal are the Stardust Fire Tribunal, the Beef Tribunal, the Flood Tribunal (Payments to Politicians) and the Moriarty Tribunal (Planning). Such tribunals make no finding of law; they simply make a finding of fact.

> *Goodman v Ireland* (1991) Ire
> In this case, a challenge to the validity of the Beef Tribunal failed. The Goodman group argued that a tribunal could not investigate matters that were the subject of civil proceeding, matters of criminal law or the private affairs of parties. The Supreme Court held that an investigative tribunal is 'a simple fact-finding operation reporting to the legislature'.

Arbitration

Arbitration is a method of settling a dispute other than by court action. It involves parties to a dispute appointing an independent third party, called an 'arbitrator', to settle the issue. The parties promise to abide by the arbitrator's decision. Arbitration clauses are common in commercial contracts, the construction industry, holiday booking agreements and partnership agreements and are known as 'commercial arbitration'. Occasionally, arbitration may be ordered by a court or provided by statute.

Arbitration is governed by the Arbitration Acts 1954 to 1998, which provide for the control of arbitration by the courts and for appeals. Generally, however, the aim of arbitration is to keep a dispute out of the courts. If there is no compliance with an arbitrator's award, the successful party may enforce the award through the courts.

When a dispute arises, the parties can pick an arbitrator and have the case decided within a matter of days. The arbitration can be as formal or informal as the parties wish. An arbitration may be very legalistic and include sworn evidence, witnesses and cross examination, or it may be simply an expert opinion on the issue in question. Arbitration has all the advantages of tribunals, i.e. it is specialised, informal, inexpensive, fast and reduces the pressure on the courts. In addition, arbitration has a big advantage when compared with either courts or tribunals: privacy. Arbitration proceedings are a matter for the parties only, so there is no negative publicity to concern a company.

CHAPTER 2

The Sources of Irish Law

Summary of chapter

This chapter deals in detail with the main sources of law in Ireland, the Constitution of 1937, case-law and legislation. The means of interpretating legislation is also covered, as is the impact on our legal system of Ireland's membership in the European Union.

The current law of Ireland is made up of a large number of types of law which have developed over the years. Our legal system is a mixture of historical law dating back to the Romans, through De Valera's Constitution of 1937, and up to cases just recently decided. Additionally, there are pieces of legislation of varying ages, laws made by the European Union and customs that have come to have the force of law, among other sources, which all contribute to our legal system.

The main sources of law can be categorized as:

* historical—Constitution of 1937;
* legal—precedent (or case-law), legislation (or statute) including delegated legislation and statutory interpretation, European Union legislation;
* subsidiary sources—no longer directly responsible for the creation of law.

Note: Subsidiary sources are not considered in this text. They include Roman law and the law of the Catholic Church, traces of which can still be seen in our legal system.

A. The Constitution of 1937, or Bunreacht na hÉireann

The Constitution is the primary source of Irish law and is superior to all other types of law. The Constitution does two major things: it sets out the institutions of State, i.e. the Dáil, Seanad, etc., and it protects the fundamental rights of the citizen.

The Institutions of the State

In the legal process, the major institutions of State are the Dáil and the Seanad, which are jointly known as the Oireachtas, the Government of the day, and the courts. The 'separation of powers', as illustrated in Figure 2.1 is a device in the Constitution that protects democracy by ensuring that no one institution has too much power. Under Article 15, the Oireachtas is the 'legislature', or law-making body. Under Article 28, the Government is the 'executive', or the body that carries out the law. Under Article 34, the Courts are the 'judicial' body, administering justice.

Figure 2.1 The separation of powers

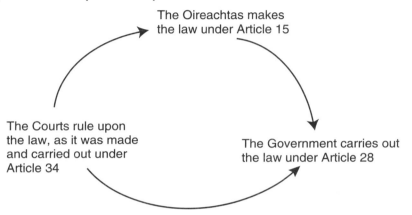

The Oireachtas makes the law under Article 15

The Courts rule upon the law, as it was made and carried out under Article 34

The Government carries out the law under Article 28

To take an example, if a new Road Traffic Act dealing with parking were passed, it would be voted in by the Dáil and the Seanad. The Government of the day would then implement the law, by dealing with procedural issues such as parking tickets. In the event of a dispute about the enforcement of the law by the Government, such as nonpayment of the fines, the issue would be heard in court. Equally, a dispute about the nature of the law, such as whether it were constitutional, would also be heard in the courts.

This is an essential feature of a democracy, that the law-making and law-implementing powers are shared among a number of groups, and the decisions of each body may be checked by an independent court.

Fundamental Rights

Some fundamental personal rights are listed in the Constitution, such as the right to vote, to equality, to free speech and to own private property. The Constitution also contains 'unenumerated rights'. These are fundamental rights that were not listed in 1937 but have been discovered through case-law over the years and are treated as implied parts of the Constitution. The following was the first such case of an unenumerated right.

> *Ryan v Attorney General* (1965) Ire
> This case established the right of bodily integrity. The plaintiff challenged the constitutionality of a piece of legislation that provided for fluoridation of tap water. The plaintiff argued that the legislation infringed her right to bodily integrity, which she argued was a right

implicit in the Constitution. The Supreme Court accepted that there was such an unenumerated right of bodily integrity. This means that there can be no interference with the body or health of a citizen, and nothing dangerous or harmful to a citizen's health may be done by the State.

McGee v Attorney General (1974) Ire
This case established the right of marital privacy. The plaintiff was a married woman who had been told by her doctor that she would be putting her life at risk if she had any more children. She decided to use contraceptives including spermicidal jelly, the importation of which was prohibited by law. The plaintiff challenged that law on the basis that it infringed her right of marital privacy. The Supreme Court held that she had a right of marital privacy, which the State should not regulate.

This development of rights makes the Constitution a living document, which was not written in stone in 1937. For example, in the *McGee* case, the Supreme Court discussed the change in public opinion in relation to contraceptives since 1937.

It is important to understand that constitutional rights are not unqualified. For example, there is a right to free speech, but it is qualified by the laws on defamation and on incitement to hatred and by censorship. Similarly, the right to vote is limited to people over eighteen, and Irish citizens in some cases.

Amending the Constitution

The Constitution represents all the people of Ireland, thus unlike ordinary legislation, it cannot be changed by the Oireachtas. It can only be changed by public referendum, which is a two-stage process. First, a proposal in the form of a bill containing no other information is initiated in the Dáil. Then, due to the sovereignty of the people, an amendment must be passed by a majority vote in a public referendum, in which the voters are Irish citizens who are entitled to vote in a general election.

In 1972 the first amendment to the Constitution of 1937 was passed to allow Ireland to join the European Economic Community (EEC) in 1973. Recent examples of amendments have been the abortion information referendum in 1992, the divorce referendum in 1996, the Northern Ireland agreement referendum in 1998, and the Nice Treaty referendum in 2002.

B. Judicial Precedent

The doctrine of precedent is also called 'case-law', or 'stare decisis', i.e. to stand by a decision. It is the most common type of law we have, as decisions made in court on a daily basis form precedents for the future.

Ireland has a common-law legal system, which is a system of largely unwritten laws that have evolved over years and cases rather than a system of preplanned and written rules. (Other common-law systems are those in

Britain and the United States.) Precedent as a source of law is the main characteristic feature of a common-law system. It is the respecting and following of past decisions in present cases.

The Reasons for Precedents

Most countries follow a system of precedent in which a decision in a case is made by following past decisions in similar cases. There are several reasons for this system.

1. Consistency or Fairness

Similar cases are treated in a similar manner, which is essential in a democracy.

2. Certainty

Due to precedent, it is easier to predict the result of a case. This is of benefit to litigants and their legal advisors.

3. Saves Time

Because most cases will be covered by an existing precedent, judges need not redecide complex points. This saves time and money in an overworked court system. If there is no similar case, a judge will create a new precedent.

4. Realistic

Precedent is often to said to be 'forged on the anvil of reality'. This simply means that each case is decided based on the reality of the actual facts involved. (This is in contrast to legislation, which is based on hypothetical fact situations.)

Operation of Precedent

Although it may appear deceptively simple, a system of precedent is in fact complex and needs certain requirements to operate properly:

- a reliable system of law reporting, so that past cases are available to lawyers and judges;
- rules for extracting the relevant information from past cases, i.e. the *ratio decidendi*;
- rules for classifying precedents into those that *must*, *may be* and *need not be* followed (which are also known, respectively, as binding, persuasive and nonbinding precedents);
- a knowledge of the courts system.

The Ratio Decidendi: A judge's decision can be any length between a page and hundreds of pages. Not all parts of this decision are relevant, only the *ratio decidendi*, i.e. the reason for the decision. This may also be called 'the rule', or 'principle', of the case. In the brief summaries of case facts in this text, what the judge 'held' is the *ratio decidendi*. Extracting the *ratio* from a decision is a very precise art, given the length of many judgements.

Obiter Dicta: Other statements of law in a case are referred to as *obiter dicta*, i.e. things said by the way. (The singular is *obiter dictum*, meaning a thing said by the way.) They are statements of legal principle that relate to facts that were not in the case or were not material to the case. *Obiter dicta* are not binding, although they may be persuasive, precedents.

For example, in a dangerous driving case, the reason for the judge's decision may be that the defendant was driving on the wrong side of the road. The judge may also comment that the decision could have been different if the defendant had to cross the white line because of an obstruction on their side of the road. This last comment is made, by the way, or *obiter dictum*. In a case of dangerous driving that does involve an obstruction on the side of the road, a later judge may draw upon the previous judge's *obiter dictum*, which is a persuasive precedent.

Famous examples of *obiter dicta* that have been followed and enshrined in law are:

- the doctrine of promissory estoppel in the decision in *Central London Property Trust v High Trees House* (1947) (see page 53 Chapter 3);
- the extension of a duty of care to statements in *Hedley Byrne & Co v Heller and Partners* (1964) (see page 257 Chapter 14).

Classifying Precedents

Precedents can be categorised into binding, persuasive and nonbinding precedents.

1. Binding Precedent

A binding precedent is one that must be followed, for example, because the facts of the present and earlier cases are identical. The decisions of a superior court are binding on lower courts.

2. Persuasive Precedent

A persuasive precedent is one that need not be followed, for example, the decision of a lower court. Decisions of foreign courts are often used as persuasive precedents in this country, particularly decisions of British courts. An *obiter dictum* from a previous case may also be a persuasive precedent.

3. Nonbinding Precedent

A nonbinding precedent is one that need not be followed by a later court because it has been 'avoided', i.e. a reason has been found to distinguish this case from the previous case.

Avoiding a Precedent

To stop the system of precedents from becoming rigid and stagnant, the courts can refuse to follow a previous case. This can be accomplished:

(1) by distinguishing the facts of the case;

(2) by declaring the *ratio* to be obscure or unclear (this will sometimes be done in older cases or when there were a number of judges who gave different reasons for their decisions);

(3) by declaring the previous decision to be too wide and thus not applicable except in narrower circumstances (sometimes, a previous decision will have reasoning that is very wide and applicable to numerous cases, and a later judge may decide to apply the case in narrower circumstances only);

(4) by declaring the previous decision to be in conflict with a fundamental principle of law (it is possible, for example, that a past decision may be contrary to the Constitution);

(5) by declaring a previous decision to be made *per incuriam,* which means that the past decision was made through lack of care, for example, where the previous judge failed to take account of a previous case or applicable piece of legislation;

(6) by declaring that a previous decision was made *sub silentio,* which means that the point decided by the judge was not argued or was silent before the court (a judge can only decide on the points of law that were argued before him or her and cannot base his or her decision on an issue that was not argued in court);

(7) where a previous decision has now been altered by legislation or overruled by a later case.

The Court's Role in Precedent

In a system of precedent, only the decisions of superior courts are binding.

With regard to decisions of the District Court and Circuit Court, as these decisions are not officially reported, they do not actually serve as precedents. However, both the District and the Circuit Courts must follow superior courts.

With regard to decisions of the High Court, this Court must follow the Supreme Court. However, the High Court is not bound by its own previous decisions, although it would tend to follow them for consistency.

With regard to decisions of the Supreme Court, this Court is not bound by its own previous decisions. This was decided in the case of *Attorney General v Ryan's Car Hire Ltd* (1965) Ire. This is to allow the highest court to have a degree of flexibility in its decision making. In addition, pre-1961 decisions are technically decisions of the old Supreme Court and need not be followed.

Note: It is very important to understand the operation of precedent because in a problem question on the exam paper, you are effectively being asked to read the facts of the case and apply or distinguish well-known past precedents to the facts in order to give your answer.

C. National Legislation

Legislation, also called 'statute law' or an 'act', is a source of law defined as law passed by the Oireachtas. There are three major issues to be studied here: primary legislation, delegated legislation and the interpretation of legislation.

In an average year, between thirty and forty pieces of legislation will be passed, and of course laws passed in previous years will still be in force. In comparison with precedent, as shown in Figure 2.2, legislation is said to be 'prospective' and to be applicable to a large number of people, whereas a decision in a case is 'retrospective' and applicable to the parties only.

Figure 2.2   Effective legislation versus effective judicial precedents

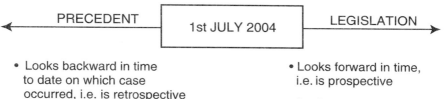

DATE OF CREATION

PRECEDENT   1st JULY 2004   LEGISLATION

- Looks backward in time to date on which case occurred, i.e. is retrospective
- Applies only to people involved

- Looks forward in time, i.e. is prospective
- Applies to a large number of people

Primary Legislation

1. Constitutional Control of Legislation

Under Article 15 of the Constitution, the Oireachtas has 'sole and exclusive' law-making power. Article 15 also states that no statute repugnant to the Constitution shall be enacted, and any repugnant statute is invalid. This latter part allows the High Court to review the constitutionality of a piece of legislation.

In addition, Article 50 of the Constitution states that any law in force in the State immediately prior to the date upon which the Constitution became operational shall continue to have full force and effect until repealed or amended by the Oireachtas. This allowed the body of pre-1937 legislation to continue in force, provided it was not contrary to the Constitution. Many old laws are still in force, such as the Sale of Goods Act 1893 and the Statute of Frauds (Ireland) Act 1695.

2. Types of Legislation

Legislation can take different forms, depending on the effect to be achieved. Legislation starts off as a bill, which can make totally new law or can alter or repeal existing laws. There are three types of bills: public, private and private members' bills.

- Public bills: These are bills that alter the general law affecting the community at large. Most bills are public bills, an example of which is the annual Finance Act.
- Private bills: These are bills that are relevant to particular issues for individuals or areas of law, an example of which is a bill that applies to a county council.
- Private members' bills: These are bills introduced by members of the Dáil but without the guaranteed support of the Government. (Usually, the Government will support a bill introduced by one of its members, and because of the position of strength of the Government, such a bill will usually be passed into law.)

There are also different types of acts:

- consolidating acts: these bring together all the statutes on one topic as if in one act, e.g. Arbitration Acts 1954 to 1980, the Companies Acts 1963 to 2003;
- codifying acts: these bring together all law in one area in a single act, e.g. Bills of Exchange Act 1882.

The difference between the two types is that consolidating acts are presumed not to change existing law, whereas codifying acts usually rebut this presumption.

3. Legislative Procedure

A piece of legislation starts its life as a bill, and when passed it becomes an Act. A bill can begin in the Dáil or in the Seanad, with the exception of those specifically stated in the Constitution as beginning in the Dáil, such as money bills.

Legislation that is initiated in the Seanad but amended in the Dáil is treated as being initiated in the Dáil.

The legislative process has five steps.

(1) The bill is printed and placed before the house.
(2) The general principles of the bill are debated (but no amendments are allowed at this stage).
(3) A specially formed committee debates the bill in detail, and amendments or alterations occur at this stage.

(4) The committee reports back to the house; amendments are also possible here.

(5) The bill is given its third and final reading at a general debate. Only verbal amendments are allowed at this stage.

The bill is then subject to a similar procedure in the other house. Once the bill is signed by the President, it becomes an 'Act' and has the force of law. However, sometimes the commencement date of the Act is specified to occur at a time after signature, to allow for publicity or for procedures to be put in place.

Delegated Legislation

Delegated legislation is secondary or subordinate legislation and consists of orders, rules and regulations made by bodies that are given power to do so under an act. The idea is that subordinate legislation fills in the details to a piece of legislation.

For example, the Tobacco (Health Promotion) Act 1988 prohibited smoking in public places as a general principles, and this has been added to over the years by specific prohibitions for various types of places such as colleges, pubs and bingo halls through delegated legislation such as the Tobacco (Health Promotion) Regulations 1990. Other examples of delegated legislation occur when a minister makes what is called a 'statutory instrument', some bodies make regulations and local authorities make by-laws. In a typical year there will be hundreds of pieces of delegated legislation introduced under the acts of that year and previous years. For example, there are currently sixty-eight pieces of delegated legislation that have been made under the Companies Acts 1963 to 2003.

Delegated legislation is commonly used because it has a number of advantages over the creation of traditional legislation, and these outweigh the disadvantages. Among the advantages of delegated legislation are the following:

(1) It saves the Oireachtas's time, as the principle is agreed to and the detail is filled in elsewhere.

(2) It allows the use of expert or technical knowledge. For example, the power to make traffic regulations in a particular suburb of Dublin may be delegated to Dublin Corporation, which will have a better understanding of the problems than a TD in the Dáil.

(3) It is flexible. Regulations can be brought in or rescinded quickly, thus speeding up the legislative process.

Among the disadvantages of delegated legislation are that:

(1) It is undemocratic, in theory, as nonelected people make the law, such as members of local authorities or civil servants. However, the Oireachtas

still controls delegated legislation through a number of mechanisms (see below).

(2) Huge amounts of delegated legislation are created annually. This makes it difficult for lawyers and the public to keep up with the changes, yet ignorance of the law is no excuse for its breach.

(3) Delegated legislation cannot be amended, only cancelled. (However, it would not really be desirable to add to or subtract from a piece of law that is already derived from another source, as the law would possibly become unclear, so this is not really a disadvantage.)

The Oireachtas controls delegated legislation. The Joint Oireachtas Committee on Legislation monitors the creation of delegated legislation. Some pieces of delegated legislation do not take effect until affirmed by a resolution of the Oireachtas. Most delegated legislation must be laid before the Oireachtas for forty days before becoming effective.

There is also judicial control of delegated legislation, i.e. the courts can examine the constitutionality of a piece of delegated legislation to see if it is within the boundaries of its parent statute. If it is not, the delegated legislation is said to be *ultra vires*, or beyond the power of the parent statute.

The Interpretation of Legislation

If a debate arises about a word or phrase used in a statute, it is for the courts to rule upon the meanings of statutes. To do this, a court may use a number of tools:

• presumptions;
• canons or rules of interpretation;
• maxims or approaches;
• aids to interpretation, internal and external.

1. Interpretative Presumptions

Presumptions are rebuttable by evidence to the contrary. For example, there is a presumption of innocence by which an accused person is presumed to be innocent until the State can prove otherwise. Examples of statutory presumptions of interpretation are that:

• a statute does not work retroactively, i.e. it is presumed not to have effect before the date on which it was passed (this means that if a statute is passed on 1 July, it takes effect from that day forward and cannot be applied to cases that occurred in June);
• a statute does not alter or repeal existing statutes, unless this is made absolutely clear;
• a statute does not interfere with private rights or deprive people of property;

- a statute does not have effect outside the State;
- all statutes are constitutional. (Unlike the other presumptions, this is a binding rule, and if it is rebutted, the statute will be declared unconstitutional and void.)

It is important to understand that all the presumptions, with the exception of the presumption of constitutionality, can be rebutted by evidence to the contrary. For example, tax legislation may have retrospective effect, and compulsory acquisition laws may provide for the State to compulsorily acquire the property of a citizen.

2. Rules (or Canons) of Interpretation

Canons of interpretation are general rules that must be followed by the courts.

The Literal Rule: In applying the literal rule, the courts simply give a word its literal, or usual, meaning. For example, a 'child' is given the usual meaning of a person under eighteen, and a 'car' is given the usual meaning of a motorised vehicle capable of transporting less than eight people.

> *Inspector of Taxes v Kiernon* (1981) Ire
> This case concerned the income tax payable by a person who was a 'dealer in cattle'. Kiernon, who was involved in intensive pig production, was assessed under the provisions applicable to cattle. He argued that this law was not applicable to him. The Supreme Court applied the literal rule and held that the word 'cattle' does not include pigs.

> *C McCann Ltd v O'Culachain* (1986) Ire
> This famous case considered the question of whether bananas could be 'manufactured' in Ireland. The plaintiff company (who marketed Fyffes bananas) imported unripened bananas into the State and artificially ripened them. The ripening process was done in specially constructed gas chambers, operated by trained staff. The bananas were then sold and exported in their ripened state. Under the Corporation Tax Act 1976, the profit on goods 'manufactured' in the State and exported was subject to a lower rate of tax. The Supreme Court held that a word should be given its 'natural and ordinary meaning', and 'manufacturing' meant the application of a process to goods. Thus the Supreme Court held that the bananas had, in fact, been manufactured in Ireland, and the plaintiff qualified for the lower tax rate.

> *Ballymac Designer Village Ltd v Louth County Council* (2002) Ire
> Under planning legislation, a planning authority had the power to give an opinion on when planning permission 'ought to be granted'. The court gave the phrase its full natural meaning even where the envisaged application would involve contravening the development plan.

The literal meaning of a word can also cover a technical meaning or a special meaning known to a class at which it is aimed.

Sometimes, the literal rules may lead to consequences unforeseen or unintended by the legislature. For example, the flick-knife displayed in the window in *Fisher v Bell* (1961) was not 'an offer for sale' under the offensive weapons legislation but an invitation to treat (see page 37 Chapter 3).

The Golden Rule: The golden rule is used to avoid giving a word an absurd meaning, for example, where the literal rule might lead to an absurdity. In the golden rule, the word or phrase in question is to be read in light of the statute as a whole, as if there were a golden thread running through the legislation to connect it all.

> *Adler v George* (1964)
> An English Official Secrets Act provided that it was a criminal offence to obstruct the security forces 'in the vicinity of a prohibited place'. A person who was found inside an RAF base was prosecuted under the Act, as the base was a prohibited place. The High Court reasoned that to give the words 'in the vicinity of' its literal meaning would result in an absurdity, as the defendant would have to be acquitted because he was *in* the prohibited place rather than in its vicinity. Instead, the golden rule was applied, giving the phrase the meaning that fitted within the statute as a whole, and the defendant was found guilty.

The Mischief Rule: The mischief rule holds that a word should be given the meaning that avoids the mischief that the statute was designed to prevent. For example, just as every piece of law is aimed at avoiding a 'mischief', so the Sale of Goods and Supply of Services Act 1980 was an attempt to avoid the mischief that the consumer would have no legal rights, and the Road Traffic Acts were aimed at preventing the mischief of undesirable behaviour on the roads. Under the mischief rule, when interpreting a word or phrase, the courts will give it the meaning that avoids the mischief.

The mischief rule is also known as the rule in *Heydon's Case* (1584). In that case, the judge stated that the court must consider what the common law was before the making of the statute, what the mischief was that the common law did not deter, what changes have been made by the Oireachtas through legislation and what reasons did the Oireachtas have for adopting this change?

The following is an example of the mischief rule in operation.

> *Gardiner v Sevenoaks RDC* (1950)
> Legislation provided for the safe storage of cinema film when it was stored on the 'premises'. The plaintiff stored film in a cave. When he was required to comply with the safety law, he argued that a cave was not a 'premises' within the meaning of the law. The court held that the mischief to be prevented was risk to people who worked in such

'premises', and thus the widest meaning should be given to the word. 'Premises' was held to include a cave.

The difference among these three rules, as illustrated in Figure 2.3, is each is wider than the previous rule: the literal rule looks at the word (or phrase) only, the golden rule looks at the word in light of the whole statute and the mischief rule looks at the word, the statute and the law before the statute was passed.

Figure 2.3 The rules of interpretation

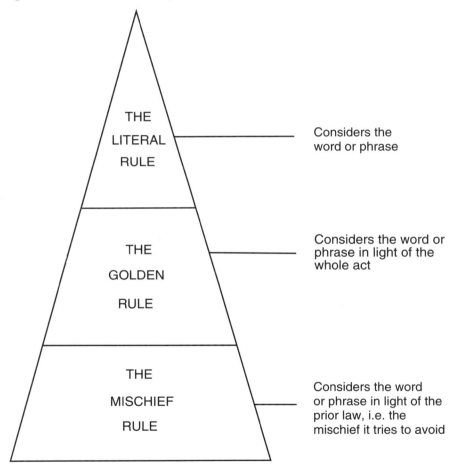

THE LITERAL RULE — Considers the word or phrase

THE GOLDEN RULE — Considers the word or phrase in light of the whole act

THE MISCHIEF RULE — Considers the word or phrase in light of the prior law, i.e. the mischief it tries to avoid

In recent years, the golden and the mischief rules have been replaced in practice by the schematic approach. In this approach, the courts consider the whole scheme of the statute, the purpose behind the legislation and the previous legal position. Thus, words can be effectively 'read into' the legislation.

Frescati Estates Ltd v Walker (1975) Ire
The Local Government (Planning and Development) Act 1963 governed the granting of planning permission to an 'applicant'. The defendant applied for and was granted planning permission for land belonging to the plaintiff company, with the intention of preventing the plaintiff from developing the land. The plaintiff argued that the word 'applicant' should be interpreted as meaning 'owner', i.e. the owner for the land for which the planning permission was sought. The Supreme Court held that the word 'applicant' should be read as 'applicant with the permission of the owner'.

3. Maxims of Interpretation

Maxims of interpretation are pithy statements of approaches to words. They are rules of language rather than rules of law.

The **Ejusdem Generis** *Rule:* When general rules are used after particular words, the general words are limited to the type of special words listed. For example, an act might refer to a licensing system for 'dogs, cats and other such animals'. The special or particular words 'dogs and cats' are followed by general words 'and other such animals'. In interpreting what 'other such animals' means, the court is limited to the types of animals specifically listed, i.e. domestic animals. Thus a licence might be required for a gerbil as an 'other such animal' but would clearly not be required for a sheep.

CW Shipping Ltd v Limerick Harbour Commissioners (1989) Ire
The Harbours Act 1946 provided for a licensing system for a 'lighter, ferry-boat or other small boat'. The plaintiff operated a tug boat, and the question was whether this was an 'other small boat' that required a licence. After discussing types of boats, the court held that a tug boat was not covered by the 1946 Act.

Expressio Unius Est Exclusio Alterius: The rule *expressio unius est exclusio alterius* means to express one thing is to exclude others not mentioned. For example, an act that applies to 'Irish citizens living in Ireland' does not apply to French citizens living in Ireland and does not apply to Irish citizens living in Britain.

Noscitur a sociis: The rule *noscitur a sociis* means a word is known by its companions, i.e. the meaning of a word is determined by the context in which it is used.

Dillon v Minister for Post and Telegraphs (1981) Ire
The plaintiff was a candidate in a general election and was thus entitled to free postage for his campaign literature. Part of his literature contained the statement 'Today's politicians are dishonest'. The defendant refused to deal with his post under the Post Office Act 1908

which prohibited the posting of material that was 'indecent, obscene or grossly offensive'. The Minister for Post and Telegraphs alleged that the defendant's literature was 'grossly offensive'. The Supreme Court held that the words 'grossly offensive' had to be read in the context of their companion words 'indecent and obscene'. The Court ruled that the plaintiff was entitled to post his campaign literature.

4. Aids to Interpretation

There are a number of simple aids to interpretation contained in each statute or available from outside sources. These are known as the internal and external aids to interpretation.

Internal Aids

(i) The long title: Each act begins with a short title by which it is commonly referred, and it also has a longer title, which gives more information about the scope of the act. For example, the Safety, Health and Welfare at Work Act 1989 also has a long title which is:

> An Act to make further provision for securing of the safety, health and welfare of persons at work, for protecting others against risks to safety and health in connection with the activities of persons at work, for the establishment of a national authority for occupational safety and health, to provide for the repeal of certain enactments, to provide for the further regulation of dangerous substances in so far as they may affect persons or property and for matters connected with the aforesaid.

(ii) The interpretation section: Each act begins with a section that defines certain relevant words and phrases frequently used in the act. For example, the Safety, Health and Welfare at Work Act 1989 defines terms including 'employee', 'employer', 'place of work' and 'personal injury' to avoid these words having to be interpreted in court at a later date.

(iii) The marginal notes: Each act is split into sections, and each will have a note in the margin briefly explaining it. These summaries can be used in making interpretations.

External aids

(i) The Interpretation Acts 1937 and 1993: These Acts contain rules of interpretation and definitions for general use. For example, references to one sex, such as 'he' or 'her', shall be interpreted to include the opposite sex, except where a statute specifically applies to one sex only, such as the legislation on maternity leave.

(ii) Dictionaries: A court can use dictionaries to find the meaning of words. This is most appropriate for finding the literal meaning. In *C McCann Ltd v*

O'Culachain, the judge in the High Court used a dictionary to find the literal meaning of the word 'manufacturing'.

D. European Union Legislation

EU History

Since Ireland joined the European Economic Community (now know as the European Union, or EU) in 1973, European law has been a source of law in Ireland. Ireland's membership required an amendment to the Constitution, to delegate some law-making power to EU, as the Constitution formerly provided that Ireland had sole and exclusive power to make its own laws.

Article 29.4.3 of the Constitution now provides that

The State may become a member of the European Coal and Steel Community . . . , the European Economic Community . . . and the European Atomic Energy Community. . . . No provision of this Constitution invalidates laws enacted, acts done or measures adopted by the State which are necessitated by the obligations of membership . . . , or prevents laws enacted, acts done or measures adopted by the European Union or by the Communities or institutions thereof . . . , from having the force of law in the State.

This effectively means that European Union law takes precedence over national law, i.e. that European Union law is superior to Irish law.

The Irish Constitution was also amended in 1987 to adopt the Single European Act, in 1992 to adopt the Maastricht Treaty, in 1998 to adopt the Amsterdam Treaty and in 2002 to adopt the Nice Treaty. These amendments were necessary because in both cases additional law-making power was being delegated to the EU that had not been agreed upon in 1972.

The European Economic Community was set up in 1957 by the Treaty of Rome. This was followed by the European Atomic Energy Community in 1957. Prior to this the European Coal and Steel Community was established in 1951. All three institutions were merged into one body known as the EEC in 1965. Since the Maastricht Treaty 1992, the union is referred to as the European Union. Following the adoption of the Nice Treaty, from 2004 there are now 20 Member States; this figure will increase as new Member States join the union.

EU Structure

There are four main institutions in the EU.

1. The Commission

The Commission is often referred to as the civil service of the EU. It currently has twenty members, including a president and five vice-presidents. There is one member from each Member State and two from France, Germany, Italy, Spain and the UK. Under the Nice Treaty, from 2005 onwards each Member State will have one Commissioner. Once the number of Member States reaches twenty-seven, the Commissioners will rotate among the Member States, who will be guaranteed at least one Commissioner in every two terms. Commissioners are appointed by governments of the Member States. Each Commissioner is assigned a portfolio, e.g. David Byrne, Ireland's current Commissioner, is responsible for health and consumer protection. Commissioners are totally independent of their Member States and represent the community interest rather than the national interest. The Amsterdam Treaty strengthened the role of the President of the Commission, giving him or her greater political authority within the Commission. The appointment of the President must be approved by the Parliament.

The Commission's role in legislation is that it has the exclusive right to initiate proposals for legislation. (However, the Council of Ministers or the Parliament can ask the Commission to draw up proposals for new laws.)

2. The Council of Ministers

The Council of Ministers is the main decision-making institution. Its membership is fluid, depending on the topic under discussion. At a Council meeting, each Member State has one member, depending on the issue being considered. A Council meeting on agriculture will be attended by the Minister for Agriculture, a finance meeting will be attended by the Minister for Finance, etc. The Tánaiste can attend any Council meeting in his or her role as Foreign Minister.

The Council is said to represent the interests of individual Member States. If a national state has a particular argument to make, it will be done at the Council level.

In relation to legislation, the Council decides whether to implement the Commission's proposals on law-making. (Although the Council does not have the right to start legislation, it can ask the Commission to propose a topic.)

3. The European Parliament

The European Parliament was formerly known as the European Assembly. It is directly elected by nationals of Member States every five years. There are currently 626 members, with an upper limit of 700. Ireland has twelve seats elected from four constituencies. The Parliament represents the principle of democracy.

The Parliament's role in relation to legislation is that it has the right to call on the Commission to initiate legislation on a particular topic. It can also reject certain types of legislation. This process is known as 'co-decision' making. Since the Amsterdam Treaty 1998 the scope of the co-decision making process has been extended, and the Parliament effectively makes laws as a co-legislator with the Council. In the final stages, both institutions must agree before new community legislation can be adopted.

4. The European Court of Justice

There are fifteen judges in the European Court of Justice, one from each Member State. The Court operates with three or five judges in each chamber to hear a case. Judges are assisted by advocates general, who have the same standing as a judge. They make reasoned submissions to the Court. The opinion of an advocate general often indicates the Court's forthcoming opinion, but the Court is free to agree or disagree. For example, in *Bosman v RFC League* (1996), a case that concerned the status of football transfers and foreign players, the Court of Justice agreed with the opinion of the Advocate General, which had been issued some months previously.

The European Court of Justice can deal with a number of types of cases.

(1) It can give 'preliminary rulings' on questions asked by national courts, under Article 177 of the Treaty of Rome. (This is a mechanism somewhat like a case stated.) For example, in *Society for the Protection of Unborn Children Ltd v Grogan* (1991) Ire, the High Court referred a question to the European Court of Justice as to whether abortion could be a 'service' under the EU rules on free movement of goods and services.

(2) It can hear direct actions between Member States and/or institutions under the Treaty of Rome.

(3) It can hear actions for compensation for damage caused by the Treaty of Rome.

Types of EU Law

Primary Source

The primary source of EU law is the Treaty of Rome 1957, which set up the European Economic Community. The treaty is like our Constitution in that it takes priority over all other forms of EU law.

Secondary Sources

There are also secondary sources of EU law.

Regulations and Directives: When the EU produces laws, they can come into effect in Ireland in one of two main ways. One option is that the law is simply presented to the Member States as a finished product, and the law takes effect immediately without the Member State having to pass any national laws. This is a regulation. These are laws that have general application, i.e. they apply to everyone. They are binding in their entirety, i.e. every piece of the law is binding in the Member State. Regulations are also directly applicable, which means that they take effect and change the law immediately. They come into force either on a stated date or twenty days after publication. There is no need for the Member State to incorporate it into national law.

Under the other method, the EU produces a piece of law that the Member States will have to implement within a period of time. This is a directive, and it is the more commonly used method. A directive states an objective each Member State must reach within a prescribed period. It is used for harmonisation programmes. For example, in contract law, the European Council of Ministers adopted the Unfair Contract Terms Directive, which was implemented in Ireland by way of a statutory instrument entitled the European Communities (Unfair Terms in Consumer Contracts) Regulations 1995.

Directives are addressed to particular Member States only. They are binding only with regard to the result to be achieved. The national state decides how to implement the directive; the choice in Ireland would be by act or statutory instrument (which confusingly are often known as regulations). There is often a delay in implementing directives, and a Member State can be liable for this.

Note: For exam purposes, an easy way to distinguish one from the other is that a *regulation* *r*equires change, whereas a *d*irective gives *d*iscretion as to how the change is introduced.

Decisions: These are types of law addressed to a particular and limited group of people, for example, one Member State or accountancy bodies in Ireland. The decision binds only the party to whom it is addressed, and it is binding in its entirety.

Recommendations and Opinions: These are nonbinding forms of law. They are usually addressed to Member States, but they can be addressed to other groups or individuals. The technical difference between them is that recommendations are made on the issuing authority's own initiative whereas opinions are given in response to a request or initiative from elsewhere.

Section B

The Law of Contract

CHAPTER 3

The Formation of a Contract

Summary of chapter

In the next four chapters we will be dealing with the law of contract. In this chapter we will cover the formation of contract with its four essential elements: offer, acceptance, consideration and legal intent.

The law of contract is the basic law governing business and commercial transactions and is also the most common type of law in private citizens' lives. A contract may be very complex, such as a multimillion pound deal to develop a shopping centre, or very simple, such as buying a newspaper.

There are five distinct parts to the study of contract law for our purposes: the formation of a contract, the contents, the validity, ending a contract and remedies for breach of contract. These will be covered in the next four chapters.

A contract is a legally binding agreement. Agreements that are not legally binding include promises, favours, gifts and moral obligations. None of these are enforceable at law. Every contract, no matter how simple or complex, has four essential elements:

1. offer;
2. acceptance;
3. consideration;
4. legal intent.

A. Offer

An 'offer' is a clear and unambiguous statement of the terms upon which the offering party (the offeror) is willing to do business. An offer must not be vague or ambiguous. An interested party must be able to understand exactly to what the contract relates. For example, a statement such as 'I'm thinking of selling my car, probably for around €10,000' is not clear enough to be an offer. By contrast, stating 'I will sell you my car for €10,500' is clear enough to constitute an offer.

Words That Are Not Offers

It is important to distinguish an offer from things that may superficially appear similar. An offer must not be confused with a mere statement of information or price, a request for tenders, an invitation to treat or advertising.

1. A Mere Statement of Information or Price

A bald statement of price or fact, such as 'those boots cost €120', is not an offer because it is not capable of acceptance. The person making the statement may not have the boots to sell or may not actually wish to sell them.

> *Boyers & Co. v Duke* (1905) Ire
> The plaintiff wrote to the defendant asking for the lowest quotation for 3,000 yards of canvas. The defendant wrote back with his lowest quote per yard. The plaintiff said that he would accept this 'offer', but the defendant refused as the price had been misquoted. The court held that 'price per yard' was 'a quotation and not an offer' subject to the plaintiff's acceptance.

> *Tansey v College of Occupational Therapists Ltd* (1986) Ire
> The court held that an information pack sent to a student was not an offer, but simply a statement of information.

Very often, if X makes a statement of price or information to Y, this will lead Y to make an offer to X on the same or similar terms. Therefore, stating the price of the boots is not an offer. However, if I then offer to buy them, a contract can take place if that offer is accepted.

2. A Request for Tenders

A request for tenders is a request for offers. For example, a State company may advertise requesting tenders for a building contract. The company is simply asking for offers to be sent to it, one of which it may then decide to accept.

3. An Invitation to Treat

Goods on display in a window, in a catalogue or on shop shelves do not constitute an offer. In fact they are invitations to treat, i.e. something that invites the potential purchaser to treat themselves, or buy the goods.

> *Pharmaceutical Society of Great Britain v Boots Cash Chemist* (1953)
> In Boots, the chain of chemists, goods were displayed on open shelving. The rules of the Pharmaceutical Society of Great Britain required a qualified chemist to be on hand at the sale of certain items.

The question was whether a contract was made when the shopper chose an item from a shelf or when he or she paid for it at the cash register. The goods on the shelf were either an offer, which the shopper accepted on taking them down, or merely an invitation to treat. The court held that a display of goods on shelves was merely an invitation to treat, and the offer was made by the customer at the cash register. Boots had a chemist available at the cash register and so complied with the law.

Fisher v Bell (1961)
A shopkeeper displayed a flick knife in his shop window. A plain-clothes police officer purchased the knife. As a result, the shopkeeper was prosecuted under Britain's Offensive Weapons Act, which made it an offence to 'offer for sale' certain offensive weapons including flick knives. The court held that this was not 'an offer for sale' under the offensive weapons legislation but an invitation to treat. (The only offer occurred when the police officer offered to buy it.)

4. Advertising

Advertising may or may not be an offer, depending on the circumstances. In many cases, an advertisement is simply seen as a source of information.

Partridge v Crittenden (1968)
An advertisement was placed in a specialist magazine offering wild birds for sale. It was an offence to sell such birds, and when the advertiser sent one to a customer, he was charged with unlawfully offering such a bird for sale. The court held that the advertisement was simply an invitaiton to treat. It was not sufficiently detailed to be an offer.

Carlill v Carbolic Smoke Ball Co (1893)
The Carbolic Smoke Ball Company manufactured a patent medicine which was advertised as being able to prevent flu, among other ailments. The company ran advertisements in newspapers stating that anyone who bought and used the Smoke Ball correctly and still developed the flu would be entiled to a reward of £100. The advertisements also stated that £1,000 was deposited in the bank, 'to show the company's sincerity'. Mrs Carlill saw the advertisement, bought and used the Smoke Ball and still developed the flu. She claimed her reward, but the company responded by stating that the advertisements were merely invitations to treat and were not meant to be legally binding offers. The English Court of Appeal held that the advertisement was an offer to the world at large and was capable of acceptance by anyone who bought and used the product according to the instructions, as Mrs Carlill had. The fact that the company had deposited money in a special account was seen as proof of legal intent, so the company could not argue that the advertisement was merely a sales

ploy. The advertisement in this case was held to be an offer because it was sufficiently clear and detailed and was thus capable of acceptance if the purchaser of the product complied with the conditions. The fact that it was an 'offer' to the world at large was relevant to the court's decision that it was, in fact, a legally binding offer, as communication of acceptance might be waived in such a case.

In all of these circumstances, i.e. statements of fact or price, requests for tenders, invitations to treat and advertising, these devices are not offers, but they open the bidding and may lead to an offer being made.

An offer can be made to various people, and these are the only people who may accept it. (Any other person may, of course, make a new offer for the goods.) An offer can be made to individuals, groups or the world at large, i.e. a group so large that it cannot be accurately quantified. An example would be an advertisement in a newspaper, if that advertisement were to be deemed to be an offer.

Forms of an Offer

An offer can take different forms. It can be oral, written or by conduct. For example, I take a newspaper from a counter and hand over the appropriate price. This is a valid offer to purchase the paper, with the acceptance also being by conduct when the shop assistant simply takes the money. An offer may also be a combination of these forms.

Normally, acceptance is in the same form as the offer, so an offer made by e-mail is normally accepted by e-mail. However, the offeror (the person making the offer) can stipulate the form the acceptance should take. For example, I might send you an offer by post but request the acceptance by fax.

Termination of an Offer

An offer does not last indefinitely. It can be terminated by lapse of time, rejection, death or revocation.

1. Lapse of Time

Many offers stay open for a specific time only, after which they lapse. For example, a special subscription rate for cable TV may be open until the end of November. If no time for acceptance is specified, an offer remains open for a reasonable time, as decided by the courts.

> *Loring v City of Boston* (1844)
> A reward was advertised and claimed four years later. The court held that the offer had lapsed because of the time that had passed.

2. Rejection

If the offeree (person receiving the offer) rejects the offer, the offer is terminated. The simplest way to reject an offer is by saying no. A rejection terminates the offer, so once an offer is rejected, the offeree cannot then attempt to accept it. (The offeree could, however, make a new offer.)

A counteroffer is also a rejection because it varies the terms of the offer. If A offers to sell her car for €10,000, and B says he will give her €8,500, that counteroffer is effectively a 'no' and terminates the original offer. This situation is illustrated in Figure 3.1.

Figure 3.1 Counteroffer

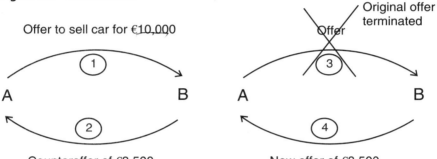

Hyde v Wrench (1840)
Wrench offered to sell property to Hyde for £1,000. Hyde said he would pay £950, but Wrench rejected this. Hyde then said that he would accept the original offer of £1,000. The court held that when Hyde attempted to vary the price, this was a counteroffer that terminated the original offer. Thus Hyde could not now accept the original offer because it no longer existed.

Of course, a counteroffer is a new offer that may be accepted, so if Wrench had been happy with Hyde's offer of £950, he could have accepted it. Equally, Wrench could have accepted Hyde's later offer of £1,000 if he so wished.

This back-and-forth bargaining can make it difficult to decide when a contract is validly formed, and this difficulty is even greater if the parties are exchanging documents or printed forms. This is sometimes known as the 'battle of the forms'.

Butler Machine Tool Co v Ex-Cell-O Corp (1979)
The sellers of machinery quoted the buyers a written price but stated that the price would rise if costs rose in the ten months before the delivery of the machinery. The buyers placed an order for the machinery on their own form, which did not allow for a price variation. The sellers then returned the portion of the buyers' form that stated that the contract took place on the buyers' conditions. The court held that the sellers' quotation

was an offer, and the buyers' response was a counteroffer. The sellers accepted the counteroffer when they returned the slip accepting the buyers' conditions. However, the court stated that there are no set rules in 'battle-of-the-forms' cases.

3. Death

If either party dies, then usually the offer dies with him or her. If the offeree dies, he or she can no longer accept. If the offeror dies and it is a contract for personal services such as gardening or employment, the offer dies with him or her. If the contract was not specifically personal, then the contract may still be formed. For example, if C accepts B's offer to sell her car before she dies, the courts may allow this contract.

4. Revocation

If the offeror revokes or withdraws the offer, the offer ends. An offer can only be revoked before it is accepted.

> *O'Donovan v Minister for Justice (2000)* Ire.
> The Department of Justice issued a job offer letter to O'Donovan, but subsequently withdrew and destroyed the letter before it reached him. On becoming aware of this fact, O'Donovan sought a court order quashing the decision to rescind the letter. The court held that an offer could be revoked.

Revocation must be communicated to the offeree by the offeror or a reliable third party. The postal rule (see below) does not apply to letters of revocation. These must arrive before the offer is validly revoked.

An offer can be withdrawn even if there has been a promise to keep the offer open for a specific period, as promises are not legally binding. An 'option agreement' is a separate contract to keep the offer open, usually made by paying a small sum to the offeror. For example, if I promise to keep my offer to sell my car to you open for a week, I can change my mind and withdraw the offer or sell it to someone else. This is because my promise is not legally enforceable. However, if you pay me €20 to keep the offer open for the week, that is a contract, or an option agreement, because of the payment of consideration. Essentially I am making a miniature contract to keep my options open in relation to the main contract, hence the name 'option agreement'. (An option agreement is like a deposit, but a deposit secures a contract, whereas an option agreement only secures time to consider the contract.)

B. Acceptance

An 'acceptance' is a clear and unambiguous agreement to the offer. No variation is allowed, as seen above in relation to counteroffers. An offer and acceptance should look as in Figure 3.2. There should be complete agreement between an offer and an acceptance; i.e. they should be two halves of the one whole. This is sometimes known as the 'mirror image' principle.

Figure 3.2 Offer and acceptance

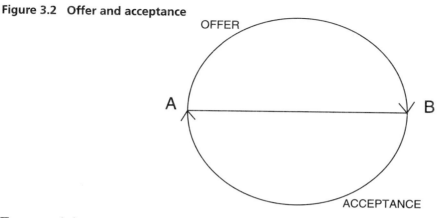

Forms of Acceptance

An acceptance can be in any form—oral, written, conduct or a combination—but it cannot be by silence or inactivity.

> *Felthouse v Brindley* (1862)
> After negotiations about the price, a potential buyer of a horse said to the seller 'If I hear no more about him, I consider the horse is mine'. The court held that this was not a proper form of acceptance. One party cannot make a contract simply because the other party does not reject it.

The Sale of Goods and Supply of Services Act 1980 outlaws 'inertia selling', which is the practice of sending unsolicited goods to a person and stating that if they are not returned, they will be deemed to have been purchased. Section 47 of the Act provides that unsolicited goods may be treated as a gift by the recipient in some circumstances.

Acceptance is usually in the same form as an offer, e.g. an offer by fax or airmail requires an acceptance by the same speedy method, according to *Entores v Miles Far East Corporation* (1955). However, the offeror is free to stipulate the method of acceptance.

Communication of Acceptance

Acceptance of an offer is not valid until is communicated to the offeror (or their agents).

> *Parkgate Investments v Shandon Park Mills* (1991) Ire
> The defendant sought to enforce an initial agreement made with the plaintiff's solicitors. The court held that there was no contract as the purported acceptance was made to the solicitor and not communicated to the plaintiff.

However, there are two exceptions to this.

1. Waiver

An offeror may make it clear by the form of the offer that he or she does not wish to receive communication of acceptance. In the *Carlill* case, for example, the court held that the form of the offer, i.e. to the world at large, made it clear that acceptance did not need to be communicated beyond the purchasing of the Smoke Ball. After the purchase, the buyer did not need to contact the company separately to accept the offer of money if the product was defective.

Most 'offers' on consumer products in which tokens are saved to get a free gift operate on this principle. For example, if a consumer saves five tokens from jars of coffee to get a free tea towel, he or she does not need to accept this offer. The form of the offer to the world at large means that the coffee company has waived its right to be notified of acceptance. However, if the coffee company did want thousands of people to give notice that they were saving tokens, the company could require this as part of the contract. (These contracts are sometimes known as 'unilateral' contracts.)

2. The Postal Rule

The postal rule is an old rule stating that communication of an acceptance takes place when a letter is *posted*. (This was because of the old practice of post offices recording all posted letters, making it easier to prove that a letter was posted than to prove that it had arrived.) Thus if a letter of acceptance is posted in Abbeyleix, that contract is formed when the letter is posted, not when the letter arrives in Dublin. This can cause injustice, in the case of loss or delay of the letter, with parties unaware that they are in a contract.

> *Household Fire Insurance v Grant* (1879)
> Grant offered to take out household insurance, and the plaintiff company accepted his offer. The company posted the letter of acceptance, but it never arrived. Grant arranged insurance elsewhere. At the end of the year the plaintiff billed Grant for one year's insurance premium. The court held that Grant was liable to pay the plaintiff because a valid contract had been formed when the letter of acceptance was posted.

A practical issue that concerns parties to a contract who are in different countries involves determining which country's laws govern the contract. Unless the parties specify the applicable law, the postal rule means that the country from which the acceptance was posted is the country where the contract was concluded.

> *Sanderson v Cunningham* (1919) Ire
> The plaintiff sent a completed insurance proposal to the defendant insurance company in London. This was an offer by Sanderson. The defendant company sent him a policy, which he signed. When a dispute arose about the insurance, the plaintiff wanted to sue the

defendant in Ireland but could only do so if the contract were concluded in Ireland. The court held that the contract was completed in London because that was where the acceptance, i.e. the policy, had been posted.

Kelly v Cruise Catering Ltd (1994) Ire
Following interviews, a Norwegian firm posted a job offer to the plaintiff in Dublin. Kelly posted a letter of acceptance in Dublin. Kelly was involved in an accident while working on board a cruise ship sailing between Mexico and the USA. The court held that Kelly accepted the contract of employment while in Dublin under the postal rule, thus the contract was formed there and could be sued upon in the Irish courts.

In *Sanderson v Cunningham* (1919), the parties could have specified that the contract was concluded in Ireland, which would be an exception to the postal rule. Parties are free to override the postal rule by providing that the contract is not formed until the letter arrives. This is normally done in practice.

The postal rule applies only to post and telegrams; it does not apply to fax or e-mail, which are considered to be instantaneous. As stated above, the postal rule does not apply to letters of revocation, which must arrive before the offer is validly revoked.

C. Consideration

'Consideration' is the price to be paid under a contract. It is what distinguishes a contract from a promise, a gift or a favour. All contracts require consideration. The only instance when an agreement without consideration can be binding is if it is in a *deed under seal*. This is a legal document that makes a promise enforceable. For example, if I guarantee a bank loan, my guarantee or promise needs to be made legally binding, or it is worthless to the bank. My signature on an appropriate form will constitute a deed under seal and will be legally binding. Another example of a deed under seal is the creation of a deed of covenant. These contracts should be in writing, clearly stating that they are intended to be legally binding, be signed and, sometimes, be witnessed.

Forms of Consideration

Consideration can take three forms: executed consideration, executory consideration and past consideration.

1. Executed Consideration

Executed consideration is a promise in return for an act. A simple example is if I state I will pay you €100 if you find my lost dog. If you do the act of finding the dog, I will fulfill my promise. If you do not, I have no obligation to pay you the money. This is used in simple everyday contracts, such as your boss promising to pay you extra if you do overtime.

Note: For exam purposes, to remember the name, remember that an act is said to be executed or carried out.

2. Executory Consideration
'Executory consideration' is a promise in return for a promise. For example, I promise to stay in your hotel in a month's time if you promise to keep a

Figure 3.3 Consideration

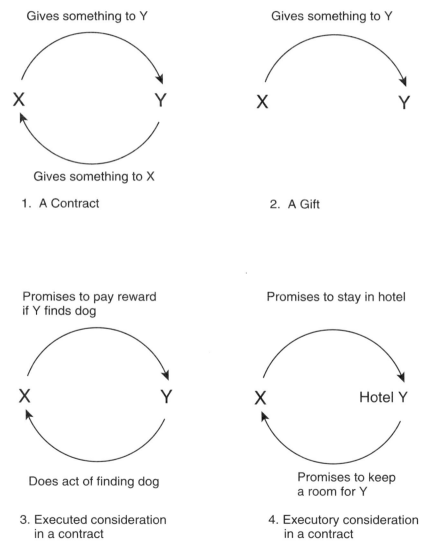

Gives something to Y

X   Y

Gives something to X

1. A Contract

Gives something to Y

X   Y

2. A Gift

Promises to pay reward
if Y finds dog

X   Y

Does act of finding dog

3. Executed consideration
   in a contract

Promises to stay in hotel

X   Hotel Y

Promises to keep
a room for Y

4. Executory consideration
   in a contract

room for me. If I fail to take the room, it would be a breach of contract on my part. Equally, if I arrive and you failed to keep a room for me, that would be a breach on your part.

Executory consideration is very useful in circumstances in which goods or services are being ordered, such as buying from a catalogue in a sale-of-goods transaction and commercial transactions such as ordering supplies. In both cases, each party gives something to the other and, in return, receives something from the other party. Consideration should look like a circle, as in parts 1, 3 and 4 of Figure 3.3. If no circle is formed, then there is no contract; i.e. there is only a one-sided promise, e.g. a gift, as in part 2.

3. Past Consideration

Past consideration is an invalid form of consideration, in that the thing that is supposed to be consideration was done in the past, with no connection to a contract. For example, A's car breaks down and her neighbour B offers to take her to work for a week until it is fixed. At the end of the week, A promises to repay B for her parking and petrol expenses. This is not a valid contract, as shown in Figure 3.4, because there is no consideration. When B offered to take A to work, this was an offer out of the goodness of her heart; there was no suggestion of a contract. When A later promises to repay B, there is no consideration for this promise, i.e. A received nothing in return, because B's acts of bringing her to work had been done in the past.

Figure 3.4 Past consideration

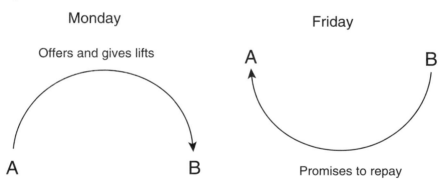

Monday

Offers and gives lifts

A   B

Friday

A   B

Promises to repay

There is no contract here because the only consideration is in the past.

Roscorla v Thomas (1842)
After the defendant had sold a horse to the plaintiff, he promised that the horse was 'free from vice'. The horse bit the plaintiff who sued for breach of warranty. The court held that the defendant's promise was not binding as the plaintiff had provided no consideration in return for it, and past consideration was not valid.

Re McArdle (1951)
Under the will of a deceased woman, her children inherited her house. Prior to her death, one of her sons and his wife had lived in the house with her and spent money improving it for the mother. The other children later promised to pay the couple for the improvements to the house but then refused. The court held that the money spent on improvements was done voluntarily, with no mention of a contract. Thus the improvements were past consideration at the time of the promise, so there was no contract formed.

The following is the leading Irish case on the issue of past consideration.

Provincial Bank of Ireland v Donnell (1932) Nth Ire
The plaintiff secured her husband's overdraft with the defendant bank (not by way of a deed under seal) in consideration of 'advances heretofore made or that might hereafter be made'. In other words, she guaranteed the loan because the bank had lent her money in the past and might do so in the future. The court held that when the woman made this promise, there was no valid consideration because the loans given to her in the past by the bank were past consideration. At the time they were given, there had been no mention of a future contract based upon the loans.

4. Exceptions to the Rule on Past Consideration

If the plaintiff's actions were requested by the defendant and payment was implied, then the court will see an exception to the rule. This is a legal fiction, based on doing fairness in a case. For example, if you work in a job where you are normally paid overtime and you are asked to work until 9 p.m. on Friday, it is implied that you will be paid for doing so.

Lampleigh v Braithwait (1615)
The defendant, who was in jail for murder, asked the plaintiff to organise a royal pardon for him. The plaintiff successfully obtained the royal pardon, and the defendant promised to repay him for his expense. The court held that this promise was legally enforceable because the defendant requested the service. The court held that there was an implied promise to pay for the requested service, as shown in Figure 3.5.

Cheques issued to pay existing debts are also an exception to the rule on past consideration under the Bills of Exchange Act 1882.

Figure 3.5 *Lampleigh v Braithwait* (1615) exception to the rule on past consideration

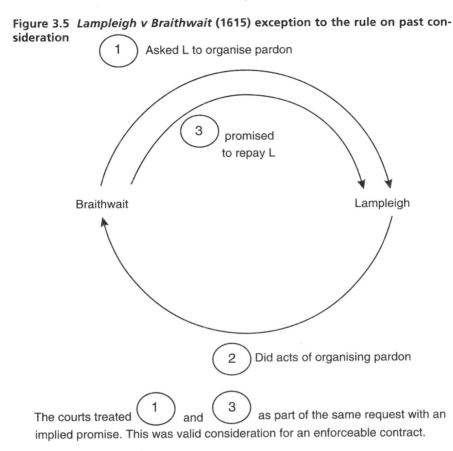

1. Asked L to organise pardon
3. promised to repay L

Braithwait

Lampleigh

2. Did acts of organising pardon

The courts treated (1) and (3) as part of the same request with an implied promise. This was valid consideration for an enforceable contract.

The Rules of Consideration

In addition to the types of consideration, there are a number of rules in relation to the operation of consideration.

1. Consideration Must Be Sufficient but Need Not Be Adequate

In other words, consideration must have some legal value, but it need not be a good price. This is a basic principle of freedom to contract. If, for example, I own a car worth €10,000, I have the freedom to sell it for €100,000 if I can find a willing buyer, and equally, I can sell it for €1 if I so wish. As long as there is *some* legal consideration, it does not matter whether it is a good bargain or not. A legal value is simply something that is capable of valuation.

Chappell & Co Ltd v Nestlé Co Ltd (1960)
Nestlé offered a free top-ten record to anyone who sent the company three used wrappers from Nestlé chocolate bars. In a dispute over the royalty fee for the records, the value of the wrappers was discussed.

The court held that there was a valid contract, the consideration for the 'free' record being the used chocolate wrappers.

This is similar to collecting tokens on breakfast cereal or teabags to qualify for a free tea towel or children's toy.

Examples of sufficient consideration would be:

- money, e.g. I give my car to you in return for €10,000;
- goods, including land, e.g. I give my car to you in return for your motorbike;
- services, e.g. I give my car to you in return for your giving financial advice to me;
- promises to do something, e.g. I give my car to you today if you promise to do my tax returns next November;
- promises not to do something, e.g. I give my car to you if you promise not to sue me for breach of contract (this is known as a promise of forbearance).

Hamer v Sidway (1891)
A nephew promised to give up smoking, drinking, gambling and swearing until he was twenty-one in return for his uncle's promise to pay him £5,000. The court held that this was a valid contract, the consideration being provided by the nephew was his forbearing from doing things he had a legal right to do.

Commodity Broking Company Ltd v Fergus Meehan (1985) Ire
In this case, the defendant's company owed money to the plaintiff, which the defendant promised to repay. The court held that such a promise could form part of a valid contract when, in return, the consideration was the plaintiff company's promise to forbear from suing the defendant. However, on the facts of the case, the court could not find any expressed or implied request by the defendant not to sue him so 'no consideration was given for the defendant's promise'.

Examples of insufficient consideration are illegal consideration, for example, a promise to pay for drugs supplied would be unenforceable, and a promise to perform a moral or religious duty.

O'Neill v Murphy (1936)
A promise by a priest to say prayers for a builder was not sufficient consideration for a contract to repair the church. This is because such duties are incapable of being valued.

A promise to perform a preexisting legal or contractual duty is another example of insufficient consideration. For example, I promise the fire brigade €100 each if they put out a fire in my house. However, the fire brigade members who put out the fire would not be entitled to the €100 each I promised them because they were already bound to put out the fire. They had a preexisting duty to attempt to put out the fire under their contract of employment. However, if the fire brigade did something new based on my request, such as rescuing my valuable painting, the members would be entitled to the money.

To take another example, if my boss is in an expansive mood and promises me a bonus at the end of the week, I am not legally entitled to it as I have provided nothing new in return by way of consideration. There is no circle of consideration, as shown in Figure 3.6.

Figure 3.6 Incomplete circle of consideration

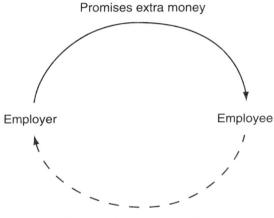

Promises extra money

Employer

Employee

Does nothing new in return

Therefore, there is no contract because there is no consideration. Employer simply made an unenforceable promise.

Stilk v Myrick (1809)
Two sailors deserted their ship in mid-voyage. In an attempt to boost morale, the captain promised to split the deserters' wages among the other sailors if they completed the voyage. The court held that this promise was not legally binding as the sailors gave no consideration in return for the promise because they were legally obliged under their contracts to finish the voyage.

Hartley v Ponsonby (1857)
A number of desertions from a ship mid-voyage meant that the ship could not sail without the remaining crew doing extra work. The captain promised the wages of the deserters to the remaining crew for sharing the extra work, and this was held to be a valid contract, as the extra work provided consideration for the promise.

However, this area is now somewhat unclear due to the controversial English decision of:

Williams v Roffey Bros & Nicholls (Contractors) Ltd (1990)

The defendants, who were the main contractors on a construction job, sub-contracted work to the plaintiffs. The sub-contractors got into financial difficulties and were unlikely to be able to finish the job. This would delay the project for the main contractor, who would be liable to pay penalties for failing to complete the work on time. As a result, the contractors offered to pay the sub-contractors additional money if they completed the contract. When the work was completed on time, the main contractors refused to pay the additional money, basing their arguments on *Stilk v Myrick* (1809).

The court held that the agreement was legally enforceable because the main contractors promised to pay extra money in return for the sub-contractors giving them the practical benefit of avoiding the penalties for late completion.

This decision is controversial for a number of reasons:

- It gives a very wide meaning to consideration as a benefit given by each party.
- It reduces the useage of the doctrine of promissory estoppel (see page 53).
- It may be considered economic duress, i.e. where one party takes advantage of the other's weakened economic situation to make a contract which should not be enforceable (see page 85).

This decision has not yet been followed in Ireland.

The Rule in Pinnel's Case (1602)

This rule states the part payment of a debt does not satisfy the whole.

The rule often causes problems for students, but it is exactly the same as the principle outlined above in relation to the fire brigade and the sailors. The rule simply means that where part of a debt is paid 'in satisfaction of the whole debt', this is not valid because no new consideration is given; the debt had to be paid anyhow. For example, if A owes €10,000 to B and is in financial difficulties, A may attempt to make a deal with B along the lines of 'I don't have the entire amount, but I will pay you €5,000 if then we can call it quits' or 'I will pay you €5,000 in full and final settlement of the debt'. If B agrees to this and promises not to sue A for the balance, this is only a promise, not a contract. B can change her mind and sue A because when B made her promise to A, A provided nothing new by way of consideration, as the money had to be repaid anyhow. Thus, part payment of the debt does not satisfy the obligation to pay the whole debt, as illustrated in Figure 3.7.

Figure 3.7 The rule in *Pinnel's Case* (1602)

Promises to accept €5,000 in 'full and final settlement' of debt

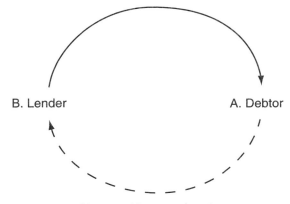

B. Lender　　　　　　　　　　　A. Debtor

Gives nothing new in return

Therefore, there is no contract because there is no consideration. Lender simply made an unenforceable promise.

Foakes v Beer (1884)
Foakes owed £2,000 to Beer. Beer promised that if Foakes paid £500 in a lump sum and the balance by instalments, she would not take 'any proceedings whatsoever' against Foakes. The question arose as to whether Beer was entitled to interest on this agreement, interest to which she would have originally been entitled. Foakes argued that Beer had impliedly given up her right to interest. The court held that Beer was entitled to receive interest because even if she had impliedly given up her right to interest, this was simply an agreement, not a contract supported by consideration.

As in the examples with the fire brigade and the sailors, if a party does something *new* in return for a promise, this may provide consideration. For example, if A owes B €10,000 payable on 1 November, A may agree to take €5,000 in full and final settlement of the debt on 10 October. There is a valid contract here, as shown in Figure 3.8, as A has made a promise and in return has received something new, i.e. the benefit of being paid early.

It is important to note that there is a potential overlap here with the doctrine of economic duress. 'Duress' means a party is threatened to get him or her to enter into a contract, and 'economic duress' is a threat to the person's business or livelihood. In a situation in which A owes €10,000 to B, and A knows that B is in financial difficulties, A may attempt to take advantage of this by saying to B 'I will give you €5,000, take it or leave it'. In these circumstances, this may be seen as an attempt to apply unlawful bargaining power to a contract, or economic duress, and the contract could be made void by B at a later date.

The rule in *Pinnel's Case* can have a very strict application in commercial cases, and as a result, the courts will occasionally vary it by the application of the doctrine of promissory estoppel (see below).

We will now consider two more rules of consideration.

Figure 3.8 Additional consideration

Promises to accept €5,000 in 'full and
final settlement' of debt

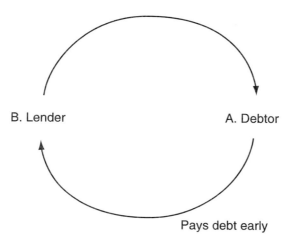

B. Lender   A. Debtor

Pays debt early

There is a valid contract because of the exchange of consideration

2. Consideration Must Be Given by a Party to the Contract

This rule is sometimes expressed as 'consideration must move from the promisee'. The logical result of this is that only a party to a contract can sue to enforce it. This is known as 'privity of contract'.

> *Tweddle v Atkinson* (1861)
> The fathers of a couple who were getting married agreed with each other that they would both pay an annual sum of money to their children. One father died without having made the promised payments, and his son-in-law sued the deceased's estate for the money owing to him and his wife. The court held that the son-in-law was not a party to the contract and, therefore, had no right to sue on it.

This is the same principle that states that if you get a present or a gift, you cannot sue the retailer if it is defective, as you were not a party to the contract. You did not provide consideration because you did not buy the item.

There are a number of exceptions to the requirement that you must be privy to a contract before you can enforce it: trust, assignment, insurance and agency.

Trust: In a trust, the parties for whose benefit the trust was created may sue the trustees, although they are not parties to the trust contract. For example, aged parents create a trust for their children that is to be administered by their accountant. After the parents' deaths, the children discover that the accountant has been defrauding them. The children, as beneficiaries of the trust, may sue the accountant as trustee, as the parents cannot enforce the contract.

Assignment: One of the parties to a contract may, with the other party's agreement, assign, or transfer, the contract to another person, who will then be able to enforce it. Leases of property are often assigned from one tenant to another, with the agreement of the landlord. In such a case, the new tenant can enforce the terms of the lease, although he or she was not a party to it.

Insurance: Under some insurance legislation, a person injured in a road traffic accident may claim against the driver's insurance, although he or she was not a party to it.

Agency: In the law of agency, an agent is given authority to contract on behalf of the principal, i.e. the hiring party. The agent must always disclose that he or she is an agent and who the principal is. However, an undisclosed principal may adopt a contract made for him or her by an agent.

3. The Doctrine of Promissory Estoppel

If A makes a promise to B, knowing that B will act upon it and B does act, A will be *estopped* from retracting her promise. 'Estoppel' is an equitable idea under which one party is stopped from changing a course of action that he or she had already indicated. Promissory estoppel was invented by the courts in an *obiter dictum* in the following case.

> *Central London Property Trust v High Trees House* (1947)
> In 1939 the plaintiff leased a block of flats in London to the defendant. In 1940, owing to the Second World War, the plaintiff agreed to reduce the rent to less than half the original amount. In 1945 the plaintiff sought to raise the rent and also to claim the unpaid portion for the last five years. (Looking at the facts so far you will see that the plaintiff made a promise to the defendant, but the defendant gave him nothing in return that could be deemed consideration, as there was already an obligation to pay the rent.) The court held that the plaintiff was entitled to increase the rent but not to claim the back rent. The court invented the doctrine now known as 'promissory estoppel', based on the equitable concepts of fairness and estoppel, i.e. to be stopped from doing something. The court held that its preference was 'to apply the principle that a promise intended to be binding, intended to be acted on and in fact acted on, is binding'.

This doctrine, however, has a very limited application: There must be a clear promise that existing legal rights will not be enforced. The plaintiff must have relied on that promise, in that it would be to his or her detriment were the promise not to be upheld. It must be unfair or inequitable for the defendant to go back on the promise. All three of these conditions are satisfied in the *High Trees case.*

Despite the doctrine of promissory estoppel, the requirement for consideration remains in most contracts. The doctrine of promissory estoppel can be used as a means of avoiding the operation of the rule in *Pinnel's Case.* However, the doctrine of promissory estoppel has been reduced by *Williams v Roffey Bros & Nicholls (Contractors) Ltd* (1990).

D. Legal Intent

The fourth essential requirement in a contract is the intention to create legal relations. In addition to consideration, this is what makes a contract legally distinguishable from a gift, a favour and a promise, which both sides know are not meant to create legal relations.

Both parties to a contract must intend it to be legally binding. Intention to create a legal relation can be expressed or implied from the circumstances. For example, in the *Carlill* case, an intention to create legal relations was inferred from the deposit of money in the bank by the Smoke Ball company.

Types of Legal Intent

The law has classified legal intent into three sets of circumstances:

- domestic and social agreements among family or friends;
- commercial contracts;
- collective agreements.

1. Domestic and Social Agreements

Agreements among family members or friends are presumed not to be contracts, unless there is evidence to the contrary. For example, if I promise to babysit for my sister's children, this is clearly not intended to create a contract. However, if I promise to babysit if she pays me €7 an hour, this is clearly intended to be a contract, due to the existence of consideration and also our implied legal intention. Equally, if I enter into a syndicate to play the National Lottery, this would be a legally binding contract because of the agreement in relation to conditions of entering and winning.

> *Courtney v Courtney* (1923)
> The plaintiff left her husband as a result of cruelty. The plaintiff returned some jewelry and her husband agreed to pay her a sum in discharge of all claims. Later the plaintiff sought a judicial separation

and her husband argued that the prior agreement meant no further proceeding could be taken. The court held that the earlier agreement was a legally binding contract.

Rogers v Smith (1970) Ire
The plaintiff was given his father's business on the stipulation that he should pay his mother's expenses and take a weekly sum from the business profits. On his mother's death he claimed the money owing to him from his unclaimed share of the profits. The Supreme Court held that in the absence of clear and unambiguous evidence, the court should not infer an intention to contract.

2. Commercial Agreements

Agreements between businesses are presumed to be contracts, unless there is evidence to the contrary. If a company's photocopier breaks down and the company next door offers to let the other company use its copies at 5 cent per sheet, this is presumed to be a contract. However, if the company next door simply says the copier can be used until the other is fixed, this would rebut the presumption. For example, in *Commodity Broking Company Ltd v Fergus Meehan* (1985) Ire, the court stated that a promise between two businesses in relation to a commercial transaction is presumed to be a contract.

'Letters of comfort' are letters giving information about a company's financial status that are stated to be nonbinding. Such letters are often given by holding companies to people dealing with their subsidiaries. The leading English case on this subject is the following one.

Kleinwort Benson Ltd v Malaysia Mining Corp Bhd (1989)
The plaintiff bank negotiated with the defendant company for a loan facility for the defendant's subsidiary company, MMC Metals Ltd. The defendant gave the bank a letter which read 'It is our policy to ensure that the business of MMC Metals Ltd is at all times in a position to meet its liabilities to you'. When MMC Metal Ltd went into liquidation, the defendant refused to ensure payment to the bank. The court held that the defendant had made no contractual promise to the bank, and the company's moral obligation to the bank was not a matter for the courts.

3. Collective Agreements

Collective bargains are agreements between trade unions or employees and employers. These may create binding contracts, depending on the circumstances. Such terms may be legally binding if they are incorporated into the contract of employment.

Goulding Chemicals v Bolger (1977) Ire
The plaintiff company negotiated with the unions in its Dublin plant when the company decided to close the facility. The defendants were

members of one union who objected to the proposals and picketed the plaintiff's premises. The Supreme Court held that the defendants were not parties to the contract and thus not bound by it. The strike was permitted.

O'Rourke & Others v Talbot (1984) Ire
The defendant company made an agreement with a group of employees that they would not be made redundant before a certain date. The court held that this 'guarantee' was intended by the parties to be legally binding, and the company was in breach of contract by making the plaintiffs redundant ahead of the specified time.

CHAPTER 4

The Contents of a Contract

Summary of chapter

In the last chapter we looked at the essential elements of a contract, i.e. the four elements that a contract must have. In this chapter we are going to look at other elements that may be part of a contract. Some contracts are required to be in writing or to be evidenced in writing. All contracts will have terms and conditions, varying according to the type of contract. Some contracts will include exemption clauses, and some standard form contracts will be subject to the EC (Unfair Terms in Consumer Contracts) Regulations 1995.

A. Forms of a Contract

As explained in the previous chapter, contracts may be in any form, such as oral, written, by conduct or any combination of these. Normally, the form of the contract is a matter on which the parties agree, but there are some specific legal rules in relation to the form of a contract.

Deeds under Seal

Deeds under seal have been dealt with in the previous chapter and are used to make a legally binding contract when there is no consideration; for example, a deed of covenant for tax purposes.

Contracts That Must Be in Writing

Some simple contracts are required by legislation to be in writing, normally for reasons of proof and protection of the consumer. Examples of these include:

- negotiable instruments (e.g. cheques, under the Bills of Exchange Act 1882);
- contracts negotiated away from business premises under the EC (Cancellation of Contracts Negotiated Away from Business Premises) Regulations 1989;
- hire purchase agreements, credit agreements and money lending agreements under the Consumer Credit Act 1995.

If these contracts are not in writing, they will not be legally binding.

Contracts That Have to Be Evidenced in Writing

Contracts that must be evidenced in writing form a separate category, which does not require that the contract itself must be in writing but that there must be written evidence of the contract. Complying with this requirement is less difficult than complying with the requirement that the contract itself must be in writing.

Under the Statute of Frauds (Ireland) Act 1695, certain contracts will only be enforceable if there is evidence of the terms in a written note or memorandum. It is important to grasp the essential point that these contracts need not actually be in writing, only that there must be some written evidence of the contract. (The object of this Act was to defeat frauds in situations where parties would make an oral contract and one would later deny it. In practice, most of these contracts would now be in writing as a matter of course, so this area arises infrequently.)

The most important of the contracts that must be evidenced in writing are:

- contracts for the sale of land or an interest in land;
- contracts not to be performed within one year;
- contracts of guarantee of debts.

Section 2 of the Statute of Frauds 1695 requires that no action shall be brought in relation to the specified contracts unless 'the agreement or some memorandum or note thereof' shall be in writing and signed by the party to be charged therewith (usually the defendant). In other words, there must be written evidence of the contract by way of a note or memorandum. The note or memorandum must refer to the 'Four Ps': the parties, the property (or subject matter), the price (or consideration) and any other particulars.

The note or memorandum need not have been created to comply with the Statute. Case-law over the years has accepted a variety of documents as suitable memorandums: correspondence from solicitors and estate agents, auctioneer's notebooks, receipts and cheques. All of these are documents that provide evidence of the contract and were not created specifically to provide such evidence. The Irish courts have even allowed two or more related documents to be joined together to provide the required information. This is known as 'joinder of documents'. If only one document is signed, the signed document must refer to the other document to which it is to be joined.

Subject to Contract

Case-law from 1979 onwards has established that a document containing the words 'subject to contract' is not sufficient to satisfy the Statute of Frauds, as this phrase indicates that no contract has been concluded. However, if the phrase 'subject to contract' was added after oral negotiations were concluded, then it will not affect the validity of a document recording the oral agreement.

Part Performance

The intention of the Statute of Frauds was to defeat frauds, but in some cases frauds were perpetrated when an oral contract was made without written evidence. In these cases one party would start to perform the contract and the other would deny that the contract ever existed. Usually there was no satisfactory note or memorandum, but there was part performance of the contract by the plaintiff. Thus the courts developed the equitable doctrine of part performance to make the contract enforceable, and the part performance was taken as evidence that the contract had been formed. For example, if A agreed to lease B's house if B installed a wheelchair ramp, but there was no written evidence of this agreement, the fact that B installed the ramp could be taken as evidence that such an agrement had been made.

Examples of acts that have been held by the courts to be acceptable part performance are entering into possession of land with the agreement of the owner, payment of rent and alteration of the land such as building an extension or planting on agricultural land.

B. Terms of a Contract

All terms of a contract must be complete and final for the contract to be legally binding. We have already seen this principle in relation to offer and acceptance, which must be complete before formal agreement is made. In some simple contracts, such as the purchase of a newspaper, the terms will be very simple, and in other contracts they will be far more complex. However, the basic principles are the same in all contracts:

- contractual terms must be distinguished from representations;
- conditions and warranties must be distinguished;
- implied and express terms must be distinguished.

Representations versus Terms

Representations are different from contract terms. These are things said in negotiations that do not become part of the contract and for which the remedy is a claim of misrepresentation. For example, if during negotiations to sell a car, the seller said that the car has never given him any trouble, this may not become part of, or a term, of the contract, but the buyer would still have an action in misrepresentation if this statement turns out to be incorrect and if it played a part in the buyer's decision to purchase the car. On the other hand, if the seller said that his car was in perfect working order, this would probably be held to be a term of the contract, and the buyer who relied on this statement would have an action in breach of contract.

The important thing to grasp is that a buyer who is misled by a statement will have a legal right of action regardless of whether the contentious precontractual statement is a representation or a term. (Breach of contract will be considered in (chapter 6.)

In many cases the distinction between terms that are part of a contract and representations that are negotiating statements is clear-cut. In other cases, however, the distinction is less clear-cut and requires analysis. Some precontractual representations do become a part of the contract, or terms. There are three rules of thumb that the courts find helpful in deciding whether a statement is a contractual term.

(1) The time at which the statement was made will be considered. The closer to the conclusion of the contract, the more likely the statement is to be considered a term.

(2) If the contract is in writing and does not contain the statement, it is unlikely to be a term.

(3) If the person making the statement had special skill or knowledge compared with the other party, it is likely to be held a term. In the above example, the statement that the car was in perfect working order would probably be held to be a term of the contract because the seller is considered to be an expert.

Remember that the buyer of a good has a remedy regardless of whether the representation is held to be a term or not.

Conditions versus Warranties

The terms of a contract may be expressed between the parties or may be implied. All terms can be classified into *conditions* and *warranties*. The difference is crucial in relation to breach of contract.

'Conditions' are vital terms in the contract and are of major importance. Breach of a condition entitles the innocent party to end, or 'rescind', the contract, and/or obtain damages. Warranties are less important terms and only allow the innocent party to obtain damages for breach. For example, if you are buying a midnight blue 2004 Volvo with sunroof and CD player, the year and the make of the car would probably be the key terms. If you were supplied with a 2002 car or a Rover, you would be entitled to get out of the contract and seek damages if appropriate. On the other hand, if the car supplied were the wrong shade of blue or did not have a CD player, this would not be sufficiently serious to allow you to get out of the contract but would allow you to claim for damages. The distinction between conditions and warranties is clearly highlighted by the following two precedents.

> *Poussard v Spiers and Pond* (1876)
> An opera singer failed to appear on the opening night of the opera. The court held that she was in breach of a condition of her contract, and as a result the contract could be ended.

Bettini v Gye (1876)
A singer failed to attend the required rehearsals for an engagement but
did attend some rehearsals and all of the performances. The court held
that he had breached a warranty or subsidiary term in his contract, and
he was ordered to pay damages.

The Sale of Goods Act 1893 and Sale of Goods and Supply of Services Act
1980 also divide the obligations of a seller of goods into conditions and
warranties, as will be explained in Chapter 7.

Whether a term is a condition or a warranty is not always clear at the time
of the contract. Some terms can remain unclassified until the court considers
the seriousness of the breach of contract. These are called 'intermediate' or
'innominate terms'. They require a wait-and-see approach, which was
adopted in the following case.

Irish Telephone Rentals Ltd v Irish Civil Service Building Society
(1992) Ire
The defendant attempted to rescind a contract for the supply of a
telephone system on the grounds that it malfunctioned. The service
supplied was not in compliance with the Sale of Goods and Supply of
Services Act 1980 in relation to services. The supply of services was
not classified into conditions or warranties but was merely described
as contract terms. The court held that where an event occurs for which
neither party has expressly provided, then it is for the court to
determine what effect the event has had. The serious defects in the
telephone system meant that the Building Society was entitled to
rescind or end the contract.

Express versus Implied Terms

In all contracts, some terms will be stated but the bulk will remain unspoken.
To take a simple example, if I buy a coffee, the express terms are that it is
coffee and that it costs €2. However, it is implied that the drink will be hot,
fit for human consumption and served in some sort of container. As another
example, consider an employment contract. The express terms might cover
the job description, payment, holidays and study leave, whereas the implied
terms would cover equality, health and safety, freedom from sexual
harassment, notice periods and redundancy, among other issues.

There are various sources of implied terms. Terms may be implied under
the Constitution, by statute, by custom or trade practice, by the 'reasonable
bystander' test and by the 'business efficacy' test.

1. Under the Constitution of 1937

For example, under the Constitution there is the right to join a trade union.
(See *Educational Co of Ireland v Fitzpatrick* (1961) Ire and *Meskell v CIÉ*

(1973) Ire in Chapter 8.C.) There are also implied terms covering natural justice, i.e. the right to be treated fairly, as in *Glover v BLN Ltd* (1973) Ire.

2. By Statute

Many statutes imply detailed terms into contracts, for example, the Consumer Credit Act 1995, the Sale of Goods and Supply of Services Act 1980 as the main source of implied terms in consumer contracts (see Chapter 7) and the Terms of Employment (Information) Act 1994 as an example of terms implied under statute in employment law (see Chapter 8).

The purpose of implied statutory terms is to protect weaker parties in contracts such as consumers, tenants and employees, by providing terms that are standard in all contracts. As a result, terms implied under statute cannot be varied by the parties, as this would defeat the intention behind the protective legislation.

3. By Custom or Trade Practice

Terms may be implied into contracts if they are customary in a particular trade or industry. Whether something is customary is a question of fact to be decided by the courts.

> *O'Connail v The Gaelic Echo (1954) Ltd* (1958) Ire
> The court held that the plaintiff journalist was entitled to holiday pay as it was customary in the Dublin area for journalists.

4. By the 'Reasonable Bystander Test'

Under the reasonable bystander test, the courts will imply a term that was so obvious that a reasonable bystander would believe it to be part of the contract, for example, that a new car would be in perfect working order. An example of this is the following case.

> *Butler v McAlpine* (1904) Ire
> A shipowner made a contract with the owner of a wharf to allow the shipowner to unload the ship's cargo at the wharf. At low tide the ship was damaged by a sack of concrete that had previously falled into the riverbed. The court held that there was an implied duty on the wharf-owner to take reasonable care to ensure that the berth was safe.

5. By the 'Business Efficacy Test'

The business efficacy test is effectively the reasonable bystander test under another name as applied to commercial contracts. The test is whether it is necessary to imply the term to give the contract the business efficacy that both parties intended it to have.

Murphy Buckley & Keogh v Pye (Ireland) (1971) Ire
The defendant hired the plaintiff estate agents to sell a factory. The agreement was that the plaintiff would be the sole agent for the sale and would be paid for introducing the ultimate purchaser to the defendant. The defendant sold the premises to a buyer who was not introduced by the plaintiff, and the plaintiff argued that it should be entitled to a fee in this case. The court held that there could be no implied term to entitle the plaintiff to a fee in this case. Such an implied term would be contrary to the express terms and would not give the contract the business interpretation that both parties intended it to have.

Express terms are given priority over implied terms because they reflect the parties' intentions. However, it is important to remember that implied statutory terms take precedence over express terms to the contrary, as explained above.

Incomplete Contracts

If there has not been agreement on all the essential terms, then there cannot be said to be a proper contract. However, if the parties do not agree on an essential term but leave it to be filled in at a later date, this may still be a valid contract. For example, I agree to buy shares and no price is specified, but we agree that I will pay the market price for the shares on Friday. This would be deemed to be a valid completed contract because the means of getting to the price is stated and certain. Other examples would be when the parties agree to have the price set by arbitration or to pay the list price for goods.

Sometimes, parties will contract 'on the usual terms'. A phrase like this indicates that the parties have done business together in the past. If both parties are happy with this, it will be a valid agreement. Phrases like this are often used when the parties have been dealing with each other for a time and have become less formal in their dealings.

C. Exemption Clauses

An exemption clause is a clause in a contract that tries to exclude or limit the liability of one party (usually the stronger party) under the contract in the case of breach. The party who puts forward or proffers the exemption clause is known as the 'proferens'.

An example of a type of exemption clause that totally excludes liability, known as an exclusion clause, is a clause in a contract for the supply of fruit which states that the wholesalers will have no responsibility in the event of their failing to supply the fruit on time. Another example is the case of *Clayton Love v B&I Transport* (1970) Ire, which will be discussed later in this section.

Another type of exemption clause, known as a limitation clause, is one that attempts to limit the liability of the stronger party. An example would be a clause in a contract to develop photographs which states that in the event of loss or damage to the films, the customer would be refunded the purchase price of the films only. Another example is the case of *Curtis v Chemical Cleaning and Dyeing Co* (1951), which will be discussed later in this section.

In general terms, the courts disapprove of such clauses because they infringe on the fundamental freedom to contract, so two strict tests have been adopted for the validity of such clauses: was the exemption clause incorporated into the contract and was the exemption clause properly constructed to cover the events that occurred? It is important to remember that an exemption clause must pass *both* tests before it will be upheld by the courts as valid.

Incorporation

A basic common-sense approach dictates that if both parties are aware of the exemption clause, then it can be said to be part of the contract. An exemption clause that is put forward after the contract was concluded can obviously not be part of the contract, as all contracts must be clear and final on agreement. However, an exemption clause may be incorporated, or become part of a contract, by signature, by prior notice of the claim or by a course of dealing.

1. By Signature

If the document or contract containing the exemption clause has been signed by the weaker party who is now complaining about the clause, the fact of signature is usually taken as sufficient proof that the clause was part of the contract. This applies even if the signing party did not read the contract, as the presumption in law is that once you have signed something you have agreed to it.

> *L'Estrange v Graucob* (1934)
> The plaintiff bought a cigarette machine from the defendant for use in her premises, having signed a document headed 'sales agreement' which excluded any implied conditions or warranties. The Sale of Goods Act 1893 did not apply to the transaction. The plaintiff gave evidence that she had not read the document before signing it. The court held that the plaintiff was bound by the terms of the agreement and that it was irrelevant that she had not read the document before signing it or that her attention was not drawn to the exemption clause.

An exemption clause is not binding if a contract was signed as a result of a misrepresentation or duress, as shown in the following case.

> *Curtis v Chemical Cleaning and Dyeing Co* (1951)
> The plaintiff left her wedding dress to be cleaned by the defendant and was asked to sign a receipt that excluded liability on the cleaners' part.

When the plaintiff questioned this, she was told that it applied to the delicate beading and sequins, which would be cleaned at her own risk. The plaintiff agreed to this. On collection of the dress, the beads and sequins were intact, but the skirt had been badly stained. The defendant argued that the exclusion clause covered such a situation. The court held that Mrs Curtis had been misled into signing the receipt, and thus it was not binding on her.

2. By Prior Notice of the Clause

The second way in which an exemption clause can become part of a contract is if the *proferens* gives the other party clear and sufficient notice of it. Common examples would be prominently displayed notices in dry cleaners attempting to limit liability for cleaning delicate fabrics or a notice at the entrance to a car park stating that the management accepts no liability for damage sustained on the premises.

Many of these cases concern the use of tickets or receipts containing exclusion or exemption clauses. Think, for example, of buying a ticket for a concert or sporting fixture. These usually contain detailed terms on the back about cancellations, refunds and exclusion of liability for accident or injury occurring at the venue. However, the purchaser never agreed to these terms when he or she made an offer based on the price of the ticket, the date and the seating, and the ticket sellers never mentioned other terms when agreeing to purchaser's offer. Thus, in legal terms, the purchaser would not have had 'prior notice' of the exemption clause, and it would not be incorporated into the contract.

> *Thornton v Shoe Lane Parking* (1971)
> The plaintiff parked his car in a multistorey car park. Outside the car park was a notice displaying the charges and also stating, 'All cars parked at owner's risk'. From an automatic vending machine Mr Thornton was given a ticket which stated, in small print, that the issue was subject to the conditions displayed on the premises. These conditions were displayed in detail on pillars in the car park and at the paying office at the exit. On collection of his car, Mr Thornton was badly injured in an accident. The court held that the contract was formed when Mr Thorton put his money into the machine (the 'parking' sign was an offer and the money was the acceptance) and the terms contained on the ticket were not part of the contract, coming after the contract was concluded.

> *Western Meats Ltd v National Ice and Cold Storage Co Ltd* (1982) Ire
> The defendant stored a substantial amount of meat belonging to the plaintiff, on condition that all goods were stored at the owners' risk. This condition was printed on the back of letters and storage documents. The defendant was negligent in labelling the stored goods and, in the run up to the Christmas period, was unable to identify the

plaintiff's goods in the store, which caused loss to the plaintiff. The court held that the defendant had failed to bring the exemption clause to the defendant's attention, and thus it was not binding. The judge stated that 'a business man, offering a specialist service, but accepting no responsibility for it, must bring home clearly to the party dealing with him that he accepts no such responsibility'.

The EC (Unfair Terms in Consumer Contracts) Regulations 1995 states that a term that has the object or effect of 'inappropriately excluding or limiting the legal rights of a consumer *vis-à-vis* the seller or supplier or another party in the event of a total or partial nonperformance by the seller or supplier of any contractual obligators' is unfair and not binding.

3. By a Course of Dealing

The third way in which an exemption clause can be incorporated into a contract is when the parties have had a prior course of dealings, that is, they have previously done business with each other on the same terms. As illustrated in the two cases below, the courts take a more lenient approach if the case concerns a business and a consumer than if the case concerns two business. However, there are no definitive rules as to what constitutes a sufficient course of dealings.

> *J Spurling Ltd v Bradshaw* (1956)
> The owner of containers of orange juice made a contract to store them with the defendant, who, on each occasion, gave the owner a document that limited the storer's liability. The juice was destroyed and the defendant sought to rely on the exemption clause. The court held that there was a sufficient course of dealings here for the exemption clause to be incorporated and, thus, binding on the parties.

> *Hollier v Rambler Motors* (1972)
> The plaintiff had left his car to be repaired by the defendant on three or four occasions over a number of years and had been given a receipt that limited the garage's liability. On the occasion in question, he was given no receipt. When the car was damaged while in the possession of the garage, the garage attempted to limit its liability on the basis that the plaintiff should have been aware of the exemption clause based on his prior course of dealings with the garage. The court held that there was no course of dealings, as a series of isolated transactions could not be held to be such.

Construction

Even if an exemption clause passes the first test of incorporation, the courts will then question whether it is properly constructed, i.e. does it cover the events that have occurred? This rule basically requires the *proferens* (or party putting forward the clause) to draft the clause correctly and exactly. The courts apply the contra proferentem rule, the fundamental breach rule and statutory regulation to see if an exemption clause was properly put together.

(1) The Contra Proferentem Rule

The contra proferentem rule means 'against the party who proffers the clause'. It effectively means that the benefit of any doubt is given to the weaker party.

> *Andrews Bros (Bournemouth) Ltd v Singer and Co Ltd* (1934)
> The plaintiff contracted to buy 'new Singer cars' from Singer and Co Ltd. An exemption clause excluded liability for 'all conditions, warranties and liabilities implied by statute, common law or otherwise'. A car with substantial mileage was supplied, and the defendant sought to avoid liability by reliance on the exemption clause. The court held the clause to be invalid because the express stipulation that the cars be new was not covered by the exemption clause on implied terms. The judge stated that if the vendor wished to be excluded from liabilities, clear language must be used.

Section 5 of the EC (Unfair Terms in Consumer Contracts) Regulations 1995 states that if there is a doubt over the meaning of a term, the meaning most favourable to the consumer shall be applied. This is the contra proferentem rule given statutory effect.

(2) The Fundamental Breach Rule (sometimes called the Core Obligation Rule)

The Irish courts will not allow an exemption clause that excludes liability for a fundamental breach of contract.

> *Clayton Love v B&I Transport* (1970) Ire
> The defendant contracted to ship the plaintiff's frozen scampi from Dublin to Liverpool. The scampi defrosted after being loaded at atmospheric temperatures. One of the two exemption clauses in the contract was wide enough to cover the defendant's negligence. The Supreme Court held that despite the parties' intentions, there could not be an exclusion clause wide enough to cover a breach of the parties' key obligations under the contract.

There is now some doubt that this decision would be followed today, as it conflicts with the fundamental principle of freedom to contract. The English courts have taken a different view, as seen in the following case.

Photo Production v Securicor Transport Ltd (1980)
In this case, the defendant company was hired to provide security for the plaintiff's factory, and the contract excluded liability for acts or omissions of the defendant's employees. One evening, a Securicor employee started a fire that destroyed the plaintiff's factory. The English House of Lords decided that an exemption clause may be wide enough to cover a fundamental breach of contract, so the exemption clause was valid.

The approach in *Photo Production* was approved by the High Court in *Western Meats Ltd v National Ice and Cold Storage Co Ltd* (1982) Ire.

This area is now subject to the EC (Unfair Terms in Consumer Contracts) Regulations 1995. The third schedule to the Act lists unfair terms including inappropriately excluding or limiting liability with respect to total or partial nonperformance of the contract.

Where the exemption clause is deemed to be invalid, the courts use the 'doctrine of severance' to remove the invalid exemption clause from the contract. The remaining terms of the contract are valid. The courts will not enter into redrafting the exemption clause for the parties. The EC (Unfair Terms in Consumer Contracts) Regulations 1995 also provides for this in relation to standard form contracts.

(3) Statutory Regulation of Exemption Clauses

A number of statutes restrict the use of exemption clauses.

Sale of Goods and Supply of Services Act 1980: Under the Sale of Goods and Supply of Services Act 1980, exemption clauses are subject to a statutory test of reasonableness. The core implied terms in sections 12–15 of the Act are there to protect the consumer and, as explained in Chapter 7, cannot be excluded in a consumer sale. However, in a nonconsumer sale, these sections can be excluded if it is 'fair and reasonable' to do so, according to section 22 of the 1980 Act. A schedule to the 1980 Act provides an indication of what is fair and reasonable (see Chapter 7).

Companies Act 1963: Section 200 of the Companies Act 1963 provides that there can be no provision in the articles of association of a company or in a contract excluding the liability of the director, secretary or auditor of a company in respect to negligence, default or breach of duty. In other words, a company cannot have an exemption clause excluding or limiting the liability of its auditor or officers.

European Communities (Unfair Terms in Consumer Contracts) Regulations 1995: The background to the directive on unfair terms in consumer contracts is that the removal of most trade barriers between the Member States of the European Union in 1992 gave the consumer easier access to a wide range of goods and services. However, it is thought that consumers are unlikely to fully utilise the European marketplace unless they are protected from unfair terms in contracts. It was against this background that the European Council of Ministers adopted the Unfair Contract Terms Directive, which was implemented in Ireland by way of statutory instrument in 1995.

The law is now contained in the European Communities (Unfair Terms in Consumer Contracts) Regulations 1995, which were made by the Minister for Enterprise, Trade and Employment. Section 2 defines the key words in the regulations. A 'consumer' is defined as a natural person who is acting for purposes that are outside his or her business; a 'seller' is a person who, acting for purposes related to his or her business, sells goods; and a 'supplier' is a person who, acting for purposes related to his or her business, supplies services.

Section 3 states that the regulations apply to any term in a contract between a seller or supplier and a consumer that has not been individually negotiated. These are sometimes known as 'standard form contracts'. Examples of contracts that have not been individually negotiated are holiday contracts, car leasing contracts and the standard terms for credit cards. It is important to understand that although standard form contracts are important, they only account for a small percentage of contracts, so this legislation does not apply to all contracts.

A term drafted in advance, which the consumer has not been able to influence, shall be regarded as not having been individually negotiated. If one term was individually negotiated, the regulations can still apply to the rest of the contract. It is for the seller or supplier to show that a term was individually negotiated.

Section 3(2) states that a contractual term shall be regarded as unfair if, contrary to the requirements of good faith, it causes a significant imbalance in the parties' rights and obligations under the contract, to the detriment of the consumer. All circumstances and other conditions of the contract must be taken into account in this assessment.

Schedule 2 of the regulations gives the test for deciding good faith. Regard must be had to:

- the strength of the bargaining position of the parties;
- whether the consumer had an inducement to agree to the term;
- whether the goods or services were sold or supplied to the special order of the consumer;
- the extent to which the supplier or seller has dealt fairly and equitably with the consumer whose legitimate interest he or she has to take into account.

Section 4 states that terms shall not be considered unfair if they are in plain intelligible language. This is for the seller or supplier to ensure and is considered to be one of the key provisions in the regulations from a consumer's point of view.

Section 5 states that if there is a doubt over the meaning of a term, the meaning most favourable to the consumer shall be applied. (There is no requirement in the directive about the size of the print to be used in standard form contracts, e.g. it is unclear if microscopic-sized terms are allowed, or if they come within the definition of unfairness in Section 3.)

Section 6 states that an unfair term will not be binding on the consumer. The rest of the contract can be severed and continue to bind the parties if that is possible.

Section 7 states that these regulations apply despite any contract term that attempts to apply the law of a non-Member State's country and to deprive a consumer of the protection under the directive. For example, it would be unfair to provide that Icelandic law applied to a contract formed in Ireland, as this would deprive the consumer of the protection of this EU legislation.

Section 8 provides for the enforcement of the regulation by the Director of Consumer Affairs.

Schedule 1 excludes some contracts and terms from the scope of the regulations, including contracts of employment.

Schedule 3 lists unfair terms in the so-called 'black list', which is not exhaustive:

- excluding legal liability for death or injury;
- inappropriately excluding or limiting liability with respect to total or partial nonperformance of the contract;
- permitting the seller to retain, without compensation, sums paid by the consumer when the seller/supplier decides not to conclude the contract;
- requiring a consumer who fails in his or her obligations to pay a disproportionately high sum in compensation (such as liquidated damages clauses).

CHAPTER 5

The Validity of a Contract

Summary of chapter

In this chapter we look at the types of contracts that can be made and contracts that are valid, void or voidable. In addition, we will consider misrepresentation, which is a defect in a contract that can lead to the remedy of rescission being awarded.

As we have seen in the previous chapter, a contract is a legally enforceable agreement. If there is not a true agreement between the parties, the contract will be said to be 'defective', or invalid.

A. Types of Contracts

Contracts can be classified into three types, according to the result of the contract. Contracts can be valid, void or voidable. It is important to understand the differences among them.

1. Valid Contracts

A 'valid' contract is one that is perfect; i.e. it is complete and regular. A valid contract is legally enforceable. The bulk of contracts are valid contracts.

2. Void Contracts

A 'void' contract is one that has no legal effect, i.e. it is null and void. It is not, in fact, a contract at all because of some defect in the agreement between the parties. An example of a void contract is one that is illegal, such as a contract to supply drugs. Although this contract may appear on its face to be a valid contract because there is offer, acceptance, consideration and legal intent, the courts will not enforce such a contract.

3. Voidable Contracts

A 'voidable' contract is one that is *able to be made void*. It is a middle ground between valid and void contracts and may go either way. A voidable contract is valid when it is made, but the weaker party may be able to avoid, i.e. get out of, the contract. For a contract to be *made void*, the weaker party must choose this course of action. Alternatively, the weaker party can affirm or accept the contract, in which case the contract remains valid. A contract will be voidable if there had been a misrepresentation.

71

B. Misrepresentation

A 'misrepresentation' is a false statement of fact made by A to B that induces B to enter into a contract with A. Misrepresentation is said to be a defect in a contract in that it enables the weaker party to seek to end the contract, or to make it void. The distinction of contractual terms and precontractual representations in Chapter 4 is relevant here, as misrepresentation deals with statements made in negotiations that are not part of the contract. A recent example of misrepresentation is

> *Doran v Delaney and Greene* (1996) Ire
> The plaintiffs bought land from the second defendants. After completion of the sale, the buyers discovered that their plot of land was landlocked. There was no access to it as it was surrounded by land belonging to another person. The buyers argued that the sellers had misrepresented this fact when their solicitor had inquired about disputes with neighbours and threatened litigation. The court held that the defendant sellers had negligently misrepresented the issue of access to the land and the plaintiffs were entitled to damages.

Elements of Misrepresentation

We will now consider the definition of misrepresentation in detail.

1. The Statement Must Be One of Fact

A fact is something that you can prove to be true or false. Certain statements that are not facts include sales talk, law, future intentions and opinion.

Sales Talk: Statements such as 'Carlsberg is probably the best lager in the world' is not a statement of fact because it is not capable of being proven true or false. This is simply sales talk, which is aimed at getting a consumer interested in a product or service.

Law: A statement of law is not treated as a fact. This is because people are assumed to know the law, even though that is an unfair standard. For example, if a buyer is told that there is no exchange on the goods he or she has just purchased, this is untrue, but it is not a misrepresentation because it is an untrue statement in relation to the Sale of Goods Act, and the buyer is assumed to know the law.

Intention: An intention cannot generally be proven true or false. However, if one party makes an untrue statement about a present intention that he or she does not have, this can be treated as a misrepresentation.

> *Edgington v Fitzmaurice* (1885)
> The directors of a company issued a prospectus, inviting the public to buy shares in the company. The directors stated that the company intended to invest the money raised in the company premises and in

expanding the business. This was completely untrue. The directors simply intended to use the money to pay off their existing debts. The court held this to be a misrepresentation. The directors' statement of present intention was treated as a fact.

Opinion: Generally an opinion cannot be said to be a fact because it cannot be proven true or false. However, the opinion of an expert will be treated as a fact.

Bisset v Wilkinson (1927)
The defendant inherited a sheep farm in Australia and sold it to the plaintiff, saying that in his opinion it would hold a certain number of sheep. When this proved incorrect, the court held that it was not a statement of expert opinion because the seller had no experience in sheep farming.

Obviously, if the seller had been selling land that he had farmed, he would be treated as an expert because he would have expert knowledge and experience of the land.

Esso Petroleum Co Ltd v Mardon (1976)
Mardon was considering leasing a new garage from Esso. The company told him that it estimated that he would sell a certain amount of petrol over a three-year period. Mardon questioned this figure and was assured that it was accurate. He took the lease but did not sell the estimated amount of petrol. In an action for misrepresentation, Esso claimed that it had simply stated an opinion and not a fact. The court held that Esso's statement was an expert opinion and therefore a fact. Esso were liable to compensate Mardon for the misrepresentation.

Doheny v Bank of Ireland (1997) Ire
The plaintiff landlord sought a credit reference about a prospective tenant from the defendant bank. The bank gave a positive reference about their client, although they knew that the client had a history of dishonesty. The bank was held liable in misrepresentation.

2. The Statement of Fact Must Be Untrue
There is nothing misleading about stating true facts.

3. There Must Be a 'Statement'
A statement can take any form: oral, written, conduct or a combination of all three. In general, silence cannot constitute a misrepresentation. There must actually be a statement made to the plaintiff.

However, the courts have developed three cases in which silence can constitute a misrepresentation or a misleading statement of fact. These are a contract *uberrimae fides*, a change of circumstance and half-truths.

*A **Contract** Uberrimae Fides:* This means a contract of utmost good faith. Such contracts require full disclosure of all material facts. Failure to disclose all information in such a contract would make the contract voidable. The main example of a contract in utmost good faith is an insurance contract. A party seeking insurance must disclose all relevant information requested, and if he or she does not, the insurance company may validly refuse to honour its side of the contract.

A Change of Circumstances: If A makes a statement to B that is true when made but becomes untrue before the parties entered into the contract, A is under a duty to tell B that the facts have changed. For example, if I enquire in a travel agency about a sun holiday and ask about pollution, the travel agent might truthfully say that there is no pollution on the beach. However, if, by the time I come to book the holiday the following day, the travel agent is aware of an oil spill on the beach, she is under a duty to tell me of the change in facts. If she does not do so, I can claim that there was misrepresentation.

> *With v O'Flanagan* (1836)
> The defendant sold his medical practice to the plaintiff. At the time of the negotiations the practice had a certain value. However, by the time the contract was concluded, the practice had become worthless because the defendant had been ill and lost all his patients. The court held that there had been a misrepresentation because the seller was under a duty to tell the buyer of the change in circumstances.

Half-truths: If a person makes a true statement but leaves out some information, this is a misrepresentation if what is left unsaid would change the effect and meaning of the statement. In the above example about a query in relation to pollution on the beach, if the travel agent replied that she had received no complaints, this is a true statement. However, if she knew that the beach was polluted, that would alter the effect of her statement and make it is misrepresentation.

> *Nottingham Patent Brick and Tile Co v Butler* (1886)
> The prospective purchasers of land asked the seller's solicitor if the land was subject to any restrictive convenants. The solicitor said that he was not aware of any, which was true, but he did not state that he was not aware of any restrictions because he had not read the documents of sale. After buying the land, the purchasers discovered that there were restrictions on uses of the land. The court held that the solicitor had made a misrepresentation because what he had left unsaid altered the effect of what he had said.

4. There Must Be Reliance on Misrepresentation

If an untrue statement of fact is made, it must lead the other party into the contract. The misrepresentation need not be the only reason the other party enters into the contract, but it must be at least one of the reasons.

> *Grafton Court Ltd v Wadson Sales Ltd* (1975) Ire
> The defendant rented the last unit in a small shopping development on Grafton Street. He was told that the centre would be of 'high quality retail type', attracting a high-spending customer. After some months, the defendant sought to get out of the contract. He claimed that, in fact, the retail units in the shopping centre were very ordinary and that he had been misled into entering the contract. The court held that although there was a false statement of fact made to him about the quality of the shop, he had not relied on the statement because all the other shops were let at the time he took his lease, and he could see that they were not of a high retail quality.

Types of Misrepresentation

The distinction among the three types of misrepresentation is important because the remedies available for misrepresentation depend on whether there was a fraudulent, negligent or innocent misrepresentation.

1. Fraudulent Misrepresentation

Fraudulent misrepresentation was defined in the case of *Derry v Peek* (1889) in which one party made a false statement:

- knowing it to be false;
- believing it to be false; or
- behaving recklessly as to whether the statement was true or false.

An example of a fraudulent misrepresentation is the deliberate lie told by the directors in *Edgington v Fitzmaurice* (1885) discussed previously in this chapter.

The remedies for fraudulent misrepresentation allow the misled party to seek recission of the contract and/or claim damages for the loss. A fraudulent misrepresentation is also actionable as the tort of deceit, in which damages are calculated on tort principles rather than on contract principles.

2. Negligent Misrepresentation

A negligent misrepresentation is a statement made believing it to be true but without reasonable grounds for such a belief. An example is the carelessness seen in the *Esso* case discussed previously in this chapter.

A 'special relationship' must exist between the parties, under the principle in *Hedley Byrne & Co v Heller and Partners* (1964), i.e. one party must be able to foresee that the other will rely on his or her statement.

The remedies for fraudulent misrepresentation allow the misled party to seek rescission of the contract and/or claim damages for the loss.

3. Innocent Misrepresentation

An innocent misrepresentation is a statement made believing it to be true with reasonable grounds for so believing. It is a 'genuine mistake'. The remedies for innocent misrepresentation are recission *or* damages at the court's discretion under section 45 of the Sale of Goods and Supply of Services Act 1980. It is a defence for the defendant to prove that he or she had reasonable grounds to believe and did believe up to the time that the contract was made that the facts represented were true.

Exclusion of Liability for Misrepresentation

Section 46 of the Sale of Goods and Supply of Services Act 1980 states that any attempt to exclude liability for misrepresentation must be justified as being reasonable by the person relying on the exclusion. For example, an exemption covering innocent misrepresentation would probably be fair and reasonable.

Rescission

Rescission is a remedy that entitles the innocent party to get out of a contract. The parties are said to return to their precontractual positions. For example, X sells Y a car for €10,000. Some weeks later Y discovers that the car is, in fact, worth less than half that due to defects that X concealed. The perfect remedy for Y would be for her to get her money back and for X to be forced to take the car back. This is how rescission works.

Exercising the right of rescission makes a contract voidable. However, the right to rescind a contract can be lost in some circumstances: delay, harm to an innocent party, impossibility of restitution and affirmation.

1. Delay

If the innocent party waits too long to rescind the contract, the court will refuse the remedy (although damages will still be available if the action is within the limitation period).

2. Innocent Party Has Acquired an Interest

If an innocent person would suffer, the courts will not rescind a contract. For example, if Y bought a building from X and now seeks to have the contract rescinded, the courts would not order this remedy if Y had leased part of the building to another person. This third person would be an innocent party who would suffer by the loss of the lease, so rescission will not be awarded.

3. Restitution is Impossible

When restitution becomes impossible, i.e. if the parties could not return to their precontractual positions, rescission will not be ordered. For example, if a partnership made a contract with Y and that partnership has since incorporated into a company, the court cannot award rescission because it would not order a business to change its legal status.

4. Affirmation

If the nonbreaching party has already affirmed or accepted the contract, the courts will not award rescission.

C. Mistake

Not all mistakes affect the validity of a contract; many are simply one party's own fault for which there is no legal remedy, e.g. buying clothes the wrong colour or size. Before the law will provide a remedy, the mistake must be fundamental, i.e. it must destroy the whole basis of the contract.

It is important to note that the law on mistake is confusing and as a result is not often raised in court.

There are three types of fundamental or 'operative mistakes', i.e. mistakes which operate to make the contract invalid.

1. Common Mistake

This is a mistake which is shared by both parties, they are in complete agreement but are equally mistaken on some fundamental point. Thus the mistake is common to both.

Figure 5.1 Common mistake

A common mistake can be of two types—a common mistake as to the existence of the subject matter or as to the quality of the subject matter.

A common mistake as to the existence of the subject matter occurs where both parties to a contract mistakenly believe that the thing for which they are contracting exists, when in fact it does not. This contract will be void.

> *Galloway v Galloway* (1914)
> A couple who were never validly married entered into a separation agreement. The court held that their separation agreement was void because the couple had made a common mistake about the existence of their marriage. (Of course, they no longer actually needed a separation agreement.)

McRae v Commonwealth Disposals Commissioners (1951)
The plaintiff purchased the salvage rights to the wreck of a boat at a certain location. After spending time, money and effort, the plaintiff discovered that there had never been any shipwreck. The defendants argued that this was a common mistake as to the existence of the subject matter. The court held that this was not a case of common mistake, as the plaintiffs only knew what the defendants told them and thus had not made a mistake. It was held that the defendants had given an implied warranty as to the existence of the ship, and therefore were in breach of contract.

The classic example of a common mistake as to the quality of the subject matter is a painting which both parties believe to be by a certain artist, but which turns out to be a forgery. It is a common mistake about the quality or value of the painting, rather than its existence. The courts will not make such a contract void unless needed in exceptional cases. Two opposite cases illustrate this:

Bell v Lever Bros (1932)
Lever Bros dismissed Bell and paid him a large severance payment. Afterwards, Lever Bros discovered that they could have dismissed Bell for misconduct without any compensation and sought to have the contract for payment declared void for common mistake. The court held that the mistake about the quality (or terms) of the employment contract was not important enough to justify rescission of the contract.

Western Potato Co-op v Durnam (1985) *Ire*
The plaintiff sold seed potatoes to the defendant, which the defendant was to cultivate and resell. Unknown to either party, the seeds were defective and not capable of producing a crop. The court held that the parties contracted under a common false assumption, which went to the root of the contract and made the contract void.

In *O'Neill v Ryan and Others* (1991) Ire, the High Court said 'the circumstances in which a shared common mistake will nullify a contract are extremely limited'.

2. Mutual Mistake

A mutual mistake is where the parties are at cross purposes and neither is aware that the other has a different view of the matter, e.g. X thinks she is buying apartment number 1 in a new block of apartments and the builders, Y, think they are selling apartment number 11.

The courts tend to resolve mutual mistakes in favour of one party or the other, rather than make the contract void. In the apartment example, the seller would be presumed to be correct, as they would know which premises they were selling.

Figure 5.2 Mutual mistake

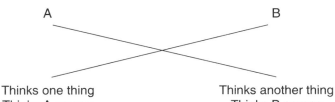

Thinks one thing   Thinks another thing
Thinks A agrees   Thinks B agrees

Tamplin v James (1880)
At the auction of a pub, James was the successful bidder. James believed he had bought the pub and the adjoining field. The sale particulars clearly stated that only the pub was for sale, but James did not inspect these. When he discovered his mistake, James refused to proceed with the purchase. The court held that the sale particulars were clear and James's mistake did not invalidate the contract. There was no mutual mistake.

If the courts cannot decide who is correct they will declare the contract void. This gives the parties the option to start again if they wish.

Raffles v Winchelaus (1864)
In London, X agreed to buy from Y a cargo of cotton to arrive 'ex Peerless from Bombay'. Unfortunately, there were two ships called 'Peerless' in Bombay with the same cargo, at the same time. Y thought the contract referred to the ship sailing in October and X thought the contract referred to the December sailing. The court held that they had no choice but to declare the contract void, as they could not decide in favour of either party.

Clayton Love v B&I Transport Ire (1970)
Clayton Love contracted with B&I for the transport of frozen scampi to England and intended the scampi to be loaded at frozen temperatures. The scampi defrosted after being loaded at atmospheric temperatures and had to be destroyed. B&I claimed both parties intended the scampi to be loaded at atmospheric temperatures. The Court held that the parties were not equally mistaken and that B&I had failed to comply with the requirement of frozen loading.

3. Unilateral Mistake

A unilateral mistake arises where only one party has made a mistake. Usually, the other party is aware of the mistake and may even have induced or led the mistaken party into it.

These are usually mistakes of identity. The courts have developed a very artificial distinction here. If the parties have contracted face to face, it is assumed that the mistaken party intended to contract with the party in front of him (regardless of anything he may have said about being rich or famous). This contract will be voidable if the mistaken party acts in time, before a resale takes place.

If the parties are not face to face, if for example they contract by letter, the courts assume that the mistaken party intends only to contract with the named party. These contracts will be void for mistake.

Figure 5.3   Unilateral mistake

• Face to face contracts – identity of buyer *not* crucial.

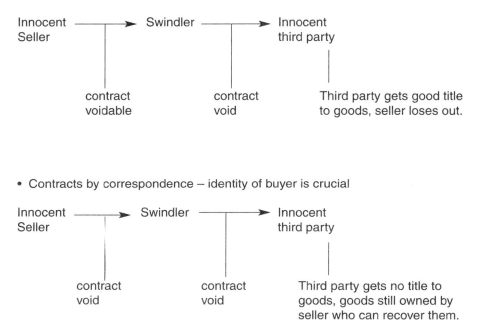

• Contracts by correspondence – identity of buyer is crucial

Face to Face Contracts

Philips v Brooks (1919)
A swindler purchased two thousand pounds worth of jewellery from the plaintiff and sought to pay by cheque. He gave his name as Mr Bullough and the sales assistant checked the address given in a directory. 'Mr Bullough' gave a forged cheque in return for a ring, which he then resold to the defendant, an innocent third party. The seller sought to recover the goods from the third party. The court had to decide whether the sales assistant had intended to contract with Mr Bullough only, or simply with the person in front of him in the shop. The court held that the assistant intended to deal with the person in front of him and thus identity was not important to the contract.

Lewis v Avery (1972)
A swindler bought a second hand car by pretending to be the actor 'Richard Green' star of the TV series 'Robin Hood'. The seller of the car

had been seeking cash but took a cheque from the actor and accepted a false Pinewood Studios pass as identification. The cheque bounced and the car turned out to have been resold to the defendant, an innocent third party. The seller sought to recover the car.

The court held that the seller had intended to deal with the person in front of him and not the actor. This is not logical on the facts, because the seller only accepted the cheque because he thought the actor was creditworthy. As in the case above, the contract was voidable and the innocent third party got good legal ownership of the car.

Contracts by Correspondence

However, if the parties do not make the contract face to face, the contract will be void, which means that an innocent third party who later buys the goods will not get good legal title to them.

> *Cundy v Lindsay* (1878)
> A swindler called Blenkarn of Wood Street ordered goods from the defendants and signed his name to look like 'Blenkiron & Co' a well known firm on Wood Street. The goods were sent on credit and resold to an innocent third party. The court held that the sellers intended to sell only to the well known firm, as they would not have accepted a postal order from an unfamiliar client. As a result the contract between the seller and swindler was void. The seller was, therefore, able to recover the goods from the innocent third party.

The outcome of Cundy is satisfactory in the circumstances, but surely the same logic should have been applied in *Philips v Brooks* and *Lewis v Avery*.

In all these cases, there are three parties: the swindler, the innocent seller and the innocent third party who rebuys the goods. Either the seller or the third party must lose out. In face to face cases the seller will lose out (as in *Lewis v Avery*) and in cases by correspondence the third party will lose (see *Cundy v Lindsay*). Obviously, the losing party has the technical option of suing the swindler for his losses, but this is not often done in practice.

4. Non Est Factum

This means 'it is not my deed', and it is an equitable relief which can be made in particular cases of mistake. If a person signs a deed or document, mistakenly believing that it was another type of document, they can claim that it was not their deed.

This relief was originally limited to people who were blind or illiterate and thus could not understand the nature of the deed they signed. It has now been expanded to all persons who sign documents which are different to what they expected, and there is no negligence on the part of the signer. It is important to note they must be mistaken about the type of document they signed, rather than just its contents.

5. Mistake in Executing a Contract

If the parties make a slip or typo in drawing up a contract after it has been agreed, the courts will simply allow the document to be rectified to reflect what the parties originally agreed.

> *Nolan v Graves & Hamilton* (1946) Ire
> The plaintiff bought a row of houses at auction for £5,500. The auctioneer mistakenly wrote the price up as £4,500. The court held that the plaintiff could not buy at the lower price, and the contract was rectified to fix the mistake.

Remedies for Mistake

The remedies for mistake are damages and/or rescission, or the remedy of rectification as is appropriate (see Chapter 6). In addition, sometimes the courts give an equitable compromise as a remedy for mistake.

Misrepresentation versus Mistake

A difficult case highlighting the overlap between mistake and misrepresentation is:

> *Leaf v International Galleries* (1950)
> The plaintiff bought a painting from the defendants, which both parties believed to be a Constable. After five years, the plaintiff discovered that it was not painted by Constable. The court held that too much time had passed to claim innocent misrepresentation in order to rescind the contract. The court stated that the correct remedy was an action for breach of warranty.

An alternative action in such a case would be a sale of goods action, although this is unlikely to be sucessful either.

> *Harlingdon and Leinster Enterprises v Christopher Hull Fine Art Ltd* (1990)
> The defendant sold an 'original' painting by Munter to the plaintiff for £6,000. The painting was later discovered to be a cheap copy worth only £100. The court held that the copy was not unmerchantable under section 14 of the Sale of Goods Act 1980 because it could still be enjoyed as a painting. It was not a sale by description because the description had to be so essential that it had become part of the contract.

D. Illegality

Certain contracts are illegal. They may be prohibited by statute such as certain types of gaming and wagering contracts. More commonly, illegal contracts may be contrary to public policy, e.g. contracts to defraud the revenue, or contracts of sexual immorality. Contracts may be illegal from the outset, such as a contract to sell drugs; or may appear to be legal but are performed in an illegal manner, e.g. a contract to supply goods which are in fact stolen.

Restraint of Trade Clauses

A clause in a contract restricting someone's free exercise of his trade or profession is a restraint of trade clause. These clauses are prima facie (on the face of it) void due to illegality. However, if such clauses can be shown to be reasonable in the interest of both parties and in the interest of the public at large, they will be valid.

The courts' attitude to restraint of trade clauses is similar to that of exemption clauses: the courts distrust restraint of trade clauses and presume them to be invalid unless they can satisfy a number of tests and will sever the invalid clause from the rest of the contract.

There are two main types of restraint of trade clauses:

Restraints on employees: a clause in an employment contract stating that when the employee leaves his or her employment, he or she cannot carry out the same type of work within a certain radius for a certain period of time. These are usually not valid.

Restraints on vendors of businesses: a clause stating that a seller cannot compete with the buyer of the business in the same type of business for certain period of time. These clauses may be valid.

A valid restraint of trade clause must satisfy three tests:

(1) Is it reasonable between the parties?

> *Skerry's College (Ireland) Ltd v Moles* (1907)
> The defendant was a shorthand teacher in Belfast. A clause in his employment contract restricted him from teaching shorthand within seven miles of Dublin, Cork or Belfast. The court held that this was not reasonable between the parties, as Moles had only worked in Belfast.

(2) Does it protect a legitimate interest of the party imposing it?

In *Skerry's College* the plaintiffs had no legitimate interest to protect in Cork or Dublin. The classic example of a legitimate interest is a secret formulae which an employer has developed.

> *House of Spring Garden Ltd v Point Blank Ltd* (1985)
> The defendant sold the plaintiffs bullet proof vests under a licensing agreement. The defendant then manufactured his own vest which breached the plaintiffs' copyright and a restraint of trade in the licensing agreement. The court held that the confidential copyrighted information was a legitimate interest which the plaintiffs could validly protect.

However, an employee's skill belongs to the employee, and the employer has no legitimate interest in it, despite having financed the development of that skill. By this standard, the restraint in *Skerry's College* relating to the defendant teaching in Belfast would not be valid today. Equally, in the sale of a business with goodwill attached, the goodwill is a legitimate interest which can be protected by stopping the seller competing in the same type of business in the short term.

(3) Is it reasonable from the community point of view?

> *Eddie Macken v O'Reilly* (1978) Ire
> The plaintiff objected to a rule of the Equestrian Federation of Ireland which required Irish competitors at international show jumping events to use only Irish bred horses. The Court held that such a restriction was reasonable from the community point of view because of the jobs in the horse breeding industry which depended on this rule. (This decision would not be made today because it is contrary to the concept of free competition under EU law).

Severance: The courts will sever an offending restraint of trade clause from a contract, leaving the rest intact. Occasionally, the courts will redraw a restraint, as in *Skerry's College*, where reference to Dublin and Cork was removed, leaving just Belfast.

The Competition Act 1991 has had a serious impact on restraints of trade, as they are now viewed as uncompetitive and are rarely upheld except in the case of vendors of businesses.

E. Capacity

Certain categories of people have a limited capacity to enter contracts. People under eighteen are minors or 'infants' according to the Age of Majority Act 1985. Minors can make three types of contract: good, bad and good until challenged, i.e. valid, void and voidable.

1. Valid Contracts

Valid contracts bind both parties. The presumption is that contracts made by a minor are not valid unless they are for necessary items, or employment.

Necessary items are defined by section 2, Sale of Goods Act 1893 as items suitable to the minor's 'condition in life'. Case law defines necessities as basic requirements of life, such as food, clothes, rent, medical services, educational fees and hire of a car. Examples of non-necessary items are expensive jewellery, furs or sports cars. The issue of whether items are necessary arises when goods or services have been supplied to a minor on credit. The minor cannot be compelled to pay if the supplies are not necessary. As a result, goods or services are rarely supplied on credit to under-eighteens, and this area is of little importance in practice.

Contracts of employment or apprenticeship, e.g. a training contract, a part-time job, are also valid contracts. These contracts must be in the minor's best interests, to avoid exploitation.

2. Voidable Contracts

Voidable contracts are those which the minor is able to avoid or get out of, either before he reaches eighteen or within a reasonable time thereafter. However, the minor can always enforce the contract against the other party.

Voidable contracts include:

(1) the renting of property;

(2) buying company shares;

(3) entering into partnership;

(4) insurance contracts;

(5) family settlements.

These are all contracts of a continuing nature, which is why the minor must act to make the contract void if he or she wishes. As a result of this law, people under eighteen are usually restricted from entering into such contracts

3. Void Contract

Under the Infants Relief Act 1874 a loan to a minor is invalid. A contract entered into when the minor is over eighteen, whereby he or she ratifies a loan contract made while under eighteen, is also invalid. As a result, lending institutions do not lend money to people under eighteen.

The law on minors' contractual capacity has little practical relevance today as business practice has restricted under eighteens from making certain types of contracts, as explained above.

F. Duress

Putting a contractual party under duress involves threatening him in order to make him enter into a contract. The threatened party cannot make a real consent to the contract as his or her will is overborne. Previously duress was limited to threats of physical violence, but duress can now include economic duress, i.e. a threat to a person's livelihood.

The Atlantic Baron (1979)
When sterling was devalued, shipbuilders who were building a new ferry for a ferry company demanded an extra ten per cent of the negotiated price by threatening to break the contract. The ferry company paid the additional price, in order to have the ferry delivered on time. They later sought to recover the additional money in court. The court held that

the ferry company was entitled to recover the money as it has been put under economic duress.

There is an overlap between the issues of economic duress and the rule in *Pinnel's Case* (see page 50). However, the rule in *Pinnel's Case* is now subject to the English decision of *Williams v Roffey Bros & Nicholls (Contractors) Ltd* (1990) (see page 50).

Duress is an equitable remedy. The contract is voidable at the option of the party under duress. The right to rescind can be lost as explained above in relation to misrepresentation.

G. Undue Influence

Undue influence may occur where the parties are in certain relationships in which the law assumes that one has power over the other, and they make a contract which is to the 'manifest disadvantage' of the weaker party. In such cases, there is a presumption of undue influence which the stronger party must rebut or disprove. A classic example of undue influence occurs where an adult child gradually emotionally pressurises an elderly parent into conveying the parent's house to the child. If the parent is then evicted, he or she is at a manifest disadvantage and can seek to have the contract set aside on the grounds of undue influence.

Examples of relationships where the presumption of undue influence arises are: parent and child, child and elderly parent or relative, religious advisor and devotee, doctor and patient. The presumption of undue influence is rebutted where the stronger party shows that he or she advised the weaker party to seek independent legal advice. If the presumption is not rebutted, the contract is voidable at the option of the weaker part. Undue influence is also an equitable concept.

The difference between duress and undue influence is that duress is a clear threat, whereas undue influence is a gradual wearing down of someone's ability to contract clearly and rationally. It is important to note that duress and undue influence can apply to gifts as well as contracts.

CHAPTER 6

The Discharge of a Contract and Remedies for Breach

Summary of chapter

In this chapter we deal with the process of ending a contract, which is known as 'discharge'. A contract can be discharged in four different ways. If a contract is discharged by a breach occurring, the innocent party is entitled to a remedy for breach of contract. The most commonly sought remedy is damages, but there are also the remedies of specific performance, injunction, rectification and rescission.

A. Discharge of a Contract

To discharge a contract simply means to bring the contract to an end. A contract may be discharged or ended in four ways:

(1) by performance;
(2) by agreement;
(3) by breach;
(4) by frustration.

Discharge by Performance

Discharge by performance is the most common way contracts end, i.e. when both parties have performed their obligations. If, for example, a painter agrees to paint a house for you, then upon completion of the job and payment, the contract has ended by performance.

The law requires that performance be *exact* and *complete*, 'exact' meaning that it has been performed as specified, and 'complete' meaning that every part of the contract has been fully performed. The courts take the view that as the contract was freely negotiated between the parties, the parties should comply with all the contract details. Therefore, parties should not agree to terms with which they are not prepared to comply. For example, in a contract to deliver one hundred red rose bushes to a garden center, it is not sufficient to deliver eighty pink rose bushes. The incorrect amount means that delivery is not complete and the colour is not exact.

We will now consider the two issues of exact and complete performance separately.

1. Exact Performance

If performance is not exactly as agreed, this gives the injured party the right to end the contract and sue for damages and/or rescission. The following case is a graphic example of this.

> *Moore & Co v Landauer & Co (1921)*
> A seller contracted to deliver 3,100 tins of pineapples to a buyer, packed in cases containing thirty tins. On delivery, the buyer received the correct overall number of tins, but some cases contained only twenty-four tins. The buyer did not suffer any loss as a result of the incorrect packaging, as the goods would be unpacked before sale, but the buyer sought to reject the goods on the grounds that they did not comply exactly with the contract. The court held the contract had not been discharged by exact performance and that the goods did not comply with the contract description under section 13 of the Sale of Goods Act 1893 (see Chapter 7).

2. Complete Performance

To require one party to completely perform his or her obligations under the contract is the basic legal standard for complete performance, and failure to complete will be treated as breach of contract. However, in some circumstances this can be a very difficult requirement with which to comply. For example, if X contracts to tile forty bathrooms in a new apartment block, and on bathroom number thirty-seven X runs out of the specified tile, it would seem very harsh if she could not receive any payment on the grounds that she failed to complete the contract. Because of situations like this, the courts have developed a number of exceptions to the rule requiring complete performance.

The Doctrine of Substantial Performance: This doctrine states that if the bulk of the work has been done, then the bulk of the price must be paid. The doctrine was developed to cover building contracts, such as the example above in which the requirement of complete performance would work unjustly on the parties. 'Substantial' performance means that the essential work has been completed, and the incomplete part is only a small percentage of the contract.

> *Hoenig v Isaacs (1952)*
> The defendant contracted to decorate the plaintiff's flat for £750 but failed to finish the work. At that stage the plaintiff had paid £400 and refused to pay the balance. The cost of finishing the work was £55. The court held that the decorator was entitled to the full contract price minus £55 because the failure to complete was insignificant.

> *Kincora Builders v Cronin (1973) Ire*
> In a building contract, a builder failed to insulate an attic as specified. The court held that this was equivalent to abandoning the contract, and thus the builder failed to prove substantial performance.

Divisible Contracts: If the contract is divisible into parts, payment for each part must be made upon performance. Alternatively, if payment for the contract is to be in a lump sum upon completion, then no money is payable if the contract is not completed. In building contracts, it is common to provide for payment at certain stages prior to completion, making such contracts divisible. An old case illustrate this very well.

> *Cutter v Powell* (1795)
> A sailor was hired for a voyage and was to be paid in a lump sum upon arrival in Liverpool. The sailor died during the voyage, and his wife claimed on a *quantum meruit* basis for the period he had worked, under an exception to privity of contract. The court held that because he had failed to finish the voyage, he was not entitled to any payment.

By contrast, if the sailor's contract had provided that he was to be paid by the month, that would be a divisible contract, and his wife would have been entitled to any wages outstanding at his death.

One Party Prevents Performance: If one party prevents the complete performance of the contract, the other party will be entitled to seek payment for the contract, either on a *quantum meruit* basis or for the full contract amount. For example, if you refuse X entry to your house when you have hired her to paint it, you cannot argue that she failed to complete the contract.

One Party Accepts Part Performance: If one party prevents the complete performance of the contract, the other party may accept partial performance. In effect, a new contract has replaced the old one. For example, I contracted to deliver one hundred rose bushes to you, but I deliver only seventy, which you accept. This is, however, subject to the rules on discharge by agreement, as discussed below.

3. Time of Performance

One final important point on performance is that the time of performance may be important. Time of performance is not generally 'of the essence' in a contract, i.e. time is not generally seen as a key issue in the contract. However, time is usually of the essence in commercial contracts. If the contract provides for the opposite, time will be treated as of the essence. The importance of time is illustrated in the following case.

> *Sepia Ltd and Opal Ltd v M & P Hanlon Ltd and Another* (1979) Ire
> The defendant agreed to sell two plots of land. In one contract there was a stipulated closing date making time of the essence, subject to the plaintiff's obtaining planning permission. The planning permission was not granted. The court held that the contract was discharged. The contract for the other plot of land, which was not subject to the planning permission requirement, was not discharged.

Figure 6.1 Discharge of a contract by agreement followed by a replacement contract

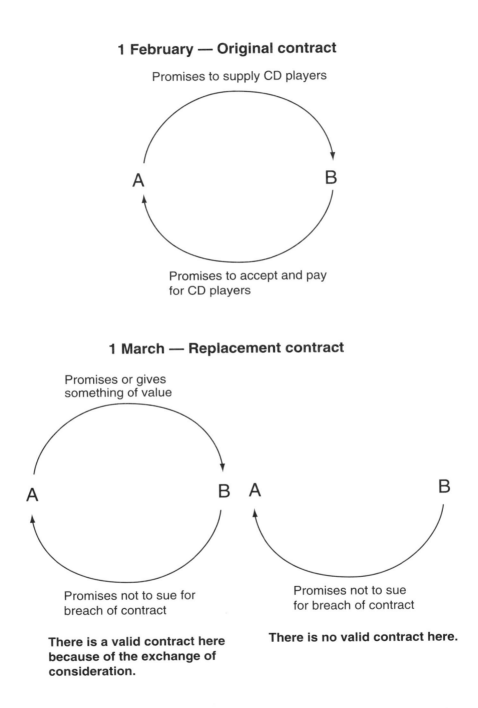

1 February — Original contract

Promises to supply CD players

A   B

Promises to accept and pay
for CD players

1 March — Replacement contract

Promises or gives
something of value

A   B   A   B

Promises not to sue for
breach of contract

Promises not to sue
for breach of contract

**There is a valid contract here
because of the exchange of
consideration.**

There is no valid contract here.

Discharge by Agreement

If, as in the above example about the roses, one party can only supply a lesser amount of goods than specified in the contract, the other party may choose to treat the contact as discharged by breach. However, in business situations, the parties are often keen to maintain good business relations, so they may often choose to end the contract by agreement instead (or agree to a replacement contract).

For example, A made a contract on 1 February to supply B with Sony CD players. On 1 March, A realises she will be unable to honour the contract. B may choose to sue A but may also agree that he will not sue her, i.e. he will end the contract by agreement. However, if B promises not to sue A, B may change his mind, as a promise is not legally enforceable. A should ensure that B's promise takes the form of a contract, in any of the ways outlined below. The essential thing to grasp here is that to end one contract you need a second separate contract, for which new consideration must be given, as shown in Figure 6.1.

There are four methods of ending a contract by agreement: waiver, novation, accord and satisfaction and contractually specified termination.

1. Waiver

A 'waiver' occurs when one party dispenses with, or intentionally gives up, his or her strict legal rights to enforce the contract. Such a promise has no consideration and will not be legally binding. However, to make such a promise legally binding, it can be put in a deed under seal, in which case the promise is binding despite the absence of consideration. Alternatively, the promise of a waiver may be enforceable if the doctrine of promissory estoppel applies.

2. Novation

A 'novation' occurs when a new contract replaces an old one on the agreement of the parties. An old contract between A and B may be replaced with a new one between the same parties or replaced with a new contract between one of the old parties and a new party. If, for example, A cannot supply Sony CD players to B, B may agree to accept JVC CD players instead. This ends the old contract and replaces it with a new contract between the same parties. Alternatively, B may agree to accept Sony CD players from C, a colleague of A's, in which case there is a new contract between one old party and one new party.

Figure 6.2   Discharge of a contract by a replacement contract of novation

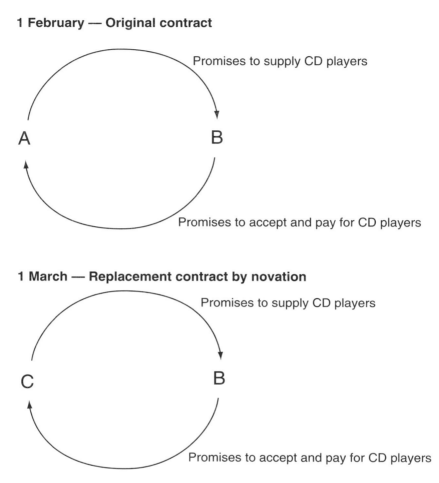

1 February — Original contract

A   B

Promises to supply CD players

Promises to accept and pay for CD players

1 March — Replacement contract by novation

C   B

Promises to supply CD players

Promises to accept and pay for CD players

3. Accord and Satisfaction

A contract may be discharged by an agreement, or 'accord', between the parties that is supported by consideration, or 'satisfaction'. This is really a discharge of a contract by mutual agreement of the parties. The consideration may be executory or executed. For example, B may promise not to sue A for breach on this occasion if A promises to give B a discount on his next order. There is an exchange of promises here, which makes this a valid contract.

4. A Contract May Provide for Its Termination by Its Terms

A contract that provides for its own termination is slightly different from the previous two categories because there is no new contract here to replace the old one. An example of a contract that provides for its own termination is an employment contract stating that either party can terminate the contract by notice. Another example is a lease of a building, which usually provides that either party can terminate the contract by giving the requisite notice to the other party. This is sometimes known as 'discharge by condition subsequent', i.e. discharge based on a condition that is known to both parties and may subsequently arise.

Discharge by Breach

Although a discharge by breach is the example of discharge with which you might be most familiar, remember that only a small percentage of contracts end by breach. It is important to remember that breach of contract gives the innocent party the *right* to terminate the contract (rescission) and sue for damages, or he or she may decide to continue with the contract and just seek damages. (The breach of contract itself does not end the contract; that is for the innocent party to do.)

We have already seen that breach may be failure to comply with a condition, which gives the innocent party the right to end the contract and seek damages; failure to comply with a warranty, which only gives the innocent party the right to sue for damages; or described as being fundamental, i.e. a serious breach going to the root of the contract. In addition to these, there are other specific types of breaches with which you should be familiar. These are: anticipatory breach and repudiatory breach.

1. Anticipatory Breach

An anticipatory breach involves one party showing, before starting performance of the contract, by words or actions that he or she does not intend to fulfill the contractual obligations. The party effectively looks into the future and anticipates that he or she will not fulfill the contract. The innocent party can choose the time at which to sue for breach of contract: the date the party was told of the anticipatory breach, the date of performance of the contract or at any time within the statute of limitations. The following case is the leading one in this area.

> *Hochster v De La Tour* (1853)
> On 2 April the defendant hired the plaintiff to act as a courier/ companion on a European tour that the defendant was undertaking on 1 June. On 11 May the defendant informed the plaintiff that his services were no longer needed as the defendant was not taking the trip. The plaintiff sued for breach of contract, and the defendant argued he could change his mind about the contract up to the date of performance, which was 1 June. The court held that the contract had been breached on 11 May, and the plaintiff could sue from that date.

2. Repudiatory Breach

A repudiatory breach of contract occurs when one party makes it clear that he or she does not intend to complete the contract. The difference between this and anticipatory breach is that in this case, performance of the contract has actually *started* when one party breaches it. The breaching party is repudiating or rejecting his or her obligations under the contract.

> *Athlone Rural District Council v AG Campbell & Son (No 2)* (1912) Ire
> The defendant contractors agreed to excavate a well for the Athlone Council. Half-way through the work, the Council said it did not want the work finished. This was held to be a repudiatory breach of contract. The contractors were entitled to damages for breach of contract or to sue on a *quantum meruit* basis.

Breach of contract can also arise during the performance of a contract, when one party fails to perform to the contract as agreed, for example, in *Clayton Love v B&I Transport* (1970) in which the frozen scampi was allowed to defrost during the voyage.

Thus a contract can be breached before the date of performance and during its performance. However, in many cases, the breach will not become apparent until after the completion of the contract, for example, a computer system that develops defects six months after installation.

Discharge by Frustration

Discharge of contract by frustration is also known as discharge by operation of law or discharge by subsequent impossibility.

A contract is said to be 'frustrated' when it becomes impossible to perform due to an intervening event that was not the fault of either party. This is a common-sense, common-law doctrine that modifies the old hard-line position that there were no acceptable excuses for non-performance of a contract. In this area it is important to be able to identify examples of frustration, recognise what is non-peformance and explain the effects a frustrating event has on a contract. The doctrine originated in the following case.

> *Taylor v Caldwell* (1863)
> In this case the defendant contracted to hire a music hall to the plaintiff. Prior to the first day of hiring, the hall burnt down accidentally, through no fault of either party. The plaintiff sought to recover the advertising expenses. The court held that the contract had ended. The defendant was not responsible for failing to provide the hall, and the plaintiff was not responsible to provide the hire price.

Frustration of contract is relatively rare and does not always fall into neat catagories.

Note: Although for exam purposes it can be helpful to use categories, remember, however, that new categories can be created by case law once the contract is impossible to perform.

1. Frustrating Events

Nonoccurrence of an Event upon Which the Contract Is Dependent: Suppose you booked a holiday to attend a sports event, such as the Olympics. If the Olympics were to be cancelled, your contract would be frustrated as it would be impossible to perform. However, if attending the Olympics was not the sole purpose of your holiday, then the contract may be able to go ahead in a modified form.

A series of cases known as the 'Coronation cases' gives us these principles. The facts of these cases revolve around contracts made in relation to the coronation of King Edward VII. The coronation was cancelled when the King became ill, leading to the frustration of the contracts that were made for the sole purpose of celebrating the coronation.

> *Krell v Henry* (1903)
> The defendant paid a deposit to hire the plaintiff's flat for the purpose of viewing the coronation procession passing below. When the coronation was cancelled, the plaintiff sued for the rest of the hire price. The court held that the contract was frustrated as its sole purpose could not take place.

> *Herne Bay Steam Boat Co v Hutton* (1903)
> The defendant hired a boat for two days to view the coronation naval review by the King and to sail around the boats. The defendant sought to get out of the contract on hearing of the King's illness. The court held that the sole purpose was not to view the King's review but also to view the assembled boats, and thus the contract was not impossible to perform.

Contracts of Employment and Personal Services: Any contract that requires personal service, such as employment and apprenticeship contracts, can be frustrated if the party providing the service becomes unable to perform it through some personal incapacity. The most common example would be illness.

> *Flynn v Great Northern Railway Co* (1953)
> The employment contract of a van driver was held to be frustrated when medical evidence proved that he would never be able to return to his job.

> *Mulvaney v Riversdale Concrete Products Ltd* (1981) Ire
> The plaintiff had been unfit for work for seven years when his employers went into liquidation. The court held that his contract of employment had been frustrated prior to the liquidation, so no redundancy money was payable to Mulvaney.

Other examples of frustrating events would be conscription into the army, being taken hostage or being a prisoner of war. Being sentenced to jail or a detention centre is a frustrating event despite the argument that it is not beyond the control of both parties.

Illegality: When a change in the law has made the contract illegal, it may be said to be frustrated. For example, if yesterday Q made a contract to sell an agricultural growth hormone to R and today legislation is passed making the sale of such hormones illegal, the contract would be impossible to perform through no fault of either party.

> *Ross v Shaw* (1917)
> An English company had made a contract with a Belgian firm. Belgium was subsequently invaded by Germany, which made the contract illegal as it would have constituted trading with the enemy. The contract was frustrated.

> *Fibrosa Spolko Akcyjnia v Fairbairn Lawson Combe Barbour Ltd* (1943)
> A British firm made a contract to make and deliver machinery to Poland. After the German invasion of Poland, the contract was held to be frustrated as it would have constituted trading with the enemy.

Government Intervention: The above example of banning agricultural growth hormones could also be described as frustration by government intervention.

> *Re Shipton Anderson & Co* (1915)
> This case occurred during the First World War, when the British government requisitioned supplies of wheat that had already been sold. The court held that the contract of sale was frustrated.

2. Nonfrustrating Events

A frustrating event must make it *impossible* to perform the contract. Therefore, it is not frustration if the contract can still be performed, regardless of whether it is now more expensive or more difficult to perform. These things are deemed by the courts to be the vagaries of business and are not sufficient to set aside a contract. Think, for example, of those Irish firms exporting largely to Britain that suffer financially due to currency fluctuations. They cannot argue that this makes their contracts impossible to perform; it must simply be accepted as the swings and roundabouts of business.

Greater Expense: The following are examples of cases of nonfrustrating events.

> *Davis Contractors Ltd v Fareham Urban District Council* (1956)
> The plaintiff contractors agreed to build a set of houses for £94,000, which they anticipated would take eight months. The contractors

encountered various difficulties with shortages of materials and workers, with the result that the job took twenty-two months to complete and cost them £115,000. The plaintiff argued that the difficulties had frustrated the contract, hoping to claim for the twenty-two months' work on a *quantum meruit* basis, which would be more lucrative. The House of Lords held that the contract was not frustrated, as it was clearly still performable.

Sullivan v Southern Health Board (1993) Ire

The plaintiff consultant, who was employed by the Health Board, sued for breach of contract, arguing that the defendant had failed to provide him with adequate resources that were necessary for him to perform his work. The defendant counterargued that the contract with the plaintiff was frustrated because the Minister for Health had failed to provide adequate funds. The court held that this was not a case of frustration as the legal basis of the contract remained the same, and the SHB was in breach of contract.

More Difficult to Perform: The *Davis Contractors Ltd v Fareham Urban District Council* (1956) case above is also a useful example of a situation in which a contract becomes more difficult to perform, but this cannot be said to be frustration.

Tsakiroglou & Co v Noblee and Thorl (1961)

One party agreed to purchase a consignment of goods that was to be shipped from Port Sudan to Hamburg, and freight charges were based on the normal route through the Suez Canal. However, the Canal was closed, and the alternative route around the Cape of Good Hope would have doubled the shipping costs for the seller and have taken much longer. The seller sought to be released from the contract on the grounds that it was frustrated. The court held that the greater expense and delay did not make the contract impossible to perform.

Self-induced Frustration: As has been clearly shown in the cases above, the frustrating event must be beyond the control of either party. One party cannot choose a course of action that leads to the frustration and then claim afterwards that it was frustration. In such a case the contract would have been performable had the party chosen a different course of action.

Maritime National Fish Ltd v Ocean Trawlers Ltd (1935)

The defendant trawling company trawled for otters on an annual basis. This activity required a licence from the Canadian Minister for Fisheries. The defendant hired a trawler from the plaintiff, to use with its own fleet of four boats. However, when it applied for five licences, it only received three. The defendant then argued that the contract to hire the plaintiff's trawler was frustrated because it would have been illegal to use it for otter trawling without a licence. The court held that the contract was not frustrated, as the defendant had chosen not to allocate the licence to the hired boat. (It was not the action of the Minister for Fisheries but the action of the defendant that led to the end of the contract.)

Where One Party Accepts the Risk of Nonperformance: If one party has acknowledged that the contract may not be performed and has accepted this risk, that party cannot later claim that the contract was frustrated.

McGuill v Aer Lingus Teoranta and United Airlines Incorporated (1983)
The plaintiffs booked a holiday with United Airlines. United Airlines had been served strike notice at that time but accepted the booking anyway. The strike took place, and the plaintiffs had to travel with a different airline, which resulted in more expense and a shorter holiday. United Airlines argued that the strike was an event beyond its control that frustrated the contact. The court held that the airline took a calculated risk in accepting the booking, and thus the contract could not be said to be frustrated. The judge did not rule on whether a strike could be a frustrating event in other circumstances.

Browne v Mulligan, Gallagher and Others (1977) Ire
The plaintiff was hired as a doctor by the defendant trustees of a hospital. The appointment was stated to be dependant on sufficient funds being available for the hospital. The hospital closed due to financial difficulties, and when the plaintiff sought compensation, the defendant argued that the contract was frustrated. The Supreme Court held that a frustrating event must be unanticipated by the parties and so not mentioned in the contract.

3. Effects of Frustration

When frustration has been established, the common law provides that the contract is at an end and neither party is liable to perform obligations that arise after the date of frustration, as in *Taylor v Caldwell* (1863). The loss is said to lie where it falls. This can be very harsh; for example, any money paid before the frustrating event cannot be recovered.

The only exception to this in which money paid before a frustrating event can be recovered is if nothing has been received in return, i.e. there has been a total failure of consideration.

Fibrosa Spolko Akcyjnia v Fairbairn Lawson Combe Barbour Ltd (1943)
One party ordered machinery to be made to order by a British company and delivered to Poland. The company paid a deposit of £1,000 with the order. Shortly before the delivery date, Germany invaded Poland and the contract was frustrated. The company that had ordered the machinery was entitled to recover its deposit. As it had received nothing in return for it, there was a total failure of

consideration. (Note however, that the company that had almost completed the manufacture of the machinery received nothing for its work, showing that this area of law is still not absolutely fair.)

B. Remedies for Breach of Contract

When a contract is breached, the innocent party has the right to sue for breach of contract and a number of other remedies that are available to him or her. By way of background, it should be explained that there are two historical systems of law: common law and equity. Common law was the system of law that operated on a case-by-case basis, which still operates in Ireland today. By contrast, equity was a system of rules based on fairness and getting an equitable result in a case. Equity was said to fill in the gaps in common law, when common law would result in an unfair decision. Equity is no longer a separate system of laws, but the effects of the old system can be seen in things like the equitable doctrine of promissory estoppel and, most importantly, the equitable remedies for breach of contract.

In most cases the remedy sought is damages, but there are also a number of other remedies available to suit specific circumstances. These are the remedies of rescission, rectification, specific performance and injunctions, all of which can be traced to the development of equity. A plaintiff can seek one of these equitable remedies *as well as* damages in appropriate cases.

Damages

An award of damages was the only remedy available at common law and so is said to be the common-law remedy. Damages, or compensation, is still the most commonly sought remedy today. As the two names for this remedy suggest, the aim is to compensate the innocent party for the damages suffered.

It is important to grasp that compensation is meant to put the innocent party in the same position as if the contract had gone ahead rather than to punish the party who breached the contract. For example, if a seller breaches a contract to supply a buyer with Christmas trees at the appropriate time of the year, the seller will have to compensate the buyer with the amount of money that the buyer would have made on the sale of the trees. This puts the buyer in the position he or she would have been in if the contract had gone ahead.

Damages are not meant to be punitive or to deliberately punish the breaching party. However, there is *obiter dicta* to suggest that the courts will prohibit someone who breaches a contract from retaining the profits resulting from that breach. This is made clear in the following case.

Hickey & Co Ltd v Roches Stores (Dublin) Ltd (No. 1) (1976) Ire
The plaintiff had a contract with Roches Stores that allowed the company to sell its fabric in the defendant's shop. Roches Stores broke

the contract because it had calculated that it would be more profitable to sell the fabric itself, even after paying compensation to Hickey. The court stated *obiter dictum* that in such a case the damages should be increased to deprive the breaching party of its profit.

The amount of damages to be awarded in any case depends on two issues: the remoteness of the damage and the measure of damages.

1. Remoteness of the Damage

The remoteness of the damage deals with how far down the line of consequences for a breach will compensation stretch. In many cases this is obvious, but in some case the facts will make it difficult for a court to decide. Rules on remoteness arise from case-law. An example will illustrate the problems of deciding whether a consequence of a breach of contract is too remote to be compensated. A has a daily standing order from B to supply fresh vegetables to B's vegetarian restaurant. One Friday, A fails to supply the vegetables, with the result that B has to purchase them in the supermarket at much higher prices. Due to the time this takes, B also has to hire additional help in the kitchen that night. The vegetables supplied by the supermarket are substandard, a number of B's customers suffer food poisoning and they make claims for compensation against the restaurant. In addition, one of the customers that night writes a very poor review of the restaurant in a Sunday newspaper, and a large number of bookings for the coming months are cancelled. The question to be asked here is whether A is responsible for all the consequences of his failing to supply the vegetables to B or whether the courts would deem some of the losses to be too remote.

The courts would decide that there should be compensation for the replacement of the vegetables and the additional kitchen help, but there would be no compensation for the losses due to food poisoning and the bad review. This is based on the principles in *Hadley v Baxendale* (1854), which is the leading case on remoteness of damages.

> *Hadley v Baxendale* (1854)
> In this case the plaintiff operated a mill in which a shaft had broken. The company gave the broken shaft to the defendant who was a carrier (courier) to take into the next town and have copied. The carrier delayed for five days before returning with the new shaft. Unknown to the carrier, the mill had no replacement shaft and had been idle during this time. The plaintiff sought compensation for the mill being out of action during the defendant's absence. It was clear that the defendant's delay was a breach of contract, but the question before the court was whether he was liable for all the losses of the mill. The court held that compensation is payable for:
>
> (1) the loss that would naturally arise from the breach (this looks at the normal facts);

(2) the loss that the parties could reasonably foresee as a consequence of the breach (this looks at any special facts of which both parties were aware).

On the facts of the case:

(1) the loss that would naturally arise from the breach is the payment of the carrier, and the mill owners were entitled not to pay him for this work;

(2) the loss that is reasonably foreseeable as a consequence of the breach could not include the mill being out of operation, as the carrier was not aware that there was no replacement shaft.

Obviously, the outcome of *Hadley v Baxendale* would have been different if the carrier had been aware that the mill had no replacement shaft. Then he would be aware of special facts, which would mean that the mill being out of operation would be reasonably foreseeable under Part (2) of the rule.

If we apply the rule in *Hadley v Baxendale* to the example of the vegetarian restaurant above, the result is as follows. Under Part (1) of the rule, the cost of replacing the vegetables in the supermarket and the cost of hiring additional staff for the night would arise naturally from the breach, on the normal facts. The presence of the restaurant critic and the consequent reduction in bookings would not come under Part (2) of the rule because it was not reasonably foreseeable as the result of the breach. If, however, the restaurant owner had made the vegetable supplier aware that a restaurant critic would be dining there on Friday night, then Part (2) of the rule would come into operation.

The following is a final case to illustrate the *Hadley v Baxendale* rule.

Victoria Laundry (Windsor) Ltd v Newman Industries Ltd (1949)
In this case the plaintiff laundry and dyeing company ordered a new boiler from the defendant, to be put into use immediately. Due to an accident, the boiler was delivered six months late. During this time, the plaintiff was offered a contract to dye soldiers' uniforms, which it had to turn down in the absence of the boiler. The plaintiff claimed the lost profit for the six months' delay and also the loss of the lucrative dyeing contract. The court held that under Part (1) of the rule in *Hadley v Baxendale*, damages could be recovered for the lost profits, which were a loss naturally arising from the failure to supply a major piece of equipment. The court also held that under Part (2) of the rule, no damages could be recovered for the loss of the one-off dyeing contract, as this was a special fact that was not reasonably foreseeable.

Once again the results of this case would have been different if the supplier had been aware that the laundry had been offered a particularly lucrative contract. Compensation will only be payable for special facts if they are known to the parties, so contracting parties should consider disclosing all relevant information.

2. Measure of Damages

The measure of damages is the second key issue in damages. The issue concerns the amount, or *quantum*, of damages to be paid, once the issue of remoteness has been settled. As stated above, the amount of damages is supposed to put the plaintiff in the same position as if the contract had gone ahead.

There are a number of issues to be considered in relation to the measure of damages: Financial and nonfinancial loss, mitigation of loss, liquidated damages, *quantum meruit* and action for the price.

Financial and Nonfinancial Loss: Most awards of damages are for financial loss, i.e. loss of money, as in the example above about the Christmas trees. These amounts are usually easily quantifiable. In certain circumstances, there are also damages for nonfinancial losses, that is, damages for nonmonetary losses or losses that are not readily quantifiable in terms of money.

> *Jarvis v Swans Tours* (1973)
> In this case a solicitor went on a skiing holiday, which the brochure stated was a 'Houseparty holiday' in a hotel providing afternoon teas, a bar and an English-speaking owner. None of these things materialised, there were no proper skis available and for the second week Jarvis was the only guest in the hotel. The plaintiff was very disappointed with his holiday and, on his return, claimed that the holiday failed to comply with the brochure. The court held that the plaintiff was entitled to damages for loss of enjoyment as well as for the lack of facilities.

> *Hynes & Hynes v Happy Holidays Ltd* (1985) Ire
> A couple was compensated for inconvenience and disruption of their holiday due to 'deplorably inadequate' conditions in their holiday apartment.

Other cases in which damages for nonfinancial loss have been recovered have been in building contracts that fail to meet the specified standards, disappointing wedding photographs and double booking of wedding receptions. It is usual in these cases for the plaintiff to seek financial as well as nonfinancial losses.

Mitigation of Loss: The innocent party to a breach of contract has a duty to mitigate or reduce his or her losses. This means that he or she must take active steps to reduce the losses of the breaching party rather than sit back and let damages accrue. In the example about the vegetarian restaurant, when A fails to deliver the supplies, B must attempt to buy the vegetables elsewhere. B should not sit back and decide not to open the restaurant that night and then claim for an entire night's lost profits from A.

Bord Iascaigh Mhara v Scallan (1973) Ire

In this case the defendant had hired a boat from the plaintiff BIM that he later abandoned in Wexford harbour. BIM left the boat in the harbour over the winter. Nine months later, the boat had seriously deteriorated, and BIM sued the plaintiff for damages. The court that held even though Scallan had breached the contract, BIM had a duty to mitigate Scallan's losses. BIM should have removed the boat from the water and rehired it to another person if possible.

Doran v Delaney and Greene (1996) Ire

The plaintiffs bought land from the second defendants. It transpired that there was no access to their land as it was surrounded by land belonging to another person. The buyers had to stop building on the land and resell it at a loss. They owed a lot of money to their builder and were unable to buy another home. In addition to proving misrepresentation by the sellers (as explained in Chapter 5), the court also held that the plaintiff's own solicitors were liable in breach of contract and tort for failing to clarify the boundaries of the land and the seller's solicitors were liable in negligence in responding to questions.

On the issue of damages to be paid by the seller's solicitors, the Supreme Court held that where property is purchased in excess of its market value due to negligence, the damages payable will be the difference between the purchase price and the market value on the day of purchase.

However, this measure of damages is not appropriate where it is reasonably forseeable that the injured party would be unable to mitigate (or cut) their losses due to lack of money. The plaintiffs were awarded compensation to enable them to build the kind of house they had intended, pay their debt to the builders and their other losses.

Liquidated Damages Clauses: Liquidated damages are damages that you can easily put a figure on, or 'liquidate', the same as financial loss. A 'liquidated damages clause' is a term in a contract that attempts to fix in advance the amount of damages payable if a breach of contract occurs.

Returning to the vegetarian restaurant example, in a contract for the daily supply of goods, the parties may realistically anticipate that at some stage in the course of their dealings, the supplier will not be able to supply the goods due to such things as bad weather or strikes. Thus the parties may have written into their supply contract a condition that if the supplier is unable to supply the restaurant, the supplier will compensate the restaurant for the cost of replacing the vegetables in a supermarket. This is a practical example of a liquidated damages clause in which the parties have anticipated a possible breach and provided for a realistic amount of damages in the event of it occurring. The benefit is that the damages are likely to be noncontentious, which means the parties will remain on good business terms.

The courts will uphold liquidated damages clauses if they are a 'genuine pre-estimate of loss', i.e. if they are a realistic attempt to anticipate the amount of damages payable. Such clauses must be drawn to the parties' attention before contracting. However, if the courts believe that the purpose of the clause was to penalise a party for breach of the contract or to deter such a breach, then it will not be valid. Such clauses are called 'penalty clauses' and are contrary to the idea that damages should neither over- nor undercompensate the innocent party. For example, if the contract for the supply of vegetables provided that in the event of A failing to supply B, A would pay B €1,500 per day, this would clearly be a penalty clause, and the courts would not uphold it.

The question of whether a clause is a valid liquidated damages clause or an invalid penalty clause is a decision for the courts, and the burden of proof is on the innocent party. The following is the leading case in this area.

> *Dunlop Pneumatic Tyre Co v New Garage and Motor Co* (1915)
> In this case the plaintiff tyre company sold tyres to the defendant garage, subject to an agreement that the garage would not resell the tyres at less than a certain price. The garage also stated, 'We agree to pay the Dunlop Pneumatic Tyre Co Ltd the sum of £5 for each and every tyre . . . sold or offered in breach of this agreement, as and by way of liquidated damages and not as a penalty.' The garage resold the tyres below the set price, and Dunlop claimed £250. The garage argued that the clause was a penalty. The court held that the main test to be used was whether the sum stipulated 'is extravagant and unconscionable in amount in comparison with the greatest loss that could conceivably be proved to have followed from the breach'. There is also a presumption that it is a penalty to have to pay a single lump sum as compensation on the occurrence of a variety of events, some of which are small and some large. On the facts the court held that the clause was a genuine attempt to specify liquidated damages, and it would be upheld.

In the *Dunlop* case, the court stated that the name given to a clause is not conclusive, but the issue of whether a clause is a liquidated damages clause or a penalty clause is for the courts to decide based on the contract.

> *Schisser International (Ireland) v Gallagher* (1971) Ire
> Gallagher's contract of employment with the plaintiff company provided that he would repay his travel and other expenses if he left his employment within three years of starting. This was an invalid penalty clause because it imposed the same liability if he left after one month, or two years eleven months.

Irish Telephone Rentals Ltd v Irish Civil Service Building Society (1992) Ire
The plaintiff rented telephone equipment to the defendant, who repudiated the contract. The contract provided that a subscriber who repudiated the contract had to pay all accrued charges and rentals due, minus a discount of thirty per cent. The defendant argued that this was a penalty clause. The court held that it was, in fact, a penalty because the plaintiff's estimated profit of seventy-one per cent was 'staggeringly large', and no attempt had been made to identify the actual loss resulting from the repudiation of the contract.

Schedule 3 of the EC (Unfair Terms in Consumer Contracts) Regulations 1995 details contract terms that are automatically unfair, such as a term requiring a consumer who fails in his or her obligation to pay a disproportionately high sum in compensation. This is very like an invalid penalty clause.

As well as a straightforward action for damages based on quantum, damages can be measured in two other ways: *quantum meruit* and an action for the price.

Quantum Meruit: Claiming damages on a *quantum meruit* basis is claiming 'what it's worth' or how much it merits. It is an alternative to general damages and is used to put the parties in the positions in which they would have been if they had never made the contract (as opposed to general damages to put the parties in the same position as if the contract had been completed).

An award of *quantum meruit* may be made when the contract has not provided for the amount to be paid and when one party is prevented from performing his or her side of the contract.

Planché v Colburn (1831)
The plaintiff contracted with the defendant publisher to write a book that was one in a series of children's books. When Planché had written half the book, the series was abandoned. He claimed that he was entitled to be paid on a *quantum meruit* basis, and the court agreed.

A similar option was open to the defendant contractors in *Athlone Rural District Council v AG Campbell & Son (No. 2)* (1912) Ire. However, if a party has the option of claiming part of the price for the contract under *quantum meruit* or all of the contract price, the party will usually claim all of the agreed contract price. Cambell & Son claimed and were awarded the entire contract price because it was not the company's fault that the contract could not be completed. This is sometimes known as 'reliance loss'.

Action for the Price: An action for the price is exactly as it sounds. If one party has failed to pay the contract price, the other party may bring an action seeking payment of the price. Obviously, this action will only be used when the innocent party is not seeking any additional damages.

Section 49 of the Sale of Goods Act 1893 provides that an action for the price may only be brought with regard to a contract for the sale of goods if the property has passed to the buyer, unless the price is payable on a specific date (see Chapter 7 on sale of goods).

Specific Performance

Specific performance is an equitable remedy, which, like all equitable remedies, is discretionary. This means that a party cannot insist on being awarded this remedy; it is for the court to decide. The court must issue an order directing the breaching party to *specifically perform* the contract as originally agreed. Specific performance will be given only when damages are an inadequate remedy. The cases in which specific performance will be given involve the sale of land and the sale of unique goods.

1. The Sale of Land

All land is considered to be unique. For example, if you contracted to buy a house at a certain price and the vendor now refuses to complete the contract, you would not be satisfied with damages as you would not necessarily be able to buy a similar house in that area at that price.

2. The Sale of Unique Goods

Specific performance will be given to enforce a contract for the sale of such items as paintings or antiques. Again, if a seller defaults on a contract to sell you a Jack B. Yeats painting, you will not be able to buy that painting elsewhere.

Specific performance will *not* be given in certain cases because damages would be an adequate remedy, and these are listed below.

1. Contracts for the Sale of Nonunique Goods

If the breaching party fails or refuses to supply goods that can be easily purchased elsewhere, damages will be an adequate remedy for the plaintiff.

2. Contracts of Employment or Personal Service

Specific performance will not be granted in a case in which an employee breaches his or her contract and leaves the employer. This is said to be because the courts will not make an order for a period of time that they cannot supervise. However, in employment law, the remedies of re-engagement and reinstatement for unfair dismissal are very similar to an order to the employer to specifically perform his or her side of the contract (see Chapter 8).

3. Contracts by Way of Deed under Seal

Contracts by way of deed under seal cannot be enforced by specific performance.

Injunction

An injunction is a discretionary, equitable remedy. It is a court order requiring the defendant to comply with a negative restriction in the contract. For example, the agreement of a wholesaler that he or she will supply to only one retailer in the Dublin area is a negative restriction, and if the wholesaler wrongfully breaches this agreement, the retailer would be able to get an injunction to stop the breach. It does not matter whether the restraint is phrased in the negative, as long as that is the result. For example, the agreement that a wholesaler will supply to only one Dublin retailer is a negative restriction, although it does not appear to be at first sight.

It is possible to get an injunction to enforce a contract of personal services, even though specific performance would not be granted in the same circumstances.

> *Warner Brothers Pictures Inc v Nelson* (1938)
> The defendant, who was more commonly known as Bette Davis, agreed to a restraint of trade clause under which she would act only for Warner Brothers and not 'engage in any other occupation' without the company's consent. Davis then contracted to act for another producer, breaching her contract with Warner Brothers. The court granted an injunction against her to stop her acting for the other producer, enforcing the negative restriction. The court also stated that it would not have granted an injunction to stop her working in any other occupation as this was too restrictive.

Injunctions can also be classified according to the time for which they are issued.

1. Interim Injunction

An interim injunction lasts only until the next sitting of the court. This would typically be granted in a one-sided application when the courts are not open. Continuing the example of the exclusive supply agreement, on a Friday night of a bank holiday weekend, the Dublin retailer discovers that the wholesaler has breached the agreement and the courts will not open until Tuesday, at which time damage may be done to the retailer's exclusive image. The retailer could apply to a designated judge on Friday night for an interim injunction, which would last until the courts open on Tuesday.

2. Interlocutory Injunction

An interlocutory injunction lasts from the initial court application until the hearing of the case, which is usually months later. Without an interlocutory injunction substantial damage might be done before the case gets a court hearing. If the Dublin retailer had to wait eight or nine months before the case came to court, the business might be seriously affected, whereas the retailer can apply for an interlocutory injunction on the date the breach is discovered, and this injunction will last until the court hearing.

3. Permanent or Fixed-time Injunction

A permanent or fixed-time injunction lasts for a definite period of time and would be given as the result of a successful court hearing.

4. Mareva Injunction

A Mareva injunction is a special type of injunction that stops the defendant from disposing of assets outside of the country, pending litigation. It is very useful in business or family law, when there is a risk that between the case being initiated and its coming to court, the breaching party might sell his or her assets or remove them from the State to avoid paying an award of damages. Like all injunctions, it is only given in very specific circumstances.

Rectification

Rectification is a also a discretionary equitable remedy. It is simply the courts' correction of a mistake in a document to reflect the parties' intentions. It is a remedy for a specific type of mistake, i.e. a simple slip or typographical error. If, for example, we agree on a sale price of €300,000 for my house, and this is mistakenly typed as €500,000, I might seek to take advantage of the mistake. You would then seek to have the contract rectified to reflect our original agreement, see page 82.

Rescission

Rescission is a remedy that entitles the innocent party to get out of the contract. The parties are said to return to their precontractual positions. For example, a computer salesperson tells me that a certain computer is guaranteed for a year, and this is one of the reasons I purchase that particular brand of computer. When the computer develops a defect after six months, I discover that it was not guaranteed, and I am presented with a repair bill for several hundred pounds. In this case I would claim that I was misled into the contract, and I would seek to set the contract aside. I would be returned the purchase price, and the seller would have to take back the defective computer.

Rescission is the main remedy for misrepresentation, and the remedy is covered in detail in Chapter 5.

C. Limitation Periods

The right to sue for breach of contract does not last indefinitely but is subject to limits under legislation. Under the Statute of Limitations Acts 1957–2000, the periods are as follows:

- six years to sue in contract;
- twelve years under a deed under seal;
- three years to sue in an action for damages for personal injury.

In all cases, the time of action is said to 'accrue', or start, on the date of the breach.

Section C

Specific Types of Contracts

CHAPTER 7

Contracts for the Sale of Goods

Summary of chapter

The main protection that the sale of goods legislation gives the consumer is the terms that must be implied into such contracts, particularly those dealing with description, merchantable quality and samples. The legislation also provides rules that the parties may follow for the passing of property in goods and the performance of a contract. There are specific remedies for breach of a sale of goods contract.

The sale of goods is probably the most common type of contract made on a daily basis. Ordinary contract law rules apply in such cases, but the position of the consumer is greatly strengthened by the implied terms in the applicable legislation, i.e. the Sale of Goods Act 1893 and the Sale of Goods and Supply of Services Act 1980.

There are three general issues in relation to the sale of goods.

First, in a sale of goods transaction, different parts of the contract may take place on different dates. For example, a contract may be formed on 1 March when A orders goods from B. The goods may be supplied by B on 15 March, and A may not pay for them until 31 March. However, once the contract is validly formed (by the exchange of executory consideration), the Sale of Goods Acts apply.

1 March	→	15 March	→	31 March
Contract formed		Goods supplied		Goods paid for

Second, the Sale of Goods Acts introduce what is known as 'strict liability', where someone, in this case the seller, is strictly liable for any breaches of law, even if the breach was not his or her fault. This is because of privity of contract under which the buyer has a contract with the seller only, and therefore the seller is made legally liable.

If a seller has to compensate the buyer for something that was not the seller's fault, then the seller may in turn sue the supplier or manufacturer, etc. from whom he or she purchased the faulty goods. The idea of making the innocent seller liable to the buyer is one of the main features of consumer protection in the sale of goods legislation, as shown in Figure 7.1.

Figure 7.1   Strict liability

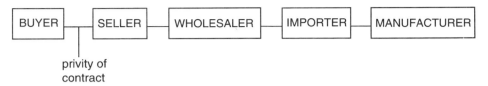

privity of
contract

Thirdly, the relationship between the Sale of Goods Act 1893 and the Sale of Goods and Supply of Services Act 1980 can be confusing. The 1893 Act was the first piece of consumer protection legislation, but it was greatly amended by the 1980 Act.

Note: For exam purposes, it is important to be accurate in referring to the section numbers and the years of the acts in question.

A. Definitions

A good starting point in the study of any piece of legislation is to define the key terms used in the area.

'Sale':   Section 1 of the Sale of Goods Act 1893 defines a 'sale of goods' as a contract by which a seller transfers or agrees to transfer the property or goods to a buyer for a money consideration called the 'price'.

'Goods':   According to section 62 of the 1893 Act, 'goods' includes all chattels personal other than things in action and money. 'Things in action' are intangible items of personal property such as debts, insurance, shares, etc. This definition does not include real property, i.e. land.
     There are four categories of goods.

'Existing Goods':   These are goods that exist and belong to the seller when the contract is made. For example, if you sell me your second-hand car, it is an existing good.

'Future Goods':   These are goods that do not exist or that the seller does not own at the time of the contract. An example would be goods made to the customer's specifications, such as clothing, or an item chosen from a catalogue, which the seller has to order, such as a new car.

'Specific Goods':   These are goods identified when the contract is made. They are often chosen from a group of similar items, e.g. 'That large cinnamon bun please'.

'Unascertained Goods':   These, also called unspecified goods, are goods identified after the contract is made. For example, when you are handed a

cinnamon bun from a selection, the specific bun you are buying was not identified until after the contract was made.

These categories are of particular relevance in relation to the rules on passing of property, as discussed later in this chapter.

'Price': Section 1 of the Sale of Goods Act 1893 refers to a money consideration called the 'price'. In fact, the price of the goods need only be partly money. This allows a trade-in as part of the purchase price. The contract may state a means of getting to the price, for example, a statement that I will buy shares at their quoted market price on Wednesday. If no price is agreed, section 8 of the 1893 Act states that a reasonable price must be paid.

'Consumer': Some of the Act's provisions apply only when the buyer is said to 'deal as a consumer'. The 1893 Act states that a buyer is dealing as a consumer if:

- he or she does not act or hold himself or herself out as acting in the course of business; and
- the other party does make the contract in the course of business: and
- the goods supplied are of a type ordinarily supplied for private use or consumption.

For example, an individual who buys a car from another individual through a small advertisement in the evening paper is not a consumer, as the seller is not in the course of business. Thus the buyer has no rights under the Sale of Goods Acts but, of course, has rights under ordinary contract law. By contrast, a person who buys a car from a car dealership will probably deal as a consumer, if he or she is buying the car for private use.

B. Implied Terms in Sale of Goods Contracts

Implied terms in sale of goods contracts are the key principles of consumer protection. In any consumer transaction, these terms form part of the contract, as a way of increasing the buyer's legal position. A seller is not allowed to contract out of these implied statutory protections.

The following are all implied *conditions*. Remember that breach of condition gives the innocent party the right to discharge, or end, the contract and to claim damages. These implied terms are in sections 10–15 of the Sale of Goods Act 1893, as amended by the Sale of Goods and Supply of Services Act 1980.

1. Section 10 of the 1893 Act: Time of Performance

The importance of the time of performance of a contractual obligation depends on the terms of the contract and on the type of contract. If the contract states that time is of the essence or important, then time is a condition of the contract, and the contract can be discharged for breach of this condition. Time is assumed to be of the essence in commercial contracts but not otherwise, unless specifically stated.

2. Section 12 of the 1893 Act: Seller has Title to Goods

The title to goods means the ownership of or property in the goods. Section 12 states that there is an implied condition in a contract of sale that the seller has the right to sell the goods and, in relation to an agreement to sell, that the seller will have the right to sell the goods, at the time property is to pass.

It is not sufficient that the seller must own the goods; he or she must also have the right to sell them, free of any rights or interference by third parties. Examples of cases in which the seller would lack the right to sell goods he or she owns would be when the goods are subject to a fixed charge or mortgage or subject to a mareva injunction. Under the Family Home Protection Act 1976, the owner of a family home cannot sell it without the consent of his or her spouse.

Sales of goods that infringe a copyright, trademark or patent would be in breach of section 12, as in the following case.

> *Niblett v Confectioner's Materials Co* (1921)
> In this case, a company sold tins of condensed milk under the label 'Nissly'. Nestlé, who produced a similar product, sought an injunction to prevent the sale of the product which the company claimed breached its trademark. The court granted the injunction because although the seller owned the goods, that company did not have the right to sell them under section 12 of the 1893 Act.

If the 'seller' has no title, the 'buyer' does not become the owner of the goods. If the buyer has to return the goods to the seller, the buyer can sue the seller for the full purchase price, i.e. no deductions for wear and tear will be made by the court.

3. Section 12(2) of the 1893 Act: Implied Warranty of Quiet Possession

The only implied warranty in the sale of goods legislation is in section 12(2) of the 1893 Act, which states that the buyer gets 'quiet possession' of the goods after sale. This means that the goods are free of any encumbrance not disclosed by the seller and that the buyer will have quiet possession of the goods except in relation to encumbrances disclosed by the seller. 'Encumbrances' are restraints on the marketability of the goods, such as a mortgage or retention of title clause. There are seven cases in which a seller who does not own goods can legally give title to a buyer; this will be covered later under the *nemo dat quod non habet* rule.

4. Section 13 of the 1893 Act: Goods Comply with the Contract Description

Section 13 provides that 'where there is a contract for the sale of goods by description, there is an implied condition that the goods shall correspond with the description'. The phrase 'description of goods' is interpreted very widely. It covers descriptions in which the goods may be future goods, such as sales from catalogues and advertisments. However, it also covers all oral statements, such as 'A pint of Guinness, please'; all packaging, labelling and photographs of goods. A description can also cover details of the product, such as its ingredients, place of manufacture, age and uses. Almost all sales will be sales by description.

> *O'Connor v Donnelly* (1944) Ire
> In this case, a request for a tin of 'John West Middle Cut Salmon' was held to be a sale by description.

If goods are inspected by the buyer before purchase, it is still a sale by description.

> *Beale v Taylor* (1967)
> A private individual advertised his car for sale, stating that it was a '1961 Triumph Herald Convertible'. After the purchase, the buyer discovered that the car was in fact made up of two different cars welded together, so that only part of the car was a 1961 Triumph Herald Convertible. The seller argued that the buyer did not rely on the description, as he had examined the car. The court held that it was a sale by description, and reliance on the description need not be the sole reason for purchasing.

In keeping with the rule in contract law that performance of a contract must be exact, the courts require strict compliance with any description of a product. There is one practical exception to this implied condition for goods 'bought as seen'. This is not a sale by description, and the buyer is not protected by the Sale of Goods Acts. This is common in auction sales.

5. Section 13 of the 1893 Act: Sale by Description and Sample

Section 13 also states that when a good is sold by sample as well as by description, it is not sufficient that the bulk of the goods corresponds with the sample if it does not also correspond with the description. For example, if a sale of carpet is by sample and the carpet is described as being 100 per cent wool, the carpet as supplied must be 100 per cent wool even if the sample was not. This protects a consumer who might not be able to appreciate the quality of a sample; the consumer also have the protection of the description. This condition applies regardless of whether the goods were sold in the course of business, so it applies in private transactions between individuals.

6. Section 14(2) of the 1893 Act: Goods Are of Merchantable Quality

Section 14(2) provides that when a seller sells goods in the course of business, there is an implied condition that the goods supplied under the contract are of merchantable quality. This is the most basic of sale of goods protections: that the goods must be saleable, or fit for the purpose for which such goods are usually bought. This is a subjective test, depending on factors such as the price of the goods, whether they are new or second hand and their description and intended purpose.

As this law is aimed at increasing consumers' rights, a good that is defective but still fit for its purposes, such as a t-shirt that runs in the wash, will be covered by section 14(2). For example, recent English cases concerning the sale of new cars have established that buyers are entitled to the 'appropriate degree of comfort . . . and of pride' in their purchases, so a defective car can be unmerchantable, even if it is still fit for the purpose of driving.

As stated in the definition, section 14 applies only to goods 'sold in the course of business'. *Caveat emptor*, or buyer beware, still applies in private sales, with a possible action in contract.

Case-law has established that 'goods' covers the goods themselves and also the packaging, instructions, labels, etc. For example, if a cup of take-away coffee is sold in a paper cup that leaks, the goods are unmerchantable under section 14.

If goods have only one purpose, they must be fit for this purpose, and the buyer need not disclose the intended purpose when the goods are purchased, as it will be deemed to be obvious. For example, tinned salmon must be fit for eating; clothes must be fit for wearing.

> *Wallis v Russell* (1902) Ire
> The plaintiff's granddaughter asked the defendant fishmonger for 'two nice fresh crabs for tea'. The defendant replied that he had only boiled crabs and selected two for the girl. The plaintiff and her granddaughter suffered food poisoning as a result of eating the crabs. The court held that the statement that the crabs were 'for tea' was a sufficient disclosure of information to the defendant to signify the intended purpose for the crabs.

This case also indicates that section 14 is not confined to manufactured goods.

If goods are multipurpose, they need be fit for only one purpose, unless their specific purpose is disclosed to the seller.

If goods have to be treated or processed in order to be usable, then the buyer must do so. For example, a buyer may be required to waterproof shoes before wear or wash cooking pots before use.

Hell v Hedges (1951)

A woman bought pork chops, and she got food poisoning when she failed to cook them properly. The court held that she did not have an action under section 14(2), as the chops would have been merchantable had she cooked them properly.

7. Exceptions to section 14(2)

There are two exceptions to section 14(2). The first occurs if defects are specifically drawn to the buyer's attention before the contract is made. For example, this would cover the sale of items marked 'shop soiled' or 'factory seconds'.

The second exception occurs if a buyer examines the goods before purchase, and the defect is reasonably discoverable. Whether a defect is reasonably discoverable is a question of fact, but the courts take a consumer-friendly approach to the interpretation of this section. The burden is on the seller to establish either of these exceptions.

A seller has no defence to section 14(2), despite the fact that flaws in goods may not be the seller's fault. This is because of the concept of strict liability. The seller may, in turn, sue the person from whom the unmerchantable goods were purchased.

8. Section 14(4) of the 1893 Act: Goods Are Fit for a Disclosed Purpose

Section 14(4) provides that when the seller sells goods in the course of business and the buyer, expressly or by implication, makes known to the seller any particular purpose for which the goods are being bought, then there is an implied condition that the goods are reasonably fit for that purpose, whether or not that is a purpose for which such goods are commonly supplied. Again, goods must be sold in the course of business to have the protection of this section.

As explained previously, if goods have one purpose, e.g. clothes for wearing, food for eating, a car for driving, the seller is assumed to know of it, and the buyer need not explicitly disclose this purpose. If, however, the goods are multipurpose, the buyer must disclose the intended purpose to come within the protection of section 14(4). Without this disclosure, it is sufficient that the goods are fit for at least one of their normal purposes.

For example, a bucket may be used for carrying water, storing rubbish or cleaning out the fireplace. Obviously, a plastic bucket could not be used for cleaning a fireplace containing hot ashes. However, if a buyer does not disclose that this is the intended purpose of his or her purchase, it is sufficient that the bucket is fit for another main use, such as holding water. If the buyer disclosed his or her intended purpose, it must be fit for this purpose.

9. Exceptions to section 14(4)

There are two exceptions to section 14(4): If circumstances show that the buyer did not rely on the seller's skill or judgement and that it was unreasonable for the buyer to rely on the seller's skill or judgement.

For example, if a buyer bought a plastic bucket for cleaning the fire, despite the seller's advice, she would have no claim against the seller under section 14(4). Equally, if a buyer did rely on a seller's opinion that a bucket could be used for such a purpose, the courts might deem this to be unreasonable.

The difference between the two parts of section 14 is that goods may be merchantable under section 14(2) but not fit for their intended purpose under section 14(4). Alternatively, goods could be fit for a specified unusual purpose but also be unmerchantable.

10. Section 15 of the 1893 Act: Goods Must Comply with a Sample

Section 15 states that a contract of sale is a sale by sample where there is a term, express or implied, to that effect. In the case of a sale by sample:

(a) there shall be an implied condition that the bulk shall correspond with the sample in quality;

(b) there is an implied condition that the buyer shall have a reasonable opportunity of comparing the bulk with the sample;

(c) there is an implied condition that the goods shall be free from any defect rendering them unmerchantable, which would not be apparent on reasonable examination of the sample.

These are three protections in section 15: the goods must match the sample, the buyer can compare them, and the goods are merchantable. There is also the overlap of goods supplied by description and sample in section 12, which states that in sales by sample and description, the goods must correspond with the description rather than with the sample. The rules on sale by sample apply to the sort of goods commonly sold by sample, such as wallpaper, material and tiles. It does not cover cases in which a sample is given, such as a food tasting in a supermarket, unless it is specifically intended by the parties to be a sale by sample.

Consumer's Rights and Breach of Implied Terms

It is important to note that an aggrieved buyer can sue for breach of as many of the implied protections as are applicable under the sale of goods legislation. For example, if I bought a vegetarian pizza and discovered that it contained meat, I could claim that the goods did not match their description, that they were unmerchantable and that they were unfit for their purpose.

Excluding Liability in Sale of Goods Contracts

As a general rule, terms implied under statute cannot be excluded in sale of goods contracts. Under section 22 of the 1980 Act, any attempt to exclude sections 13–15 shall be void if the buyer is a consumer. If the buyer is not a consumer, it is still not possible to exclude section 12 on title, but the other sections can be excluded if it is fair and reasonable to do so. An example would be a sale by a wholesaler to a retailer of substandard merchandise at a low price. Liability can be excluded in that sale but not when the retailer sells them to consumers. Under section 11 of the 1980 Act, it is an offence to try to exclude liability by displaying notices attempting to restrict the rights of a buyer under sections 12–15 or by publishing statements to that effect or by supplying goods or documents that bear such a statement.

Sections 13–15 of the 1893 Act are implied terms that cannot be varied by the parties. The rest of the Act is a guideline that parties *may* apply but that they are also free to alter to suit their own needs. This is because sections 13–15 are to protect consumers, whereas the rest of the Act may apply in nonconsumer transactions, e.g. between two business with equal bargaining power.

C. Passing of Property

'Property' in goods is the same as ownership and title. As explained at the begining of the chapter, in many sale of goods transactions the formation of the contract, performance and payment may be spread over a period of weeks or months. This may give rise to difficulties in deciding whether the buyer or the seller owns the goods at any stage during that time. The property, or ownership, of the goods is different from possession. The party who currently has the goods in his or her possession does not necessarily own them. It is important to identify when property passes because of issues of risk, and liquidation or bankruptcy.

Risk: Risk passes with ownership. Whoever owns the goods is responsible for insuring them. This can be important when, for example, the goods are being transported from the seller's place of business in Dublin to the buyer's premises in Abbeyleix. If the goods are damaged in transit in a road accident, it will be crucial to determine which party owned them and had the responsibility of insuring them at the time of the damage.

Liquidation or Bankruptcy: Who owns the goods can be important in a liquidation. On liquidation of a company, a liquidator will make a list of the company's assets and a list of creditors. Goods that do not belong to the troubled company cannot be included in the list of assets, even if in they are in the possession of the company. In the case of the bankruptcy of either the buyer or seller, it is necessary to know whether the goods belong to the Official Assignee in Bankruptcy.

The parties need to know if the special buyer/seller remedies in the Sale of Goods Acts apply to them. To do so they must be able to tell if title to the goods, rather than just physical possession, has passed from one party to another.

1. General Principles on the Passing of Property

Section 16 of the 1893 Act provides that in a contract for the sale of unascertained goods, no property in the goods passes to the buyer unless and until the goods are ascertained (see rule 5 below).

The parties may make rules to decide when property passes from seller to buyer. According to section 17, in a contract for the sale of specific goods, the property passes at the time the parties intend it to pass. The courts consider the terms of the contract, the conduct of the parties and the circumstances of the case to decide on the parties' intentions. Section 17 allows the operation of retention of title clauses, whereby the parties stipulate when property passes.

2. Section 18 of the 1893 Act

If the parties do not specify when they wish the property to pass, the rules in section 18 of the 1893 Act will apply to them. This section is split into five rules, which cover all situations.

Rule 1: When there is an unconditional contract for the sale of specific goods in a deliverable state, property passes when the contract is made. In this case, a 'deliverable state' is a state in which the buyer would be bound to accept delivery. It is immaterial that the time of payment and/or delivery are postponed. For example, if I buy a newspaper, an unconditional contract is formed under which the newspaper is in a deliverable state. The property then passes when the contract is made. This is the case in the bulk of simple contracts.

Rule 2: When there is a contract for the sale of specific goods and the seller is bound to do something to the goods to put them into a deliverable state, the property passes when such thing is done and the buyer has notice of it. For example. if I buy a set of shelves that are to be painted a particular colour, when the shelves are painted and I have notice of this, the property passes to me

Rule 3: When there is a contract for the sale of specific goods in a deliverable state and the seller must do something to fix the price, the property does not pass until such act or thing is done and the buyer has notice that it has been done For example, if I buy all the turf remaining in a shop, the seller may have to weigh the goods to set the price. When this has been done and I have notice of this, property passes to me.

Rule 4: When goods are delivered to a buyer on approval or on a sale or return, the property will pass to the buyer when he or she

(a) signifies his or her acceptance to the seller: or

(b) does any other act adopting the transaction: or

(c) retains the goods beyond the time fixed for return or retains them beyond a reasonable time.

For example, if I buy drinks for a party from an off-licence on a sale or return basis, I am deemed to have property in those goods that I have made it clear I am buying, whether I do this through:

(a) telling the seller what I accept; or
(b) consuming the drinks; or
(c) retaining them beyond a certain time.

Rule 5: When there is a contract for the sale of unascertained or future goods by description and goods of that description in a deliverable state are unconditionally appropriated to the contract, either by the seller with the assent of the buyer or by the buyer with the assent of the seller, the property in the goods then passes to the buyer.

'Unconditionally appropriated to the contract' means that the goods are identified as the contract goods. The assent or agreement may be express or implied and may be given before or after the goods are identified. For example, if I order a piece of furniture to be made to my specifications, property only passes to me when the completed furniture is set aside with my name on it and I am notified that it is ready.

These rules may appear difficult, but they can be simplified for purposes of recall as in Figure 7.2. In each case, think of the type of goods, the condition that has to be fulfilled and whether the buyer has been notified that the condition has been fulfilled. In practice, however the rules on passing of property are distorted by insurance, i.e. the goods may be insured by someone other than the owner and by a retention of title clause.

3. Retention of Title

Retention, or reservation, of title is a practical way of avoiding section 18, in keeping with the freedom to do so under section 17. In a contract of sale, the seller may specify that he or she retains title in the goods until they are paid for, even if the buyer resells or alters the goods. If the buyer then goes into liquidation, the seller can repossess the goods as he or she still has title to them. If a buyer goes into liquidation and there is no retention of title clause, the liquidator will sell the unpaid seller's goods and give the proceeds to someone else, usually a secured creditor. Retention of title clauses are used to prevent this from happening.

Figure 7.2   Passing of property under section 18 of the 1893 Act

SECTION 18 RULE	TYPE OF GOODS	TYPE OF CONTRACT	WHEN PROPERTY PASSES
1 ➤	Specific and deliverable goods	➤ unconditional	➤ when the contract is made
2 ➤	Specific goods ➤	the seller must put goods in a deliverable state ➤	when the seller has done so and the buyer has notice
3 ➤	Specific and deliverable goods	➤ the seller must measure the goods to get the price ➤	when the seller has done so and the buyer has notice
4 ➤	Specific or ascertained goods	➤ a sale or return contract	➤ when the buyer signifies the goods they accept
5 ➤	unascertained ➤ or future goods	sale by description	➤ when goods fitting the description are identified as the contract goods and the buyer has notice

Retention of title clauses may be simple or complex. A complex one would cover a situation in which the buyer resells or uses the goods, as in the first case on these clauses.

> *Aluminium Industry v Romalpa* (1976)
> Romalpa bought tin foil from the plaintiff manufacturer. The tin foil and the proceeds of sale remained the plaintiff's property until the buyer had paid for them. Romalpa went into receivership. The company still had some of the foil, and the suppliers had not been paid. The court held that the condition of sale was valid, thus the receiver was not entitled to the tin foil nor to the money raised in its sale. These were not assets of the company but remained the property of the plaintiff.

Romalpa clauses were followed in Ireland, as seen in the next case.

> *Sugar Distributors Ltd v Monaghan Cash and Carry Ltd* (1982) Ire
> Retention of title clauses were standard in contracts between parties at the time that the plaintiff supplied sugar to the defendant. These clauses were usually printed on the back of delivery dockets and invoices and referred to on the front. The court held that this was sufficient to incorporate the retention of title clause into the contract, so the unsold sugar in the possession of the liquidator was the plaintiff's property.

Retention of title clauses are very widely used commercially. They are often mistakenly seen as a sale of goods remedy, when, in fact, they are a preventative measure used by the seller to safeguard his or her position.

D. 'Sale' by a Nonowner

Nemo dat quod non habet means no one can sell what they do not own. This is usually known as the *Nemo Dat Rule*, which applies to 'sales' by a person who does not own the goods.

Section 21 of the 1893 Act states that where goods are sold by a person who is not the owner thereof and who does not sell them under the authority or with the consent of the owner, the buyer has no better title to them than the seller had. This is in keeping with section 12 of the 1893 Act, which requires a seller to have title to the goods he or she sells. However, there are seven exceptions under which the buyer can get title although the seller did not own the goods sold.

1. Agency

Under section 21 an agent may sell goods with the consent of the principal. This rule applies only to mercantile agents, i.e. ones who buys and sells goods for other people in the ordinary course of business.

2. Estoppel

If the true owner of goods leads others to believe that a third party owns the goods, the true owner is estopped from taking action if the third party sells the goods. For example, if to avoid a court action for maintenance, I tell people that my brother owns my car, I cannot complain if he sells it. In such a case, the buyer will get title. I created the impression that my brother owned the car, and I am now estopped from denying it.

3. Market Overt

Under section 22 when goods are sold in an 'open public market' (the forerunner of shops), a buyer who buys 'in good faith' (i.e. innocently) and 'without notice that seller lacks title' will get title. The goods must be of a type normally sold in the market and the sale must take place during daylight. This law has limited practical use and was repealed in England in 1994.

4. Sale under Voidable Title

Under section 23 when the seller has a voidable title that was not avoided at the time of the sale, a person who buys in good faith without notice that seller lacks title gets good title. For example, if I sell my car to X and X gives me a cheque that bounces, my contract with X is voidable, i.e. I am able to make it void. However, if before I avoid the contract, X sells the car to Y, then Y will get good title to the car. It is a sale under a voidable title, and if

Y bought the car in good faith and without notice of X's lack of title, then Y gets good title to the car.

5. Resale by Seller in Possession

Under section 25(1) if goods are left in the possession of a seller and resold to a second buyer, the second buyer gets good title. For example, a person buys heavy goods and tells the shop that the goods will be collected later. If while the goods are being held, they are accidentally resold to a second person, the second person gets the legal title to the goods, even though they were not the shop's property to sell. Although this may seem unfair, it is practical in such cases in which the shop may have no way of contacting the second purchaser, who may have paid in cash.

6. Resale by Buyer in Possession

Under Section 25(2) if a buyer has possession, has not yet received title to the goods but resells them, the second buyer gets good title. Very often in commercial contracts, a buyer may have physical possession of goods for which he or she will not receive title for some time. In these circumstances, if the buyer resells the goods to another party, this second transaction is legally valid. This section of the 1893 Act allows people who buy goods subject to a retention of title clause to resell them. (However, in practice it is common to specify in a retention of title clause that the goods may be resold.)

7. Special Powers of Sale

A court or statute may order or allow persons such as dry cleaners, hotel operators, etc. to sell goods they possess but do not own. This is usually lost or unclaimed property.

E. Performance of a Sale of Goods Contract

The seller's key obligation is to deliver the goods to the buyer or to a specified location. The buyer's obligations are to accept and pay for the goods. Part II of the 1980 Act provides rules for performance of these obligations, but these rules *may* be varied by agreement of the parties.

1. Delivery

According to section 62 of the 1893 Act, delivery is the transfer of possession of the goods from one person to another. For convenience, delivery can take four forms:

(1) physical transfer of the goods;

(2) transfer of the means of control of the goods, e.g. keys to a car;

(3) transfer of title documents to the goods, e.g. a bill of lading;

(4) by attornment, under which a third party who holds the goods for the seller acknowledges (or 'attorns') that she now holds them for the buyer.

The place of delivery is generally the buyer's place of business or residence. If the goods are specific and both parties know that they are at some other place, then delivery is to be at that place.

The time of delivery is generally said to be 'of the essence' in commercial contracts. If no time of delivery is stated, delivery must take pace within a reasonable time and at a reasonable hour, according to section 29 of the 1893 Act. Section 29 also states that the seller is responsible for the expense of getting the goods into a deliverable state.

Delivery of the goods and payment are concurrent conditions.

2. Incorrect Delivery

Incorrect delivery gives various options to the buyer. If excess goods are delivered, the buyer may:

(1) reject the goods;
(2) accept and pay for the contract amount; or
(3) accept and pay for the entire amount.

If insufficient goods are delivered, the buyer may:

(1) reject the goods; or
(2) accept and pay for the insufficient amount.

If delivery is mixed, i.e. includes goods of a different type, the buyer may:

(1) reject the goods; or
(2) accept and pay for the contract goods.

The buyer may not accept the different goods, although he or she could make an offer to the seller for the different goods.

3. Instalments

The buyer is not obliged to accept delivery in instalments and may reject goods so delivered, according to section 31 of the 1893 Act. However, the parties may contract for delivery by instalments. In such a case, if payment is to be made after each instalment, the contract is said to be severable.

In a severable contract, if one or more instalments are defective, the buyer may be able to claim for damages or may be able to rescind the contract. Which of these options the buyer has depends on the number of defective deliveries and the likelihood of the defect reoccurring.

4. Acceptance

The buyer's first obligation under section 27 of the 1893 Act is to accept the goods. Acceptance can take three forms.

(a) The buyer informs the seller that the goods have been accepted.

(b) The buyer acts as if the goods have been accepted. Examples of this would include using the goods and reselling them.

(c) The buyer, without good and sufficient reason, retains the goods for a reasonable length of time, without telling the seller that the goods have been rejected.

It is very important to note that once the buyer has accepted the goods, she can no longer rescind the contract for breach. Thus section 20 of the 1980 Act states that where the goods, which he or she has not previously examined, are delivered to the buyer, he or she is not deemed to have accepted them unless and until he/she has had a reasonable opportunity of examining them for the purpose of ascertaining whether they are in conformity with the contract.

For example, a buyer who has been driving a new car for six months before she becomes aware of a defect would be held to be still examining the goods and would not yet have accepted them. Equally, if the buyer had the car repaired by the seller a number of times before finally seeking to have it replaced, the act of seeking repairs would be an indication that she had not yet accepted the car. Obviously, a seller may rightly refuse to accept the goods if they are defective.

5. Payment

The buyer is also obliged to pay for the goods, usually, as stated above, concurrently with delivery. Although time of delivery is 'of the essence', time of payment is not. Thus nonpayment on the due date does not give the seller the right to rescind the contract, only the option of seeking damages. Such damages could include additional costs and interest, at the courts' discretion. Inordinate delay in payment may, however, give the seller the right to resell the goods as if the buyer had abandoned the contract.

The usual method of payment is cash. Case-law has established that when a cheque is dishonoured, this does not count as payment. In import and export of goods, 'irrevocable letters of credit' may be used as a means of payment. These documents are enforceable against the bank or against the buyer for the price.

Remedies

In a sale of goods, specific legislative remedies exist in addition to ordinary contract remedies. The remedies are split into those of the buyer and the seller against the goods and against the person, as shown in Figure 7.3. Remedies against goods are known as 'real remedies', and remedies against a person are known as 'personal remedies'.

Figure 7.3 Remedies in a sale of goods contract

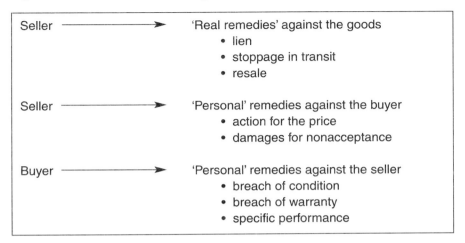

Seller ⟶ 'Real remedies' against the goods
- lien
- stoppage in transit
- resale

Seller ⟶ 'Personal' remedies against the buyer
- action for the price
- damages for nonacceptance

Buyer ⟶ 'Personal' remedies against the seller
- breach of condition
- breach of warranty
- specific performance

1. Remedies of an Unpaid Seller against the Goods

The seller's remedies against the goods are only given to 'an unpaid seller', which is a seller who has not been given the price or has been given a cheque that has been dishonoured. Remember that the buyer will often have ownership of the goods before she has physical possession of them. Some of the seller's rights are against the goods that may still be in her possession.

Lien: Under section 41 of the 1893 Act, an unpaid seller has the right to retain the goods in his or her possession until payment for them has been received. This right exists:

(a) when the goods are not sold on credit;

(b) when the goods are sold on credit but the credit period has expired;

(c) when the buyer has become insolvent.

A lien is simply a right to retain possession of the goods until payment is received not a right to end the contract or resell the goods. It is a right to retain goods owned by another person, so a lien cannot be used until ownership has passed to the buyer.

Stoppage in transit: Under section 44 of the 1893 Act, the buyer must be insolvent before the seller can exercise this right. It is a right that applies when goods are in transit between the seller and the buyer. The unpaid seller may issue an order to the carrier of the goods to stop delivery.

The right of stoppage ends:

(a) if the goods are delivered to the buyer or agent;
(b) if the carrier acknowledges to the buyer or agent that the goods are now held on behalf of the buyer;
(c) if the carrier wrongfully refuses to make delivery to the buyer or agent.

After the unpaid seller exercises the right of stoppage, he or she may then often exercise a lien over the goods.

Resale: Under section 48 of the 1893 Act, the unpaid seller has a right to resell the buyer's goods:

(a) if the goods are perishable;
(b) if the seller notifies the buyer of her intention to resell and the buyer fails to respond within a reasonable time;
(c) if the seller has specified a right of resale in the contract, which also means she has a right of resale at common law.

If the resale causes financial loss to the seller, he or she may sue the buyer for the outstanding amount. For example, a seller contracts to sell fruit to a buyer for €500. The buyer does not accept the goods, and when the seller resells the goods, he or she only gets €350. The original buyer is liable to pay the seller the €150 lost on the resale. In such a case, the third party who bought the goods from the seller on a resale would receive good title to them.

It should be noted that although all three remedies are separate, it may be possible in some circumstances to exercise all three, i.e. stop the goods in transit, exercise a lien for payment and ultimately resell the goods.

2. Remedies of an Unpaid Seller against the Buyer

Action for the Price: This remedy is used when ownership of the goods has passed to the buyer, who then wrongfully refuses or fails to pay for them according to the terms of the contract. It can also be used when the price is not paid on the specified day, regardless of the date of delivery and of the fact that ownership has not yet passed to the buyer.

Damages for Wrongful Nonacceptance: If the buyer wrongfully refuses or fails to accept and pay for the goods, the seller may seek damages. Damages for nonacceptance will usually be higher than an action for the price because the damages may include any additional expenses such as transportation and storage. If there is an available market for the goods, the amount of damages is usually the difference between the contract price and the market price on the day the goods should have been accepted. All issues of damages are assessed under the principles in *Hadley v Baxendale*

(1854), i.e. damages for the loss naturally resulting from the breach and also special damages in exceptional cases.

3. Buyer's Remedies against the Seller

Breach of Condition: As we have seen in contract law, a breach of condition gives the buyer the right to discharge the contract, i.e. reject the goods. This is the most commonly used remedy of consumers who are complaining about the quality of goods. A buyer can also seek damages if appropriate.

Breach of Warranty: A breach of warranty, such as quiet possession in section 12(2), gives the buyer the right to claim damages only. Because of this, a buyer may be deemed by the courts to still be 'testing' the goods some months after purchase and to not yet have accepted the goods.

Specific Performance: This may be awarded at the discretion of the court when damages would not adequately replace the goods.

F. Consumer Protection

Small Claims

The practical problem with sale of goods cases has been the expense of going to court over a relatively inexpensive item when the seller would not provide a remedy under the Sale of Goods Acts. A Small Claims Procedure was started in the District Court to remedy this and has been applicable throughout the country since 1993. 'Consumer claims' in relation to goods and services not exceeding €1270 can be handled through an exchange of documents by the District Court Registrar. The cost is €9. Most cases are settled through negotiation, but cases can proceed to the District Court, where both sides pay their own expenses. The scheme is very successfully and increasingly widely used.

CHAPTER 8

Contracts of Employment

Summary of chapter

In this chapter we will look at the contract of employment, starting with the distinction between employees and independent contractors. Then we will look at the formation and sources of employment contracts in Irish law. We will then look at the key implied terms of health and safety, and equality. Finally we will look at the different ways in which an employment contract may be terminated—by wrongful dismissal, unfair dismissal and redundancy—and the rights of employees in these cases.

Employment law is governed by ordinary contract principles, which we have covered, and also by specific legislative regulations dealing with the employment relationship. To begin, it is neccessary to explain the employer–employee relationship and its importance.

A. Employees versus Independent Contractors

The first issue to grasp in employment law is the distinction between employees and independent contractors. Most employment relationships are organised into one of these forms, and the distinction is crucial.

An 'employee' in legal terms is someone who is under a contract *of* service. This contrasts with an independent contractor, or self-employed person, who is under a contract *for* services. This distinction is often obvious. The example most-often used is that a chauffeur is an employee who has a contract of service with his or her boss, whereas a taxi driver is an independent contractor who has a contract to provide services for his or her passenger. Obviously, the employer of a chauffeur has ongoing legal responsibilities in relation to such issues as salary and conditions of employment. The taxi's customer, on the other hand, has no responsibilities apart from payment for the service.

However, not all cases are as clear-cut as the chauffeur–taxi driver distinction. Over the years, the Irish courts have developed a number of tests for distinguishing between employees and independent contractors. Prior to looking at this, we will consider why the distinction is so important.

Reasons for the Distinction

1. Statutory Protection

Statutory rights are given only to employees. For example, only employees with a contract of service may claim under the Unfair Dismissals Acts 1977 to 2001.

Note: Very often, the first point in an exam answer on employment will be to state that the issue you are about to discuss applies only to employees.

2. Vicarious Liability

To be 'vicariously liable' for the wrongs of another means that one person is legally liable, even though that person did not commit the wrong. In most cases, an employer is vicariously liable for the wrongs of an employee because the employer benefited from the risk created by the employee and also because, in practical terms, the employer has more money and usually has insurance. However, an employer is not vicariously liable for the wrongs of an independent contractor, except in exceptional cases.

3. Preference in Winding Up

When a company is in receivership or liquidation, debts to employees are treated as preferential debts under section 285 of the Companies Act 1963 and will be paid before floating charge holders.

> *In Re Sunday Tribune (in Liquidation)* (1984) Ire
> During the liquidation of the *Sunday Tribune*, the question of the status of three workers arose. The first was a part-time subeditor working on a shift basis. The second was Mary Holland, a weekly columnist, who was paid a weekly fee and was required to attend editorial meetings. The third was a regular contributor of commissioned articles. All three worked for other businesses and, as a result, were permitted by the Revenue Commissioners to pay PRSI as if they were independent contractors. The court held that the first worker was an employee and used the control test (defined below) to reach this decision. Mary Holland was also held to be an employee, as she was an integral part of the newspaper. The third worker was not an integral part of the paper but was a classic independent contractor who sought work from the paper. The first and second workers were paid money due to them as preferential creditors, but the freelance journalist was not.

4. Tax

Employees are on tax schedule E and have PRSI deducted at source. Independent contractors are self-employed and make their own tax returns under schedule D.

5. Trade Union Representation

In some circumstances only those under contracts of service are represented by trade unions.

> *Lambe Brothers (Dublin) v Davidson* (1978) Ire
> The defendant had worked for the plaintiff as a painter for a number of years, working regular hours. The plaintiff had never paid tax or PRSI for the defendant. The plaintiff offered to make Davidson an employee, but he refused 'to clock in'. When his contract ended, the defendant began to picket the plaintiff's premises. The court, applying the reality test (discussed below), held that Davidson was not an employee and was therefore not entitled to the protection of the Trade Disputes Act 1906 in relation to his picketing.

The Legal Tests

Given the importance of the distinction between employees and independent contractors, the courts have often been faced with deciding the status of a given worker. A number of tests have been developed over the years.

1. The Control Test

In *Roche v Kelly* (1968) Ire, the judge stated that 'the principle and determining test is the master's right to direct servants as what is to be done and how to do it'. This test was developed in the nineteenth century, when the parties were still known as master and servant. It is still used in cases of vicarious liability.

There are a number of problems with the control test. It is not suited for skilled workers who are told what to do but have discretion and responsibility in how they do it. This point was made in *In Re Sunday Tribune* (1984), in which the judge stated, 'The control test is no longer of universal application. In the present day when senior staff with professional qualifications are employed, the nature of their employment cannot be determined in such a simplistic way.'

The control test is also not suitable for the 'servant of two masters', i.e. an employee of A is contracted out to B, who is responsible for the employee's wrongs while contracted out. For example, if you are injured while on audit, who is responsible, your employer or the firm you were auditing?

> *Minister for Labour v PMPA Insurance Ltd* (1986) Ire
> The Minister prosecuted PMPA for alleged breaches of the Holidays (Employees) Act 1973 in relation to a temporary typist hired by PMPA under an agreement made with Alfred Marks Bureau (Ireland) Ltd. The contract provided that Alfred Marks was the employer and paid the wages, whereas control, direction and supervision was with PMPA, i.e. a classic example of a servant of two masters. The court held that

it did 'not regard the facts as establishing any contract, express or implied between PMPA and the employee', and thus PMPA had not breached the holidays legislation.

This area of law has now changed. The Unfair Dismissals (Amendment) Act 1993 and the Terms of Employment (Information) Act 1994 deem an employee working for an employer through another body or employment agency to be employed by the person for whom the work is being done. The definition of employment agency is very wide and does not require that the supplier of labour actually trade as an employment agency in order for A's workers subcontracted out to B to be deemed to be employed by B.

2. The Integration Test

The integration test was formulated by the legal academic Otto Kahn-Freund and judicially adopted in England by Lord Denning in *Stevenson, Jordan and Harrison v MacDonald and Evans* (1952). The issue considered was whether the worker was integrated into, or part of, the employer's business. The courts considered whether the worker was a vital part of the operation of the workplace. This test was considered in Ireland in *Kirwin v Dart Industries and Leahy* (1980) Ire (see below) and also in *In Re Sunday Tribune (in Liquidation)* (1984) Ire.

> *Kelly v Irish Press* (1985) Ire
> Kelly had been a soccer correspondent with the *Irish Press* since 1952, submitting eleven weekly columns during the season. His work was calculated at twenty-four hours a week. Kelly was also a civil servant. The Sports Editor had ultimate control of the piece, and copyright rested with the newspaper. The Circuit Court decided that he was not an employee of the *Irish Press* because the newspaper could not stop him working elsewhere and because he did not work for the entire year.

This decision highlighted the inaccuracy of the integration test because, obviously, Kelly was an intergral, or important, part of the *Irish Press*.

The integration test is also inappropriate for small businesses, where there is little scope for employee integration.

3. The Mixed Test

The mixed test was developed in the following case, the facts of which illustrate the difficulties of pigeon-holing a particular working arrangement.

> *Ready Mixed Concrete v Minister for Pensions* (1968)
> The contract of a lorry driver for the plaintiff company stated that he was self-employed. He owned, insured and maintained his own lorry, but Ready Mixed Concrete had helped to finance its purchase. He wore a uniform, and the lorry was painted in the company's colours. He could delegate the driving and was paid per mile driven. The issue

arose as to whether he was an employee for whom Ready Mixed Concrete would have to pay pension contributions to the defendants. The court ruled that all terms of the relationship should be considered and, in so doing, decided that the driver was, in fact, an independent contractor.

The problem with the mixed test is that it leads to adding and subtracting of issues, rather than taking an overview. Control also plays an important part in the mixed test, as it is the first factor considered. Thus the Irish courts have adopted the following test.

4. The Reality Test

The reality test was first used in the following case.

> *Kirwan v Dart Industries and Leahy* (1980) Ire
> Dart Industries was the international organisation that manufactured Tupperwear. Leahy was the distributor for a certain part of Ireland. Kirwan sold Tupperware for Leahy. She was given a car by Leahy, which was taxed and insured but for which Kirwan paid the running costs. Kirwan earned commission on the sales of the Tupperwear dealers she trained. In determining her status, the Employment Appeals Tribunal looked at the reality of the situation. Kirwan had some freedom as to her work, but ultimate control rested with Leahy. Kirwan was an integral part of the company's distribution. The car was an inducement to succeed. In deciding that Kirwan was under a contract of service, the Tribunal stated the proper approach was to 'consider the reality of the situation, consider all the aspects, no single one is decisive'.

The reality test is different from the mixed test because in the mixed test, the element of control is treated as the most important of the range of factors. In the reality test, all factors are considered equally, and an overview is taken. There is no exhaustive list of factors for the court to consider. However, some examples of the factors to which the court or tribunal may look are:

- method of payment of wages;
- whether tax or PRSI is deducted at source;
- whether the worker provides his or her own tools or equipment;
- whether the worker is viewed as being an employee by the other employees;
- the degree of financial risk taken by the worker;
- whether the worker has his or her own helpers;
- whether the worker has an opportunity to profit from sound management in the performance of the task.

In summary, all tests may still be used, but in complex situations the reality test is considered most suitable. Recently the Revenue and the courts have become increasingly likely to hold a worker to be an employee rather than a self employed contractor.

Mahon v Henry Denny & Sons (Ireland) Ltd (1997) Ire
The plaintiff was a supermarket food demonstrator with Denny's, which was a wholly owned subsidiary of Kerry Foods. She was paid £28 (€35.50) per day plus mileage. Kerry Foods provided all her food and equipment for demonstration and her uniform. Mahon was under twenty-four hours notice to work. If she arrived at a supermarket to find her demonstration cancelled, she had to be available for an alternative demonstration; if none was available she would receive only her mileage allowance.

Mahon's contract provided, 'You will not be an employee of Kerry Foods, you will be providing it with your services as an independent contractor, as and when you are required, during the terms of the contract'. She was responsible for her own tax affairs and was not insured for any damage or injury she might sustain or cause while working for Kerry Foods. The contract was renewed annually.

In the Supreme Court it was held that Mahon was an employee rather than an independent contractor, despite the contract which she had signed to the contrary. Among the features the judge highlighted were:

- the worker did not provide any independent input into her job;
- the worker did not provide any equipment or investment;
- the worker could not alter her level of earnings through improving efficiency of management.

Additional Employee Issues

1. Label on Employment Irrelevant

It is important to note that it is for the courts or tribunal to determine whether a contract is 'of service' or 'for services'. The intention of the contracting parties or the label given to the relationship is not determinative, as seen in the *Mahon* case.

2. Taxation Issues

The Revenue Commissioners take a strict view of what constitutes an employee, and if they believe that arrangements with contract staff are a sham implemented to avoid taxation, the employer may become liable to pay PRSI for the 'consultant'. In addition, the worker may face a tax bill. An employment contract aimed at defrauding the Revenue may not be enforced by the courts.

Lewis v Squash (Ireland) Ltd (1983) Ire
The plaintiff was employed by Squash (Ireland) Ltd. He moved from being an employee to the status of a self-employed contractor. His wages thus became consultancy fees, with a large payment for 'expenses'. Later, Lewis claimed that he had been unfairly dismissed. The Employment Appeals Tribunal held that the intention of both parties to defraud the Revenue meant that the contract was illegal and would not be enforced by the EAT.

However, the Unfair Dismissals Act 1993 now provides that, notwithstanding the contraventions of law, a dismissed employee is entitled to have his case heard to conclusion. However, the court or EAT is required to notify the Revenue Commissioners (or the Minister for Social Welfare if the case involves an employee working and drawing the dole simultaneously).

3. Office Holders

There is also the distinction between employees and office holders. An office holder is someone who holds a position created by statute, such as a company director, the holder of a senior public sector position or the Garda Commissioner, as in *Garvey v Ireland* (1981) Ire. The same tests are used for determining whether such a person is an employee or not. Many officer holders are excluded from such legislation as that covering unfair dismissals. All public-sector office holders are taxable under schedule E regardless of their status.

4. Regular Part-Time Employees

It is important to understand that whether a worker is part-time or full-time has nothing to do with the distinction of employees and independent contractors as seen in the *Mahon v Denny* case. Part-time workers are treated the same as full-time under the Protection of Employees (Part-Time Work) Act 2001. The aims of the act are to facilitate and to improve the quality of part-time work. The act guarantees that part-time workers may not be treated less favourably than full-time workers. A full-time employee is defined as an employee who is not a part-time employee, and a part-time employee is defined as an employee whose normal hours of work are less than the those of a comparable employee.

The rights that now apply to such workers are under the following acts, where part-time workers have the same rights as full-time workers:

- Terms of Employment (Information) Acts 1994 and 2001—written notice of terms of employment;
- Minimum Notice and Terms of Employment Acts 1973 to 2001—minimum notice;
- Maternity Protection of Employees Act 1981 and Maternity Protection Act 1994—maternity leave;

- Unfair Dismissals Acts 1977 to 2001—protection against unfair dismissal;
- Redundancy Payments Acts 1967 to 2001 and Protection of Employees (Employer's Insolvency) Acts 1984 to 2001—statutory redundancy;
- Organisation of Working Time Act 1997—maximum forty-eight-hour week for most employees and twenty days of annual leave. Part-time employees are entitled to a lesser amount.

It is important to realise that certain rights have always applied to part-time workers, such as equality and health and safety.

5. Fixed Term Contracts

A contract of service given to an employee can be open ended or fixed term. Previously, fixed term contracts were often rolled over by employers in order to get around the Unfair Dismissals Acts. Typically, employment contracts were for a period of under twelve months, with a break of two months, followed by another fixed term contract. The Unfair Dismissals (Amendment) Act 1993 now provides that if a fixed term or specified purpose contract expires and an employee is offered another fixed term contract within three months, the employer may have to justify the dismissal if the second contract is not renewed. The aim of this provision is to stop employers offering successive fixed term contracts, either with or without a break. This legislative change has greatly reduced the flexibility and use of fixed term contracts.

6. Agency Staff

Difficulties can arise in determining the legal status of a 'servant of two masters', i.e. where an employee of A is contracted out to B. A key legal question is who is responsible for a worker's wrongs while that worker is contracted out.

As a result of *Minister for Labour v PMPA Insurance Ltd* (1986) Ire, see page 134, this area of law has changed. The Unfair Dismissals (Amendment) Act 1993 and the Terms of Employment (Information) Act 1994 deem an employee working for an employer through another body or employment agency to be employed by the person for whom they are doing the work. Thus, staff contracted from agencies have gained some security of employment against the company where they work.

The definition of employment agency in the legislation is very wide and does not require that the supplier of labour actually trades as an employment agency, so that A's workers subcontracted out to B may be deemed to be employed by B.

> *Bourton v Narcea Ltd and AIBP* (1995) Ire
> AIBP were a meat processing plant. They required boners for seasonal work, which they hired from Narcea. Bourton was employed by

Narcea as a boner. Following a row between Bourton and an employee of AIBP, AIBP refused to allow Bourton into their plant. Narcea sought to move him elsewhere, but he refused and subsequently claimed Narcea had unfairly dismissed him. He later included AIBP in his claim.

The court held that Bourton was an employee of AIBP under the Unfair Dismissals (Amendment) Act 1993 (although his case failed because he lacked the requisite service). Thus in this case Narcea who did the actual dismissing were treated as the agency, and AIBP were deemed to be the employer who had to justify the fairness of the dismissal.

7. Company Directors

Regardless of whether company directors are employees or independent contractors, their service contracts cannot be for longer than five years at a time. Five-year contracts can be renewed in their last six months. Any term longer than five years must be approved by the shareholders. Under section 5 of the Companies Act 1990 a shareholder is entitled to inspect a copy of a director's service contract.

B. Formation of the Contract of Employment

A contract of employment has the same essential elements as any contract, for example, a job advertisement is an invitation to treat. A person may offer him or herself for the job, and an employer may accept this. All employment contracts are a mixture of express and implied terms from various sources.

The Terms of Employment (Information) Acts 1994 to 2001 provide that an employer must give an employee a written statement of the terms of employment within two months of starting work. This written statement must include:

- the full name of the employer and employee;
- the address of the employer;
- the place or places of work;
- the job title or the nature of the work;
- the date of commencement of employment;
- the duration of a temporary or fixed-term contract;
- the pay intervals and the rate or method of calculating remuneration;
- the hours of work;
- the paid leave;
- the terms and conditions relating to sickness or injury;
- the pensions and pension schemes;
- the periods of notice of termination of employment;
- reference to any relevant collective agreements.

Failure to comply with the Act can result in an employee being paid up to four weeks' wages as compensation on hearing before the rights commissioner and appeal to the Employment Appeals Tribunal.

Remember that a valid employment contract may be formed orally, but written terms are useful for information and proof.

C. Sources of Contracts of Employment

Employment contracts are unusual in that very often more is implied into the contract than is expressly stated. Typically, a contract of employment is composed of both express terms and implied terms:

* from the Constitution of 1937;
* from common law;
* from statute;
* from collective bargaining.

Express Terms

Express terms will usually be the key terms from an employee's point of view, e.g. payment and hours of work, and these terms will usually be discussed at an interview or upon a job offer being made to a potential employee. Express terms may include mobility clauses whereby an employee agrees to relocate as required by the employer or restraint of trade clauses that prohibit the employee from competing with the employer (by working for a competitor or by opening his or her own business) for a period after the employment ends. Restraint of trade clauses are usually invalid under competition law.

Express terms cannot exclude implied statutory terms. When a statute provides for a statutory minimum, an employer cannot pay employees less than this but is free to give them more. For example, an employer must give employees the statutory minimum redundancy pay but may give them a greater amount than that to which the statute entitles them.

Implied Terms

1. Terms Implied by Bunreacht na hÉireann 1937

Article 40.6.1(iii) of the Constitution guarantees the right of freedom of association. This has been tested in relation to the right to join a trade union in a number of Irish cases.

> *Educational Co of Ireland v Fitzpatrick* (1961) Ire
> This case established the freedom of association. The plaintiff employed union and nonunion staff. In an attempt to compel the employer to hire only union members, the union members picketed the plaintiff's

premises, and the plaintiff sought an injunction to remove them. The Supreme Court ruled that freedom of association meant that employees could join the union of their choice.

Meskell v CIÉ (1973) Ire

This case established the right of disassociation. In an attempt to simplify bargaining, CIÉ dismissed all their employees and automatically re-employed them if they joined a particular union. The plaintiff refused to join the specified union, and the Supreme Court held that he could not be compelled to do so. The court in this case also stated that constitutional rights were superior to common-law rights.

Other constitutional guarantees that are relevant to trade unionism are the freedom of expression in Article 40.6.1(i) and freedom of assembly in Article 40.6.1(ii). The right to earn a livelihood is enshrined in Article 45 of the constitution. Arguably the unenumerated constitutional right of bodily integrity could be applied to health and safety in the workplace. A constitutional term in relation to fair procedures in employment was implied in the following case.

Glover v BLN Ltd (1973) Ire

The contract of the plaintiff director provided that he could be dismissed if guilty of serious misconduct that, in the opinion of the board, would injure the business of the company. The plaintiff was dismissed for such misconduct, but the board did not inform him of the complaints made against him. The Supreme Court held that there had been a breach of natural justice in the failure to give reasons, and as a result Glover was entitled to damages for wrongful dismissal.

2. Terms Implied from Common Law

Until the passing of statutory regulation, common law was the main way that employment law developed, with the courts implying terms into contracts. The courts used the custom test and the reasonable bystander test to strengthen the position of the employee.

Generally, implied common-law terms are split into the duties of the employer and those of the employee. The employer's duties are to pay, to provide work, to secure the employee's safety, to cooperate and to not misrepresent the employee's abilities in a reference.

Duty to Pay (if this is not an express term): If an employee is unpaid, he or she can claim constructive dismissal or, alternatively, redundancy through being put on short time if that is the case.

The Payment of Wages Act 1979 allows an employer to pay wages other than by cash.

> *Nolan v Telecom Eireann* (1985) Ire
> The plaintiff failed to get an injunction to prevent the defendant from paying wages by cheque. The court held that the balance of convenience favoured paying by cheque.

Section 4 of the Payment of Wages Act 1991 provides that the employer shall give an employee a written statement of his or her gross wages and deductions. Section 5 prohibits any deductions from wages unless authorised by statute, a term of the contract or the consent of the employee.

Duty to Provide Work: This is not traditionally a common-law duty, but it was suggested in the following case.

> *Byrne v RHN Foods* (1979) Ire
> The plaintiff was allowed into the workplace but was given no work to do and was effectively shunned by all the employees. She resigned and successfully claimed constructive dismissal (to be discussed later).

The courts have held that a duty to provide work exists in exceptional circumstances, such as:

* when employment is paid on a commission or piece-work basis;
* when employees are undergoing training or apprenticeship;
* when the employee's reputation is as important as the payment.

> *Clayton, Herbert and Jack Waller Ltd v Olivier* (1930)
> The defendant, Laurence Olivier, was moved from a leading role in a film to a supporting one, but his payment remained the same. He successfully proved that the resulting loss of publicity was damaging to his reputation.

This ruling could be extended to apply to any employee with a reputation to protect, in regard to his or her future employment prospects.

Duty to Provide for Employee's Safety: This was traditionally a common-law duty, and an employer's common-law liability remains. However, health and safety legislation now also regulates this area (see page 145). An employer's failure to have regard for this duty has justified constructive dismissal.

Mutual Duty to Cooperate: This is an overall duty judged on the circumstances.

Duty Regarding References: There is no duty on an employer to provide a reference for an employee, although should an employer gives an unjustified positive reference, a subsequent employer who hires on the basis of it may sue for negligent misrepresentation. Equally, an unjustified negative reference may give an employee an action in the tort of defamation.

The employee's implied common-law duties are to exercise skill and care, to obey orders, to be faithful and honest and to cooperate.

Duty to Exercise Skill and Care: As in all legal relationships, this depends on the facts.

Duty to Obey Orders

> *Hartery v Welltrade (Middle East) Ltd* (1978) Ire
> The plaintiff was an accountant with the defendant company. Serious difficulties with the company's contracts in Libya developed, and the plaintiff refused to return from his holidays to deal with them. On his return to work, he was dismissed. Hartery failed to show that this was a wrongful dismissal. The court held that in a genuine emergency, the order to return to work was not unreasonable because of the possible grave consequences for the company if the problems were not resolved.

In the *Hartery* case, the court emphasised the duties of an employee as well paid as the plaintiff. Thus the duty to obey reasonable orders varies according to the circumstances and position of the employee.

> *O'Donoghue v Carroll Group Distributors Ltd* (1982) Ire
> The plaintiff worked for the defendant cigarette company at its distribution centre for Munster. The plaintiff's van bore prominently displayed no smoking stickers. When the plaintiff refused to remove the stickers, she was warned and then dismissed. The Employment Appeals Tribunal held that the stickers were embarrassing and possibly detrimental to the defendant's business and that her dismissal for failure to obey instructions was lawful.

Only lawful orders must be obeyed.

> *Morris v Henleys (Folkstone) Ltd* (1973)
> An employee who was dismissed for refusing to falsify petrol consumption figures was successful in claiming wrongful dismissal.

Duty of Fidelity or Honesty: The employee must account and care for the employer's property, information, money, etc. This duty covers the taking of bribes and making secret profits. It may also cover the confidentiality of information and employment with rival companies. This duty can be seen as part of the overall duty to cooperate.

Duty to Cooperate: This is a duty on both parties. It is mainly used in addition to one of the other duties discussed above. This could have been raised in *Byrne v RHN Foods*.

The importance of implied terms is that their breach can lead to discharge of the employment contract and a common-law action for wrongful dismissal. Breach of an implied term can also justify constructive dismissal.

3. Terms Implied under Collective Bargaining

The results of collective bargaining between trade union or employee representatives and employers are usually expressly incorporated into the contract of employment. Alternatively, they may be adopted by agreement, for example, when an agreed pay rise is given to the workforce. The legal status of collective bargains in Ireland is the subject of much debate (see Chapter 3). The Supreme Court in *Goulding Chemicals v Bolger* (1977) Ire suggested *obiter dicta* that collective bargains are legally enforceable between the parties.

Under the Industrial Relations Act 1946, parties can register a collective bargain with the Labour Court and it will be legally binding, although this is rarely done in practice.

4. Terms Implied by Statute

Some of the statutes that imply terms into employment contracts are listed at page 232 in relation to the protection of regular part-time workers. The Safety Health and Welfare at Work Act 1989, and the Employment Equality Act 1998 are two major instruments of statutory protection of employees.

D. Safety and Health in the Workplace

Specific Legislation

The major piece of legislation here is the Safety Health and Welfare at Work Act 1989, which reformed previous decades of legislation. However, other pieces of legislation covering this area still remain in force, e.g. Mines and Quarries Act 1965, and Dangerous Substances Acts 1972 and 1979.

Safety Health and Welfare at Work Act 1989

The main provisions are:

Duties of Care: A general duty of care is owed by employers, self employed, employees and people in control of premises. The duty also extends to designers, manufacturers, importers and suppliers of articles used by the above people, and to the designers and builders of the place of work (sections 10 and 11). Case law has not yet tested how extensively this will be construed.

These categories of persons are much wider in scope than the old employer-employee categories covered in previous legislation. However, most of the Act is restricted to employees—a person is deemed to be an employee unless the contrary is shown. This definition includes trainees apart from school or college students.

Under section 6 (General Duties of Employers) an employer is under a duty to:

- provide a safe place of work;
- provide a safe means of access and egress;
- provide a safe plant and machinery;
- provide a safe system of work;
- provide information, instruction, training and supervision;
- provide suitable protective clothing or equipment where it is not reasonably practicable to eliminate hazards;
- prepare and revise adequate emergency plans;
- ensure safety and prevent risk in connection with articles or substances;
- provide welfare facilities;
- obtain the services of a competent person to ensure the safety and health of employees.

Under section 9 the duties of an employee are:

- to take reasonable care for his or her own safety and that of others;
- to co-operate with the employer to comply with safety regulations;
- to use protective clothing or equipment provided;
- to report hazards.

Failure to comply with duties imposed under the above sections does not give rise to a right of action in any civil proceedings. These sections are essentially criminal in nature, i.e. they must be enforced by the Health and Safety Authority. However, the Regulations issued under the Act will give rise to such rights, and rights existing prior to 1989 continue to exist, e.g. an action in negligence.

The Safety Statement

The employer must provide a safety statement, which is the employer's detailed management plan on health and safety including a statement of general policy, identification of workplace hazards and assessment of the risks to health and safety. The safety statement must be brought to the attention of employees and must be revised as necessary. There is no obligation on the employer to consult with the employees regarding the safety statement. The safety statement is admissible in evidence in civil and criminal proceedings.

Under section 158 of the Companies Act 1963 the director's report at the annual general meeting of a company must contain an evaluation of the implementation of the company's safety statement during the period of the report.

The Safety Representative

The employees may elect a safety representative who has the right to represent the workforce in dealings with the employer, the Health and Safety Authority and the inspectors. Safety representatives have the right to paid leave for training courses, a right to investigate accidents and dangers, and a right of information from the employer necessary to ensure safety and health.

Accident Prevention

Part III of the Act establishes the National Authority for Occupational Safety and Health, more commonly known as the Health and Safety Authority. It has five main functions:

* to enforce the legislation;
* to promote safety and accident prevention;
* to produce codes of practice on safety;
* to provide advice and information;
* to conduct and publish research.

This is supervised by the Minister for Enterprise, Trade and Employment.

Enforcement

Enforcement of the action is by criminal sanction. The Health and Safety Authority has an enforcement role under the Act. The authority has the power to enter and search, take statements and confiscate goods. The Act provides for the appointment of inspectors, who can also issue improvement and prohibition notices, the issue of which is appealable to the District Court. An improvement notice specifies any defaults to be remedied and, if necessary, the measures to be followed. The authority can apply to the High Court ex parte for a prohibition order to close a place of work or part of it when it is deemed unsafe.

Section 30 provides for the issue of codes of practice by the Authority. The codes provide practical guidance for employers. Although failure to comply will not render a person liable under civil or criminal law, the codes are admissible in evidence and represent good practice. These codes will therefore prove significant in future legal proceedings.

If an accident occurs where a worker is out of work for three days or where the worker dies as a result of a work related injury, this must be reported to the Health and Safety Authority.

Common Law Liability for Safety

An action in the tort of negligence still exists for workplace injuries. An injured employee must show that the employer owed him a duty of care which was breached, causing loss to the plaintiff. As with all tort law, the duty of care owed by an employer to an employee and vice versa, will vary with the circumstances.

> *McKeever v Dundalk Linen Co* (1966) Ire
> A fifteen-year-old was injured on his first day at work. The court held that it was negligent not to supervise him, because of his age and inexperience.

Four Safety Standards

These four standards were developed by the courts at common law:

1. A Safe Place of Work

Where the employer does not own or occupy the premises on which employees must work, the duty of care will depend on the circumstances.

2. Safe or Competent Staff

This duty to ensure staff are safe and competent applies in all circumstances, including hiring, supervision and firing.

> *Hough v Irish Base Metals Ltd* (1967) Ire
> The plaintiff was injured on his first day of work, when another employee kicked a gas burner at him 'for divilment'. The employers were not liable.

3. Safe and Proper Equipment

The employer must provide and maintain safe equipment, protective clothing and other requirements as needed.

4. Safe System of Work

Safe system of work is a separate and cumulative category. A system of work includes all reasonably incidental tasks and facilities, e.g. breaks, provision of first-aid kit etc. The plaintiff in the *Hough* case based his action on lack of a safe system.

E. Discrimination in Employment

Discrimination in employment is the area of greatest legal regulation, apart from dismissal.

Employment Equality Act 1998

The Employment Equality Act 1998 radically reformed the law on equality in the workplace, by repealing the Equal Pay Act 1974 and substantially repealing the Employment Equality Act 1977. The old law dealt only with discrimination on the grounds of sex or marital status, whereas now the grounds for discrimination have been substantially expanded to include:

- gender;
- marital status;
- family status (including caring for a child or disabled person);
- sexual orientation;
- religion;
- age (eighteen to sixty-five, or in vocational training over school leaving age);
- disability;
- race;
- membership of the Travelling community.

Discrimination on any of these grounds is prohibited.

The Act covers direct and indirect discrimination in relation to:

- access to employment;
- conditions of employment;
- training or experience for or in relation to employment;
- promotion or regrading;
- classification of posts.

Contracts and collective agreements will be void if they discriminate within the terms of the Act. Advertising which is discriminatory within the Act is prohibited.

The Act also deals directly with the issue of vicarious liability—an employer will be liable for an act done by an employee in the course of his or her employment. However, in proceedings brought against an employer, it will be a defence for the employer to prove that he or she took reasonable steps to prevent such acts.

Equality between Men and Women

Men and women shall at any time be entitled to equal pay for equal work, for the same or associated employers. Where the employees are working for associated employers, the contracts of employment do not have to be the same, although the terms must be reasonably comparable. The definition of like work covers work that is identical, similar and equal in value. Under the previous equal pay act, a case on equal in value was:

Four Female Employees v Irish Aviation Authority (1998) Ire
Four female 'Communication Assistants' employed by the defendant
claimed that they were entitled to equal pay as two male 'Radio
Officers' because the work done was equal in value when compared
under a number of headings. The male workers were paid nearly
£9,500 (€12,062) more per year. The Labour Court held that the jobs
were equal in value and the four women were awarded £100,000
(€127,000) each in back pay.

A general equality clause in relation to gender issues is implied in contracts of
employment. An employer will be allowed to operate differences between
contracts of employment where the difference is based on grounds other than
gender. Indirect discrimination is also included. Indirect discrimination
covers non-essential requirements for a job which a higher percentage of
one sex can comply with, e.g. an age limit may discriminate against women
who have taken time off work to rear children. Positive action to eliminate
the effects of past discrimination against women is allowed.

For the first time in Irish legislation, sexual harassment is specifically
provided for in the 1998 Act. An employer may be liable where an
employee is sexually harassed by the employer, another employee or a
client or customer of the employer.

Butler v Four Star Pizza Ltd (1995) Ire
The defendant employer was held vicariously liable when they failed
to act following complaints by one staff member that she had been
sexually harassed by another employee.

However, the definition of sexual harassment imposes an objective test
of what a reasonable person would find offensive, rather than a
subjective test of what the actual employee found offensive.

There are some exceptions where discrimination is provided for in certain
cases including:

- grounds of authenticity for entertainment, e.g. a male model;
- the performance of duties outside the state where laws or customs could
  not reasonably allow for a person of another sex to do the duties, e.g. a
  male engineer required for Saudi Arabia;
- duties involving personal services, e.g. a personal nurse;
- sleeping or sanitary facilities for employees are on a communal basis and
  it is unreasonable to expect the employer to provide separate sleeping
  facilities.

Exceptions are made for benefits conferred on women in relation to
pregnancy, maternity and adoption.

Exceptions are also made in certain circumstances for the Gardaí, Navy
and prison service.

Equality Generally

In relation to other grounds, the Act provides for an entitlement to equal treatment and pay. It prohibits direct and indirect discrimination on such grounds. It also provides that harassment of an employee on one ground will constitute discrimination by the employer. Positive action is allowed for persons over fifty, those with a disability or members of the Travelling community.

An employer may not discriminate against a person on the disability ground where the person requires special facilities if the cost of providing the facilities will not give rise to undue hardship.

It is lawful to impose requirements in relation to residence, citizenship, proficiency in Irish on Gardaí, members of the defence forces, civil servants, officers of local authorities and teachers.

There is a specific exclusion of discrimination by religious, educational or medical institutions where the institution is controlled by a religious body and the discrimination is essential for the ethos of the institution.

Enforcement

A new office of Director of Equality Investigations within the Labour Relations Commission has been established by the Act. Complaints of discrimination under the Act must be made within six months of the occurrence. The parties may be referred to binding mediation if they do not object. If it is a matter of dismissal, it is referred directly to the Labour Court. An individual may refer the matter directly to the Circuit Court.

The director may:

(1) order compensation of up to three years arrears of remuneration;

(2) order the equal remuneration;

(3) order compensation for the effects of discrimination;

(4) order equal treatment in whatever respect is relevant;

(5) order a person to take a course of action.

The Labour Court may order (3)–(5) above, and may order re-instatement or re-engagement with or without compensation. The Circuit Court may make similar orders to the Director, and may order re-instatement or re-engagement with or without compensation.

The Act also provides for a new Equality Authority. The new Authority will be able to refer matters to the Director of Equality Investigations. It will be entitled to seek injunctions and will be able to refer collective agreements to the director. It will be entitled to develop codes of practice, carry out equality reviews and take proceedings in cases of discriminatory advertising.

F. Maternity, Adoptive and Parental Leave

Maternity Protection Act 1981

The aim of the Maternity Protection Act 1981 is to provide for maternity leave with protection of employment for female employees. The social welfare scheme provision is eighteen weeks at tax free seventy per cent of gross earnings. Some employers 'pay' their female employees on maternity leave, i.e. they top up the social welfare money by paying the employee's salary as normal and having her reimburse the employer with the social welfare money. An employer is not obliged to do this. An employee may take an additional eight weeks unpaid leave.

During leave, there is no break in continuous employment. Maternity leave is not dependent on returning to work, and an employee who intends to do so must give formal notice of that intention. An employee should return to her old job, or one equivalent in grade and location. To exercise her right of maternity leave, an employee must observe the time limits and procedures set out in the Act for notice of leave. Cases go the Employment Appeals Tribunal, with an appeal to the Circuit Court and, ultimately, the High Court.

Maternity Protection Act 1994

The Maternity Protection Act 1994 provides as follows:

- leave on health and safety grounds where there is a risk to the health and safety of an employee. Employees who have recently given birth (in the last eighteen weeks) or who are breast-feeding up to twenty-six weeks after the birth have this right, if the Safety, Health and Welfare at Work Act 1989 requires it;
- leave of an employed father from his employment on the death of the mother during her maternity leave;
- time off work for ante-natal and post-natal care, providing appropriate notice is given;
- protection of employment rights during a period of leave and natal care absence.

Adoptive Leave Act 1995

Adoptive leave is available to an adopting mother or a sole male adopter who is in employment. The leave is fourteen consecutive weeks of adoptive leave from the beginning of the placement of the child, and an additional eight weeks' unpaid adoptive leave. The fourteen week period normally qualifies for a social welfare benefit as with maternity leave. Absence on leave is not counted as a break in continuous service.

An adoptive parent must give four weeks' notice of expected date of placement, and confirm this as soon as possible. In the case of foreign adoptions, an eligible employee must give their employer a copy of the declaration of suitability and eligibility, issued pursuant to the Adoption Act 1991, before the start of adoptive leave. They must also give an expected date of placement. Particulars of placement must be furnished as soon as possible thereafter. Leave can thus be taken prior to the adoption, to allow the adoptive parent to go abroad.

On the death of an adoptive mother, the adoptive father may take the balance of the leave, as under the Maternity Protection Act 1994.

A married, adoptive father is not entitled to leave despite the following decision which was taken under the old Employment Equality Act 1977:

> *O'Grady v Telecom Eireann* (1997) Ire
> Telecom Eireann implemented adoptive leave for female civil servants in 1983. The leave was for ten weeks with pay. Mr O'Grady and his wife adopted a child in Romania in 1991. He applied for the adoptive leave scheme and was refused. Mr O'Grady argued he had been denied adoptive leave while a female comparator had been given it. His argument was that there was no biological reason to restrict adoptive leave to women, and this constituted sexual discrimination under the Employment Equality Act 1977.
>
> The Labour Court held that Mr O Grady had been discriminated against under the Employment Equality Act 1997 by being treated less favourably than a woman in similar circumstances. The Supreme Court said Telecom's scheme treated adoptive mothers more favourably than adoptive fathers and was thus discriminatory.
>
> There is currently no legislative intention to introduce adoptive leave for married men.

Parental Leave Act 1998

The Parental Leave Act 1998 introduced unpaid leave for parents. It applies to both men and women, in relation to their children born or adopted on or after 3 June 1996. Each parent with one year's continuous service is entitled to fourteen weeks leave for each child, which must be taken before the child is five (subject to modification in the case of an adopted child). Each parent has a separate right to take leave. The leave is not transferable. A woman's parental leave does not affect her right to maternity leave.

An employee must give six weeks' notice of intention to take leave. An employer may postpone leave if it would have a substantial adverse effect on the business, but must agree to a date within six months. After parental leave, an employee should return to his old job, or one equivalent in grade and location. Employment rights, except remuneration and superannuation benefits, are unaffected during leave.

The Act also introduces Force Majeure leave which gives all employees a right to limited time off for family emergencies caused by accident or illness. This leave is paid, and separate from parental leave. Force Majeure leave is limited to a maximum of three days in twelve months or five days in thirty-six months. The leave applies where, due to an injury or illness of a close family member, the immediate presence of the employee is indispensably required at the place where the family member is. A 'family member' is a child or person to whom the employee is in loco parentis, a spouse or person with whom the employee is living as husband and wife, brother, sister, parent or grandparent.

The Carer's Leave Act 2001

This act introduced a new entitlement for employees to take temporary unpaid carer's leave for sixty-five weeks to care personally for persons who require full-time care and attention. The employee is entitled to return to work afterwards with no deterioration in his or her conditions of employment. There is no requirement that the carer and person cared for be related; no specific relationship is required.

Protection of Employees (Part-Time Work) Act 2001

The Protection of Employees (Part-Time Work) Act 2001 extends the protection of maternity leave, adoptive leave, parental leave and carer's leave to part-time employees.

G. Ending Contracts of Employment

We will begin by looking at the implied statutory terms on terminating a contract of employment.

Strict contract theory can be applied to the discharge of an employment contract, i.e. discharge by performance, breach, agreement and frustration. However, in general, the categories of lawful dismissal, summary dismissal, constructive dismissal, wrongful dismissal and unfair dismissal are used. These will first be explained in brief and then in detail.

Definitions

Lawful Dismissal: An employee can be lawfully dismissed by notice. The required notice may be in the contract of employment or it may be the statutory minimum in the Minimum Notice and Terms of Employment Acts 1973 to 2001.

Summary Dismissal: This is dismissal without notice. Section 8 of the 1973 Act provides that in cases of 'misconduct', employees may be dismissed without notice.

Constructive Dismissal: This refers to an employee who leaves his or her employment as a result of the employer's behaviour in repudiation of the contract. This is treated as dismissal rather than redundancy.

Wrongful Dismissal: This is dismissal in breach of the contract of employment. It is an alternative action to unfair dismissal. The most common example of wrongful dismissal is dismissal without adequate notice, where the employer has no reason for summary dismissal.

Unfair Dismissal: The Unfair Dismissals Acts 1977 to 2001 give a right of redress in cases of unfair dismissal. Prior to this, an employee who was dismissed for an arbitrary reason but who was given notice or payment had no legal action.

1. Lawful Dismissal

A contract is lawfully terminated by notice. The required notice may be in the contract of employment or it may be the statutory minimum in the Minimum Notice and Terms of Employment Acts 1973 to 2001. Section 4 of the Act provides that employees with thirteen weeks of continuous service must be given notice as follows:

Continuous Service	Notice
Less than two years	one week
two to five years	two weeks
five to ten years	four weeks
ten to fifteen years	six weeks
over fifteen years	eight weeks

Section 6 provides that an employee must give one week's notice, regardless of length of service (unless the contract provides otherwise). 'Notice' is not defined in the Act, but clear dates must be given. The rights of an employee during the notice period are the same as normal in relation to such things as holidays and sickpay.

2. Summary Dismissal

Summary dismissal is dismissal without notice. Section 8 of the 1973 Act provides that in cases of 'misconduct', employees may be dismissed without notice. 'Misconduct' was defined in *Carvill v Irish Industrial Bank Ltd* (1988) Ire as 'actions or omissions of employees inconsistent with performance of the express or implied terms of their contract'. Examples would include theft, arson, assault and breach of confidentiality. Basically, the employee's behavior leads to a situation in which he or she can be dismissed on the spot; i.e. it would seem ridiculous for the employer to have to give notice. Summary dismissal may be lawful or wrongful depending on the facts.

3. Constructive Dismissal

Constructive dismissal occurs when an employee leaves the workplace but is treated as having been dismissed because the employer's conduct has made it impossible for the employee to stay. Thus the dismissal is not actual but said to be 'constructed'. Examples of circumstances justifying constructive dismissal are the employer's breaching an essential procedural requirement such as the provision of work or pay, failure to provide a safe system of work or the poisoning of the work environment, as in cases of sexual harassment. If an employee were constructively dismissed, he or she would be able to claim for either wrongful or unfair dismissal.

4. Wrongful Dismissal

Wrongful dismissal is dismissal in breach of the contract of employment. It is an alternative action to unfair dismissal. The most common example of wrongful dismissal is dismissal without adequate notice, in which the employer has no reason for summary dismissal. It is also in breach of contract if a dismissal is in breach of disciplinary procedures stated in the contract.

> *Allied Irish Bank v Lupton* (1984) Ire
> The plaintiff's contract expressly excluded summary dismissal and provided for set procedures in the case of dismissal, which were not followed in the plaintiff's case. The court held the dismissal to be invalid, as the procedures were 'expressed in unequivocal terms in the contract'.

A dismissal for unconstitutional reasons as in *Meskell v CIÉ*, would also be a wrongful dismissal, as would a dismissal in breach of the implied constitutional term of natural justice, as in *Glover v BLN*.

As wrongful dismissal is an action based on contract, ordinary contract remedies apply. Specific performance is traditionally not given for two reasons: because of the difficulty in supervising such an order; and the court's reluctance to force parties to work together when the relationship may have broken down irretrievably. (Remember, however, that the statutory remedies for unfair dismissal are very similar to specific performance.) However, the refusal to give specific performance as a remedy has been modified in recent years.

> *McCann v Irish Medical Organisation* (1989) Ire
> The plaintiff was general secretary of the Irish Medical Organisation (IMO). He sought an injunction restraining the defendant from terminating his service and appointing another person to his position. The High Court granted an interim injunction to the plaintiff restraining the defendant from appointing another to his job, which is similar to ordering the IMO to honour his contract of employment.

The remedy of declarative relief is used to declare the dismissal null and void. It is used in breaches of fair procedures and the Constitution.

Damages are the most commonly awarded remedy. The award can include damages for loss of reputation and, for high earners, is often greater than an award in relation to unfair dismissal.

Garvey v Ireland (1981) Ire

The plaintiff was the Commissioner of the Garda Síochána. He was dismissed without warning by the Government of the day and was not given any reasons or opportunity to contest the dismissal. The Supreme Court held that the dismissal was 'void and ineffective' because the Government has failed to act fairly or in accordance with the principles of natural justice. Garvey was awarded damages partly to compensate for the damage to his feelings and reputation and partly to punish the Government in punitive damages for acting as it did.

5. Unfair Dismissal

The legislation in the area of unfair dismissal gives a right of redress in cases of unfair dismissal. Prior to this, an employee who was dismissed for an arbitrary reason but who was given notice or payment had no legal action. The law is contained in the Unfair Dismissals Acts 1977 to 2001.

Dismissal is defined in section 1 of the Unfair Dismissals Act 1977 and does not include resignation, frustration or the expiry of a fixed term contract but does include constructive dismissal.

Section 2 of the 1977 Act excludes certain people from claiming under the Acts:

• people of retiring age;
• those employed by a close relative in a private house or farm where both reside;
• members of the defence forces and gardaí;
• FÁS trainees and apprentices;
• those with written contracts of training or probationary periods;
• those with less than one year of continuous service.

It has been estimated that these exclusions cover twenty per cent of the workforce.

To claim under the Act, an employee must prove:

(a) that he or she is under a contract of service;
(b) that he or she has one year of continuous service. (However, in some cases one year's service is not required; the claim can be made at any time);
(c) that he or she was dismissed.

The employer must then prove that the dismissal was not for an unfair reason. In practice this determination is left with the Employment Appeals Tribunal, so there is no real shifting of the burden of proof.

If an employee is not justified in leaving the workplace, it will be treated as a resignation, and this is a question for the courts to decide on the facts.

Futty v D & D Brekker (1974)
A supervisor in the defendant company said to the plaintiff, 'If you don't like the job, f . . . off.' Mr Futty took this to mean that he was dismissed. The court held that bad language was not uncommon in the workplace, and the words meant 'get on with the job'. The employee was not justified in treating it as a case of constructive dismissal.

Fair Grounds for Dismissal

Once it has been established that a dismissal took place, the employer must then show that it was not unfair. Section 6(4) lists the fair grounds, which are capability, competence, qualifications, conduct, redundancy, statute or other substantial grounds.

1. Capability

'Capability' refers to the claimant's physical or mental ability to do the job. The Employment Appeals Tribunal considers the employee's blame or lack of blame as irrelevant.

2. Competence

'Competence' covers poor work performance.

3. Qualifications

'Qualifications' refers to formal employment requirements. A dismissal of a driver who lost his or her licence would not be unfair, nor would the dismissal in the case of any missing certification, as in *Ponnampalam v Mid Western Health Board* (1979) Ire (see below), be unfair.

4. Conduct

Conduct is the most commonly used ground in the Act. Conduct that justifies dismissal is the same as misconduct, explained above. This is now interpreted to include conduct outside of the workplace if it damages the employer.

Flynn v Sisters of Holy Faith (1985) Ire
The plaintiff was a secondary school teacher employed in the defendant's convent school. The plaintiff gave birth to a baby while living with a separated married man, and was dismissed shortly afterwards following complaints from parents. The Employment Appeals Tribunal found that there had been no unfair dismissal, and the decision was appealed to the Circuit Court and to the High Court. The High Court held that there had been no unfair dismissal. Costello J. stated 'It seems to me perfectly clear that the appellant's dismissal did not "result" from her pregnancy . . . . [I]t resulted from her refusal to terminate a relationship of which the respondents had complained . . . . [H]er conduct violated her obligations to the school.'

5. Redundancy

'Redundancy' is defined in the Redundancy Payments Act 1967. However, redundancy may be unfair if it is selective.

> *Quilty v Cassin Air Transport (Dublin) Ltd* (1982) Ire
> The plainitff was made redundant from the defendant company while she was on maternity leave. The court held this to be unfair.

> *Dillon v Wexford Seamless Aluminium Gutters* (1980) Ire
> The plaintiff was made redundant from his job with the defendant. The court found that he had been selected because of his trade union activities, which made the dismissal unfair.

6. Contravening Statute

A driver who has had his or her licence revoked could fairly be dismissed, as his or her continued employment would be in breach of the Road Traffic Acts.

> *Ponnampalam v Mid Western Health Board* (1979) Ire
> An Indian doctor was employed by the defendant. His continuing employment as a surgeon required the sanction of Bord na n'Ospideal under the Health Act 1970. When this was not forthcoming, the plaintiff was dismissed because his continued employment was illegal under the Act.

7. Other Substantial Grounds

Section 6(6) states that a dismissal will not be unfair if there are 'other substantial grounds' to justify it. However, because section 6(4) covers so many cases, it is difficult to imagine any other grounds that are not covered. A similar provision in the English unfair dismissals legislation was used to dismiss a woman when it was discovered that she was married to the manager of a firm of competitors.

Fair versus Unfair Dismissals

Even where the dismissal is fair, the employer should give reasons and comply with fair procedures. Failure to do so can make the dismissal unfair.

Section 6(1) states that all dismissals are deemed to be unfair unless the employer can show otherwise. The specific unfair reasons for dismissal as stated in section 6(2) are trade union involvement, religious or political opinions, race or colour, pregnancy-related issues, legal proceedings against the employer, sexual orientation, age or membership in the travelling community.

1. Trade Union Membership or Activities

Dismissal for reason of trade union membership or activities is actionable at any time. There is no requirement to have one year's service.

> *Williams v Gleeson* (1978) Ire
> The plaintiffs were told to choose between the union and their jobs. Their subsequent dismissal for continuing union membership was held to be unfair.

2. Religious or Political Opinions

> *Merriman v St James Hospital* (1986) Ire
> The plaintiff was dismissed after she refused, on religious grounds, to bring a crucifix and candle to the bed of a dying man. The Circuit Court held that this was an unfair dismissal.

3. Race or Colour

Racial discrimination was suggested by the Indian doctor in *Ponnampalam*, above, but the case was decided on another point.

4. Pregnancy or Connected Matters

It is unfair to dismiss an employee for pregnancy or connected matters unless the employee is unable to do her work or it becomes unlawful to continue to employ her. This is, however, subject to the decision in *Flynn v Sisters of Holy Faith* (cited above).

Dismissal for reasons of pregnancy is actionable at any time. There is no requirement to have one year's service.

5. Exercising Statutory Rights

An employee cannot be dismissed for exercising his or her statutory rights to maternity, adoptive, parental or carer's leave, or to the National Minimum Wage. Dismissal for these reasons is actionable at any time. There is no requirement to have one year's service.

6. Involvement in Legal Proceedings against an Employer

An obvious case in which an employee could be victimised is one in which the employee is involved in legal proceedings against the employer. For example, an employee takes an equality action against the employer or a claim for compensation for an accident in the workplace. It would also apply to an employee who has been involved in legal proceedings through giving evidence against his or her employer for another party.

7. Sexual Orientation

The Unfair Dismissals Act 1993 added sexual orientation as an unfair reason.

8. Age

The Unfair Dismissals Act 1993 added age as an unfair reason.

9. Membership of the Travelling Community

The Unfair Dismissals Act 1993 added membership in the travelling community as an unfair reason.

Procedures

To bring a claim, an employee must give notice in writing within six months of the dismissal to the employer and to a rights commissioner. The 1993 Act provides that in exceptional cases, this period may be extended to twelve months. The case could then be referred to the Employment Appeals Tribunal. The 1993 Act introduced the important procedural change that an employee may now go directly to the Employment Appeals Tribunal without reference to a rights commissioner, which is a useful time-saving amendment.

Under the 1977 Act, when a breach of the Income Tax or Social Welfare Acts had occurred, the employee was not entitled to claim a remedy for unfair dismissal. Since the 1993 Act, the tribunal and the courts will now deal with such cases, notwithstanding the contravention of the law, and there is no obligation on the tribunal or the courts to report the breaches to the relevant authorities.

Remedies

The remedies available for a successful action of unfair dismissal are reinstatement, re-engagement and compensation.

1. Reinstatement

Reinstatement is the return of the employee to his or her former job, with no break in continuous service. It is effectively as if the dismissal never took place. Under the 1993 Act, the employee will benefit from any improvements in terms and conditions that occurred after he or she was dismissed. This remedy can be seen as analogous to specific performance of the employment contract.

2. Re-engagement

Under the remedy of re-engagement, the employee is given a new but equivalent job to the former job he or she held. It may be used when the Employment Appeals Tribunal feels reinstatement would be impossible. The Employment Appeals Tribunal has discretion to award re-engagement from the date of dismissal.

3. Compensation

Damages are payable for up to 104 weeks of remuneration. This is the most widely awarded remedy, which may be given in addition to the other remedies or on its own. The award can cover actual and prospective loss.

When an employee can take an action in wrongful dismissal or an action in unfair dismissal, he or she can only choose one. Most employees choose the unfair dismissals route because it is easier to prove, the Employment Appeals Tribunal is cheaper than a court and the available remedies are wider, as shown in Figure 8.1.

Figure 8.1 Differences between wrongful and unfair dismissal

	UNFAIR DISMISSAL	WRONGFUL DISMISSAL
Source of action	• Unfair Dismissals Acts 1977 to 2001	• Breach of contract
Hearing	• Employment Appeals Tribunal	• Ordinary courts
Remedies	• Reinstatement • Re-engagement • Damages	• Damages

H. Redundancy

Redundancy is governed by the Redundancy Payments Acts 1967 to 2003 and the Protection of Employees (Part-Time Work) Act 2001.

Definitions

Redundancy is defined in section 7 of the Redundancy Payments Act 1967. 'Redundancy' is held to have occurred if the dismissal arises when:

(a) the employer ceases to carry on business for which the employee was employed or in the place where the employee was employed;

(b) the requirements for the employee have ceased or diminished;

(c) the employer has decided to carry on business with fewer or no employees, whether by requiring the work that the employee had done to be caried on by other workers or otherwise;

(d) the work that the employee had done is to be done in a different manner for which the employee is not properly qualified or trained;

(e) the work that the employee had done is to be done by a person also capable of doing other work for which the employee is not properly qualified or trained.

Put more simply, the test for redundancy is whether the employee's job has ceased to exist. If the job still exists, it is not a redundancy.

Vaux & Associated Breweries v Ward (1968)
A fifty-seven-year-old female bartender was dismissed from her job in the plaintiff's pub and was replaced by a younger woman wearing a 'bunny girl' costume. The woman claimed redundancy pay, and the court held that it was not a case of redundancy as her job still existed.

Statutory Redundancy

To claim statutory redundancy under the Redundancy Payments Act 2003, a claimant must prove that he or she:

- is under a contract of service;
- is between sixteen and twenty-six years of age;
- has been employed for two years continuously; and
- has been dismissed for reason of redundancy.

Redundancy pay is calculated as follows:

- two week's pay for each continuous year of employment;
- plus one week's pay.

A week's pay is the 'normal weekly remuneration', subject to a maximum figure of €507.90 per week. Statutory redundancy payments are tax-free. (Employers get a rebate of sixty per cent from the Department of Enterprise and Employment, which must be claimed within six months of the redundancy.)

An employee may be able to claim redundancy without being dismissed if he or she is put on 'short time' for four weeks, i.e. if he or she earns less than half the usual weekly amount or does half the usual weekly hours due to lack of work. If this is temporary and the employee is told so, the employee can claim redundancy after four consecutive weeks or six broken weeks on short time in a thirteen-week period.

An employee may also claim redundancy if the employee is 'laid off' for four weeks, which occurs when there is no work at all, although the employer believes that it is temporary and has told the employee so. These option are not popular in a time of high unemployment.

Section D

Company Law

CHAPTER 9

The Characteristics of a Company

Summary of chapter

In this chapter we introduce the concept of corporate personality by discussing the other legal formats a business might take and the different types of companies. The characteristics of a company are explained, particularly the concept of separate legal personality and when this personality may be set aside by the lifting of the 'corporate veil'.

A. Defining a Company

The first point in a study of company law is to define exactly what is meant by a company. The definition in the Companies Act 1963 states that a company means a company *formed and registered* under this Act or an existing company. Since the passing of the subsequent Companies Acts, a company can be said to be an association formed for a business purpose and registered under the Companies Acts 1963 to 2003. This simply means that a company is formed in accordance with all the companies legislation in place at the time. For example, a company formed in 1968 would be a company formed under the Companies Act 1963, a company formed in 1868 would be a company that existed when the 1963 Act was passed and a company formed in 2003 would be a company formed under the Companies Acts 1963 to 2003.

The 'Companies Acts 1963 to 2003' is the collective name for the eleven pieces of legislation relating to company law. These are referred to in the following chapters in an abbreviated form: for example, the Companies Act 1963 is the CA 1963, and the Companies (Amendment) Act 1983 is the C(A)A 1983.

This process of forming and registering a company in accordance with legislation is known as 'incorporation', and once incorporated, the company has an identity of its own, known as a 'separate legal personality'. These are the essential features that set a company apart from the other trading formats open to a person setting up a business.

B. Different Trading Formats

There are three basic trading formats: a company, a sole trader and a partnership.

Company

One choice open to a person setting up a business is to form, or 'incorporate', a registered company. There are different types of registered companies, depending on the uses to which they are to be put. The most common type of company in Ireland, and the one we will consider most carefully, is the private company limited by shares, the typical 'Murphy and Co Ltd'.

The key feature of a company is that it is a legal entity (or person) in its own right, legally different from the people who own it. This is also known as a 'separate legal personality'. The advantage of limited liability results from this.

Sole Trader

The sole trader was the traditional method of doing business in Ireland until the second half of the twentieth century. A sole trader is simply an individual who sets himself or herself up in business. There is no specific law governing sole traders, although they are covered by general law such as the law of contract. A sole trader has no separate legal personality, and any profits or losses made by the business are borne by the sole trader, which is seen as the greatest risk of this form of business. Many people still operate as sole traders. For example, barristers cannot trade other than as sole traders.

Partnership

Partnerships are still a relatively common method of doing business in Ireland, and for some professionals such as accountants and solicitors, it is the only allowable business format. A partnership is defined by the Partnership Act 1890 as an association of two or more parties carrying on a business in common with a view to a profit. A partnership is similar to the coming together of two or more sole traders, with all partners sharing the profits and losses. A partnership has no separate legal personality either.

The primary differences between a partnership and a company are shown in Table 9.1.

C. Effects of Incorporation

There are three main consequences of incorporation, which can also be seen as the advantages of incorporation.

1. Separate Legal Personality

The company becomes a legal person in its own right, distinct from the shareholders and management. This was seen in the famous case of *Salomon v Salomon & Co Ltd* (1897) (see section E below). Separate personality means that the artificial legal person, the company, can do almost everything a human person can do; it can make contracts, employ people, borrow and pay money, sue and be sued, among other things.

Table 9.1 Partnerships versus Companies

Characteristic	Partnership	Company
Name	'Murphy and Partners' 'Murphy and Company'	'Murphy & Co Ltd' 'Murphy Plc'
Size	two to twenty partners fifty partners for accountants and solicitors	one to fifty shareholders for a private company seven or more shareholders for a public company
Separate Legal Personality	None	Personality that is distinct from its shareholders. A company can own property, employ people and have a bank account
Liability	All partners have unlimited liability *Exception:* limited liability for one partner under the Limited Partnership Act 1907	Limited liability for all shareholders up to the limit that they owe on their shares
Succession	Partnership dissolves on death of one partner *Exception:* If agreement otherwise specifies	Perpetual succession with new members taking over when a shareholder dies
Management	Partners acting jointly	Directors manage on behalf of shareholders
Shares	None Partners' interest cannot be transferred without the consent of other partners	Freely transferable *Exception:* Restricted transfer on shares of a private company
Regulation	Partnership agreement is optional	Memorandum of Association and Articles of Association are mandatory
Legislation	Partnership Act 1890 Limited Partnership Act 1907	Companies Acts 1963 to 2003

2. Limited Liability

Once incorporated, a company's members enjoy limited liability, provided that their shares are fully paid up and it is a limited company. For example, if a company goes into liquidation owing €100,000, the debt is the debt of the company, not of the shareholders. The shareholders' debts are limited to any money they owe for the purchase of their shares.

3. Perpetual Succession

A corporation once formed will continue until such time as it is wound up. The fact that a member, even one holding one hundred per cent of the company's shares, dies has no effect on the legal existence of the company.

However, there are some potential disadvantages of forming a company, although in practice the advantages greatly outweigh these.

1. The Costs of Incorporation

The cost of incorporation, currently €60 plus one per cent of the value of the issued share capital, and the annual cost of administering a company may be a deterrent to a very small business.

2. Complex Regulation

The Companies Acts have made the regulation of a small company unnecessarily complex, so some businesses may prefer to stay as sole traders or partnerships.

3. Disclosure

A company is less private than a sole trader or partnership, as a certain amount of information has to be made available to the public. (However, allowances are made for a small private company in relation to what it needs to disclose.)

4. Capital Maintenance

There are strict rules on capital maintenance in a company, dealing with the withdrawal of capital or profits from a company. Such rules do not apply to sole traders or partners.

5. Cessation of Business

If a company wishes to cease business, it must be formally wound up, unlike a sole trader or partnership, which simply goes out of business.

D. Types of Companies

A registered company may be limited or unlimited. A limited company may be limited by guarantee or by shares. A company limited by shares may be a private or public company. A comparison is shown in Figure 9.1.

1. An Unlimited Company

An unlimited company is very similar to a partnership in that the company members, like partners, are liable for the debts of the company. They may be liable without limit or liability may be limited to a certain figure, e.g. €10,000. A person may choose to form such a company to avail of a corporate structure, for example, when buying property. Also, unlimited companies do not have to attach accounts to the annual return, so it has a privacy advantage. Unlimited companies are relatively rare in practice, totaling approximately 3,000 companies in Ireland.

Figure 9.1 Types of companies

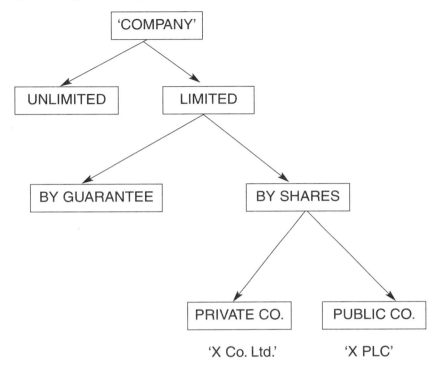

2. A Company Limited by Guarantee

A company limited by guarantee is a company that guarantees to pay its debts up to a certain limit in the event of the company being wound up. This format is often used for charities, clubs and nonprofit organisations. Usually the members do not provide money to the company on formation or during its life, so it is suitable for companies that wish to get legal personality and limited liability but do not need to raise money from its members. There are approximately 8,500 companies limited by guarantee in Ireland.

3. A Company Limited by Shares

A company limited by shares is the most common type of company, accounting for ninety per cent of all companies. In this type of company, the liability of shareholders for the debts of a company is limited to any amount unpaid on their shares. Normally, when shareholders buy shares, they pay for them fully, so they then have no liability to the company if it goes into debt. (It is similar to my buying and paying for a CD player. If the seller then goes into liquidation, I have no responsibility to pay them any more money.) Limited liability is the reason most people form a company limited by shares. This type of company is often simply referred to as a 'limited company'.

4. Public and Private Limited Companies

When forming a company limited by shares, there is a choice between forming a private or a public company. The modern public limited company was created by the Companies (Amendment) Act 1983.

Section 2, C(A)A 1983 defines a public limited company as 'a company which is not a private company'. The requirements of a public limited company are that:

(1) the memorandum must state that it is a public company (section 5, C(A)A 1983);
(2) the name must end with the words 'public limited company' or 'cuideachta phoibli teoranta' (section 4, C(A)A 1983);
(3) the nominal value of the share capital must be at least €38,092 (section 19, C(A)A 1983).

A company that does not comply with these requirements is a private company.

A public company may be created in three ways:

- it may have been originally created as a public limited company before 1983;
- it may be created as a modern public limited company under the 1983 legislation;
- it may have been reregistered from a private company to a public limited company.

There are approximately 130,500 private companies in Ireland and almost 1,000 public companies.

It is important to remember that not all public companies are quoted on the Irish Stock Exchange. In fact, of the public companies in Ireland, less than one tenth of these are listed on the exchange. Companies listed on the stock exchange are often called 'publicly quoted companies', or 'market companies'.

There are a number of other differences between private and public companies, as shown in Table 9.2.

5. Group Companies

Sometimes companies may be organised into a group. There will be one holding company that holds shares in other companies, known as 'subsidiaries'. (A company can own shares in the same way as a human can, due to its separate legal personality.)

Group companies are used where a company has a diverse series of interests or wants to separate its areas of business for management and administration reasons.

Table 9.2 Private versus public companies

Characteristic	Private	Public
Reason for formation	To benefit from separate legal personality and limited liability	To raise capital from the public
Type	Pub, shop or dry cleaner	Company with a national or international dimension, e.g. Waterford Wedgewood plc Bank of Ireland plc Guinness plc
Nominal value of share capital	None	€38,092
Commencement documentation	Certificate of Incorporation	Certificate of Incorporation and Certificate to Commence Trading
Transferability of stock	Restricted	Freely transferable
Number of shareholders	one to fifty	Minimum seven
Requirement to provide financial information	Some exceptions for small- and medium-sized companies	Required
Term of director	May be 'for life'	Limited term

The Companies Act 1963, section 155 defines the relationship of holding and subsidiary companies. A company is a subsidiary of another if that other company:

(a) is a member of it and controls the composition of the board of directors; or

(b) holds more than half in nominal value of its equity share capital; or

(c) holds more than half in nominal value of its shares carrying voting rights (other than voting rights arising only in specified circumstances); or

(d) the first-mentioned company is a subsidiary of any company that is the other's subsidiary.

6. One Person Companies

Since the EC (Single Member Private Company) Regulations 1994, it is possible to incorporate a private limited company with only one shareholder. (Prior to 1994, private companies were required to have two shareholders.)

E. Corporate Personality

As explained above, the most notable feature of a company is that it is separate at law from its shareholders, or is a separate legal person. The 'veil of incorporation' is the rather poetic term given to this separation of the company from its shareholders or members. This separation of a company from its members was established in the House of Lords in the following famous case.

> *Salomon v Salomon & Co Ltd* (1897)
> Mr Salomon had a boot manufacturing business which he decided to incorporate into a private limited company. He sold his business to the newly formed company, A Salomon & Co Ltd, and took his payment by shares and a debenture or debt of £10,000. Mr Salomon owned 20,000 £1 shares, and his wife and five children owned one share each. Some years later the company went into liquidation, and Mr Salomon claimed to be entitled to be paid first as a secured debenture holder. The liquidator and the other creditors objected to this, claiming that it was unfair for the person who formed and ran the company to get paid first. However, the House of Lords held that the company was a different legal person from the shareholders, and thus Mr Salomon, as a shareholder and creditor, was totally separate in law from the company A Salomon & Co Ltd. The result was that Mr Salomon was entitled to be repaid the debt as the first secured creditor.

In this case, Mr Salomon was the major shareholder, a director, an employee and a creditor of the company he created. It is quite common in Ireland for one person to have such a variety of roles and still be a different legal entity from the company.

> *Lee v Lee's Air Farming Ltd* (1961)
> In this case, Mr Lee formed his crop spraying business into a limited company in which he was director, shareholder and employee. When he was killed in a flying accident, his widow sought social welfare compensation from the State, arguing that Mr Lee was a 'worker' under the law. The State argued that Mr Lee was self-employed and thus not covered by the legislation. The court held that Mr Lee and the company he had formed were separate entities, and it was possible for Mr Lee to be employed by Lee's Air Farming.

The following case is similar to *Salomon* and *Lee*, but the principle of separate personality worked to the disadvantage of the plaintiff.

> *Battle v Irish Art Promotion Centre Ltd* (1968) Ire
> The defendant company was involved in legal proceedings but did not have enough money for legal representation. The plaintiff, who was the major shareholder and managing director of the company, sought to conduct the company's defence. The court held that while a human

person can represent him- or herself in court, a legal person such as a company can only be represented by a solicitor or barrister.

The principle in *Salomon's Case* that a company is a legally different person from those who control it represents the current law in Ireland. For example, if I form a company called 'Murphy & Co Ltd' in which I own one hundred per cent of the shares and am a director and employee, legally speaking the company and myself are two distinct people. The 'corporate veil' surrounds the company of Murphy & Co Ltd and prevents outsiders challenging the operation of the company. However, although the principle of separation is central to company law, there are a number of situations when the company and its members can be identified together and treated as the same. These are the exceptions to the rule in *Salomon's Case*, when the corporate veil is lifted and the reality of the situation is examined.

F. Lifting the Corporate Veil

The corporate veil can be lifted in two ways: by specific provision in legislation and by discretion of the courts. Although the cases when the veil has been lifted vary with the facts of the cases, there are said to be three main reasons why this may be done:

(1) to enforce the provisions of company law;
(2) to avoid fraud;
(3) to deal with a group of companies.

Legislative lifting of the veil is usually for purposes of enforcing company law, whereas the courts usually lift the veil to prevent fraud.

Lifting the Veil by Legislation—Automatic

When it is specified in the Companies Acts that the corporate veil will be lifted, there is no discretion, and the veil will be lifted automatically.

1. Minimum Membership

Section 36, CA 1963 provides that if the number of shareholders of a public company is reduced below the statutory minimum of seven and the company trades for more than six months, every shareholder who knows that the company is trading with less than the minimum shall be liable for the debts of the company during that time. (Since the passing of the EC (Single Member Private Company) Regulations 1994, section 36 CA 1963 no longer applies to private companies.)

2. Failure to Use Proper Name

Section 114, CA 1963 provides that if a company fails to affix its name properly on its place of business, letters, documents and bills of exchange, the company and every officer of the company will be liable to a fine. (The officers of a company are the directors and secretary.)

> *Durham Fancy Goods v Michael Jackson (Fancy Goods) Ltd* (1968)
> The defendants endorsed a cheque made out to 'M. Jackson (Fancy Goods) Ltd'. The court held that the plaintiffs had accepted an incorrect version of the name, thus could not rely on section 114.

> *Lindholst & Co A/S v Fowler* (1988)
> The defendant was a director of the Corby Chicken Co. Ltd. He signed cheques referring to the 'Corby Chicken Co.' and was liable under section 114.

3. No Certificate to Commence Trading in a Public Limited Company

Section 6, C(A)A 1983 provides that the directors of a public company will be jointly and severally liable when a public limited company trades without a certificate to commence trading (however, such contracts are still valid).

4. Fraudulent Trading

Section 297, CA 1963 (as inserted by section 138, CA 1990) states that if in the course of a liquidation it appears that 'any person was knowingly a party to the carrying on of any business of the company with the intent to defraud creditors or for any fraudulent purpose, they may be personally liable without limit for the debts of the company'. Fraudulent trading is not defined by statute and is very difficult to prove because it must be shown that the directors, in incurring the debts in question, knew that the company would be unable to pay them.

5. Reckless Trading

Section 297, CA 1963 (as inserted by section 138, CA 1990) provides for personal liability without limit for any officer of a company who was knowingly a party to the carrying on of company business in a 'reckless' manner. An officer in this context includes an auditor, liquidator, receiver, shadow director, director or secretary. The reckless trading provisions may be used when the company is unable to pay its debts and is in liquidation or examinership.

Section 297 defines 'reckless trading' as occurring when a person was a party to the carrying on of the business and, having regard to the general knowledge, skill and experience that might reasonably be expected of a person in his position, ought to have known that his actions or those of the company would cause loss to the creditors or he was a party to the contracting of a debt by the company and did not honestly believe on reasonable grounds that the company would be able to pay the debt when it fell due. It is a defence to have acted honestly and reasonably in relation to the conduct of the affairs of the company.

Application for fraudulent and reckless trading can be made to the High Court by a company's receiver, examiner, liquidator, creditor, or the Director of Corporate Enforcement (see Chapter 16).

6. Tax Offences

Legislation dealing with Income Tax, Corporation Tax and Capital Gains Tax contains many instances where the corporate veil may be lifted to treat companies and their owners together.

Lifting the Veil by the Courts—Discretionary

The cases that deal with the courts' lifting of the veil do not fall into neat categories, but many of the cases have a common thread. In these cases, the court will have considerable discretion in deciding whether to lift the veil of incorporation.

1. When the Company Was Formed for Fraudulent Purposes

Gilford Motor Co v Horne (1933)
The defendant was subject to a restraint of trade clause in his contract of employment with the plaintiff, which bound him not to solicit the plaintiff's customers if he left the company. On leaving his employer, Horne set up a company and used this format to solicit customers from his former employer. The court held that the company was formed for an improper purpose, i.e. to defeat an employment contract, and thus the court could lift the veil of incorporation and identify Horne with the new company. (Note: such a restraint of trade would be unlikely to be upheld today).

Jones v Lipman (1962)
Lipman made a contract to sell his house to Jones and then wished to get out of the contract. He formed a company, conveyed the house to it and then claimed he could no longer sell the house to Jones. The court held that this company was formed as a 'device or sham' to frustrate the sale contract, and an order of specific performance of the sale contract was granted to Jones.

Roundabout Ltd v Beirne (1959) Ire
In order to break a trade dispute about union membership, the owners of a pub set up a new company called Roundabout Ltd and conveyed the pub to it. The pub's employees continued to picket the premises, and the new company successfully got an injunction to remove the picketers employed by the pub. The court held that the strikers were not employed by the new company and thus could not picket its premises. The judge described the formation of Roundabout Ltd as 'a legal subterfuge' but a legitimate one.

However, it could be argued that the company was formed to break contracts of employment and the constitutional right of trade union membership and, thus, was a sham formed for a fraudulent purpose. This case would probably not be decided in this way today.

2. Group Companies

The courts will lift the veil in cases of group companies to reflect the economic and commercial realities of a situation.

> *Power Supermarkets Ltd v Crumlin Investments Ltd and Dunnes Stores (Crumlin) Ltd* (1981) Ire
> The plaintiff, the Quinnsworth chain of supermarkets, leased a large unit in a shopping center from Crumlin Investments Ltd. The lease contained a restrictive covenant whereby Crumlin Investments Ltd covenanted not to allow another grocery as tenants in the center. Subsequently, Crumlin Investments Ltd sold the center to Cornelscourt Shopping Centre Ltd, which was part of the Dunnes Stores group of super-markets. Each of the retail units in the Dunnes Stores Group was operated as a separate company, although they were all controlled by the Dunne family. A new company, called Dunnes Stores (Crumlin) Ltd (the second defendant), was formed and began to operate a supermarket in the shopping center. The High Court held that Dunnes Stores (Crumlin) Ltd was bound by the restrictive covenant, although it was not a party to it. The judge stated that 'a court may, if the justice of the case so requires, treat two or more related companies as a single entity so that the business notionally carried on by one will be regarded as the business of the group, if this conforms to the economic and commercial realities of the situation.'

> *The State (McInerney & Co Ltd) v Dublin County Council* (1985) Ire
> A subsidiary company served a land purchase notice on Dublin County Council in respect of land owned by its holding company. Dublin County Council objected on the grounds that the subsidiary was not the 'owner' of the land under the relevant planning act. The subsidiary argued that it was part of the holding company, but the High Court refused to allow this argument, stating that 'the corporate veil is not a device to be raised or lowered at the option of the parent company or group. The arm which lifts the corporate veil must always be that of justice.'

> *Lac Minerals Ltd v Chevron Minerals Corporation of Ireland Ltd and Others* (1995) Ire
> The first and third defendants were members of the Chevron Group of Companies. They contracted with the second defendant company to exploit mineral rights. The plaintiff company made a contract with the third defendant, Transocean Chevron Corporation Ltd, and subsequently

dealt with all three defendant companies and with the Chevron Group. In a complicated action over the terms of the mineral rights in a contract, the plaintiff sought to lift the corporate veil surrounding the third defendant and to show that it could be identified with the Chevron Group. The High Court stated that to lift the corporate veil in relation to a group of companies, two requirements must be satisfied.

(i) The acts of one company must be factually identified with another company.

(ii) There must be circumstances where justice would be served only if the court ignores the distinction of the separate companies.

The court held that the affairs of the first and third defendants were dominated by the parent company Chevron, and thus, the court lifted the veil of incorporation.

Allied Irish Coal Supplies Ltd v Powell Duffryn International Fuels Ltd (1998) Ire
The defendant company was one of twenty-five subsidiaries of Powell Duffryn plc. The plaintiff sought to treat the defendant and its parent as part of a single economic entity, as part of a breach of contract action against the subsidiary. The Supreme Court held that this argument was totally at variance with the principle of separate legal personality, and there were no grounds for lifting the corporate veil.

3. If the Court is Exercising Discretion
The court's exercise of discretion is simply a catchall category to cover cases that do not easily fit into either of the above categories.

Re Bugle Press (1961)
There were three shareholders in Bugle Press Ltd. Two of the shareholders who each owned forty-five per cent of the shares wanted to buy out the owner of the remaining ten per cent of the shares. The two major shareholders formed a company with a share capital of £100, which then made a take-over bid for Bugle Press Ltd. The two major shareholders accepted this bid and then served notice on the third shareholder compelling him to sell his shares under the take-over procedures in the English Companies Act. The court held that this was 'a bare-faced attempt' by the majority shareholders to remove the minority through the formation of a company, and this device failed. The take-over bid could not go ahead.

Re Murph's Restaurant Ltd (1979) Ire
In this case, three shareholder–directors ran a restaurant together. They had years of experience running restaurants and working together prior to forming the company. The company was run on a

very informal basis. Two of the shareholder–directors fell out with the third and removed him from the company. The third shareholder then sought to have the company wound up on the grounds that he had been treated oppressively or unfairly. The court held that the removal of the shareholder–director repudiated a relationship that was based on mutual trust and confidence and was more like a partnership than a company. As a result of this analysis, the judge felt that it was 'just and equitable' to lift the corporate veil and wind up the company.

Reynolds v Malocco trading as 'Patrick' (1998) Ire
The plaintiff sought an injunction to prevent publication of a defamatory magazine article. The courts considered the reality of his recovering damages from a newly formed company with a £2 (€2.53) share capital, by lifting the corporate veil and looking at the reality of the situation.

The decisions of *The State (McInerney & Co Ltd) v Dublin County Council* (1985) and *Lac Minerals Ltd v Chevron Minerals Corporation of Ireland Ltd and Others* (1995) can also be seen as the court's exercising its discretion based on the justice of the case.

CHAPTER 10

The Formation of a Company

Summary of chapter

This chapter deals with the practice and procedures of how a company is formed. The emphasis is on the company's two main documents of incoporation: the memorandum and articles of association. In the memorandum of association, the two most problematic clauses are the name clause, and the objects clause which outlines the company's aims in business. If a company exceeds the scope of its objects clause, its actions will be said to be *ultra vires* the company, or beyond its powers.

A. Pre-incorporation Issues

The typical Irish company is a small family business with shareholder–directors formed to take advantage of limited liability. To incorporate such a company, documents must be prepared and lodged with a fee in the Companies Registration Office, located in Parnell Square and presided over by the Registrar of Companies. Such a company may be formed by a Mr or Ms Salomon, who would do the preparatory work before seeking to have the company registered. Alternatively, the individuals could pay a solicitor, accountant or company formation specialist to incorporate the company for them. It is also possible to buy a ready-made company 'off the shelf'. When a public company is being formed, the initial sale of shares to the public, or 'flotation', will be done through an issuing house and will be subjected to detailed scrutiny and regulation.

Promoter

The person who forms the company is know as the promoter. A company promoter was defined in *Twycross v Grant* (1877) as 'one who undertakes to form a company with reference to a given project, and to set it going and who takes the necessary steps to accomplish that purpose'.

In the last century, promoters were a specialised group of professionals who set up the new limited companies, and there are a number of cases of frauds perpetrated by promoters on the persons for whom they were setting up the company. Today, as explained above, the promoter is likely to be the person who decided to set up the business or a member of a recognised professional body, so there is less risk of fraud.

Promoters are under the usual duties to use due skill and care in the performance of their duties. In addition, they are said to owe fiduciary duties to the company they are forming. A fiduciary duty is a duty to act in the best interest of another. It would cover the avoidance of a conflict of interests and the making of full disclosure of profit or interest. A typical nineteenth-century fraud by a promoter was the sale of his own property to the newly formed company at a hugely inflated price. If a promoter was found to be in breach of his duty to a company, the contract could be rescinded and damages recovered. This problem rarely arises with modern companies.

Pre-incorporation Contracts

A promoter may have to make contracts on behalf of a company that has not yet been formed. If a company is incorporated on 1 March, the promoter may have leased premises or hired staff in February, before the company came into existence. Such contracts are known as pre-incorporation contracts.

The problem is that a company has to make its contract through an agent, and an agent can only act on behalf of an existing principal. This situation gives rise to a potential problem with preincorporation contracts, as an agent (the promoter) cannot make contracts on behalf of a non-existent principal (the company).

To avoid this problem, section 37, CA 1963 provides that a company can adopt or ratify a preincorporation contract made on its behalf after it has been incorporated. However, the company is not bound to ratify such a contract, and in such a case the promoter would be personally liable on the contract. To cover the possibility that the company might not ratify the contract, the promoter will usually seek to exclude personal liability for any contracts she or he made on behalf of the company. As this is obviously unsatisfactory to the party contracting with the promoter, few preincorporation contracts are made in practice other than in Mr or Ms Salomon-type one-person companies.

B. The Registration Procedure

The promoter prepares the documentation and presents them to the Registrar of Companies along with the appropriate fee. If everything is in order, the Registrar issues a 'Certificate of Incorporation'. If the company is a public limited company, a 'Certificate to Commence Trading' will also be issued. The incorporation is advertised in *Iris Oifigiúil* (an official government publication used for making information public).

The documents that must be registered are:

(1) the memorandum of association;
(2) the articles of association;
(3) form A1.

The memorandum of assocation is the company's constitution, covering its key issues. The articles of association are the internal rules and regulations for the functioning of the company. These will be considered in detail later. Form A1 is a prescribed form, containing details of:

(a) the particulars of the first directors and secretary (who must also sign the form);

(b) a statutory declaration by the solicitor engaged in the formation of the company or by a person named as director or secretary that there has been compliance with the registration requirements of the Companies Acts 1963 to 2003;

(c) a statement of capital, detailing the classes of shares, nominal value and number of shares authorised and issued.

If the company is a public limited company, it must register with a minimum authorised share capital of €38,092. The documents must be accompanied by a registration fee of €60 plus one per cent of the value of the issued share capital.

If the documents are in order, the Registrar must issue the Certificate of Incorporation. This is the equivalent of a company's birth certificate. The Certificate of Incorporation proves:

- that the company has been registered;
- whether it is a private or public company;
- that there has been compliance with the requirements of the Companies Acts 1963 to 2003.

If the company being formed is a public limited company, it must also receive a Certificate to Commence Trading under section 6, C(A)A 1983. This is a statutory declaration stating:

- that the nominal value of allotted shares is not less than €38,092;
- the amount of paid up allotted capital (which must be at least twenty-five per cent of the nominal value of allotted shares);
- details of any preliminary expenses;
- details of any benefits to a promoter.

It is an offence to trade without the Certificate to Commence Trading, but any contracts made by the company are still valid. The corporate veil may be lifted, and a company may be struck off for failure to get the certificate, as explained in Chapter 9.

C. Documentation Requirements

Publicity

One of the prices to be paid for limited liability is that a company must provide information about itself to the public. The main sources of such information are:

(1) The company's file at the Companies Registration Office in Parnell Square. (A company must file a number of documents on formation and then on an annual basis. Any person can access this information and obtain copies of it for a small fee.)

(2) The company's statutory registers and books, which must be kept at the company's registered office. (Some of these are available to the public, and some are only available to company shareholders.)

(3) *Iris Oifigiúil*. (The Companies Acts require certain notices, such as the incorporation of a company and liquidation, to be published in *Iris Oifigiúil*. In addition, some notices are required to be published in a daily newspaper.)

(4) The letterheads and documents of a company, which give basic information about the directors, the registered number of the company and the address of its offices.

Statutory Registers and Books

The following documents must be kept at the registered office of a company:

(1) the register of members under section 116, CA 1963;

(2) the register of debenture holders under section 91, CA 1963;

(3) the register of directors and secretaries under section 195, CA 1963;

(4) the register of directors' and secretaries' interests in shares under section 59, CA 1990;

(5) the register of interests in shares in public limited companies under section 80, CA 1990;

(6) a directors' conflict of interest book under section 194, CA 1963;

(7) copies of instruments creating charges under section 109, CA 1963;

(8) the books containing minutes of general meetings and directors' meetings under section 145, CA 1963;

(9) the books of account under section 202, CA 1990.

Company Accounts

A company is obliged to maintain a number of basic records.

1. Books of Account

Section 202, CA 1990 (replacing section 147, CA 1963) requires every company to keep 'proper books of account' to record and explain the transactions of the company. These must comply with the requirements of legislation and give a true and fair view of the company's financial situation. These are known as 'primary records' and are available only to the officers of a company.

2. Balance Sheet and Profit and Loss Account

Balance sheets and profit and loss accounts are made available to company shareholders at general meeting. Again, under section 149, CA 1963, they must comply with legislation and give a true and fair view of the profit or loss of the company for the financial year. The balance sheet and profit and loss accounts must include the information contained in the schedule to the C(A) A 1986.

3. Accounts to be Filed in Companies Registration Office

Since the Companies (Amendment) Act 1986, some information about private companies must be made available to the public. This is known as the 'annual return'. Small- and medium-sized companies, based on certain features, are given concessions in relation to that which be published under the 1986 Act as shown in Figure 10.1. In this case, a small private company is one satisfying two of three conditions:

- a balance sheet total of less than €1.9 million;
- a turnover of less than €3.81 million;
- an average number of less than fifty employees.

A small company files an abridged balance sheet and certain notes to the accounts rather than a profit and loss account.
   A medium-sized company must satisfy two of three conditions:

- a balance sheet total of less than €7.62 million;
- turnover of less than €15.24 million;
- an average number of less than 250 employees.

A medium-sized company files a profit and loss account that begins at gross profit, i.e. such companies need not disclose turnover and cost of sales.
   A large private company is any company that does not come within the above two categories.

Figure 10.1 Company accounts

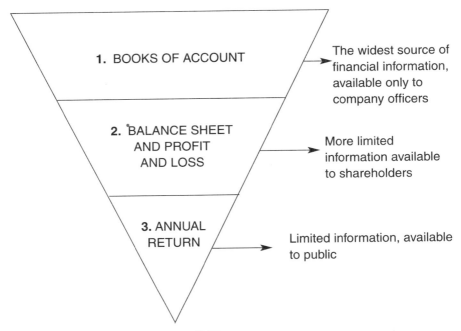

Companies Registration Office

The role of the Companies Registration Office is as a central office of the State to deal with issues under the Companies Acts, such as the incorporation of new companies, statutory filing of company information, registration of charges and other functions under separate legislation. A computerised file on each company is maintained and can be accessed by the public. Each company is under a duty to file information in the Companies Registration Office for inclusion in its file, most notably its annual return. Failure to do so can result in a company being struck off. Each year thousands of companies are struck off the Register, and individual directors are prosecuted for personal failure to ensure filing of statutory documents.

The office of the Registrar of Companies was created by the Joint Stock Companies Act 1844. The Registrar is in charge of the Companies Registration Office and its staff of approximately one hundred and twenty. The Companies Registration Office Website is at www.cro.ie.

D. The Memorandum of Association

The memorandum of association is the fundamental document of a company. It is equivalent to a company's constitution and contains the key information about a company. A company's memorandum is said to be for external use. This means that outsiders might be interested in reading what it contains. For most people seeking information about a limited company, the first step would be to consult the company's memorandum in the Companies Registration Office in Parnell Square.

According to section 6, CA 1963, the obligatory clauses in the memorandum of association are:

(1) the company's name;

(2) its objects;

(3) a limited liability clause;

(4) a capital clause;

(5) an association clause.

Name Clause

The name a company chooses is usually that by which it is referred. A company may choose a name that identifies the type of business in which it is involved, such as Murphy Printers Ltd, or a name that identifies the company with the major shareholder–director, such as Eavan Murphy Ltd. Alternatively, the company may choose an unusual name to catch the public's attention, such as Zenith Ltd. However, the company must also consider a number of legal limitations on the choice of name.

1. Form of Name

Section 6, CA 1963 states that the name of the company must end with the words 'limited', 'public limited company' or the Irish equivalents. However, if the Minister for Enterprise, Trade and Employment is satisfied that a limited company is to be for the promotion of commerce, art, science, religion, charity or any other useful purpose and its profits will be used for the promotion of its objects, then the Minister may allow the company to dispense with the words 'limited' or 'public limited company' under section 24, CA 1963. Examples are the Irish Cancer Society, Parentline and the Zoological Gardens of Ireland. Between ten and twenty companies per year are licensed to omit 'limited' from their name.

Under section 6, CA(A) 1983, it is an offence for anybody other than a 'plc' to trade under a name ending in 'public limited company'.

2. Undesirable Names

Section 21, CA 1963 states that no company shall be registered by a name that, in the opinion of the Minister for Enterprise, Trade and Employment, is undesirable. Guidelines from the Minister show that undesirable names could be:

• an offensive or blasphemous name;

• one that implies State sponsorship;

• one that uses the words 'bank', 'society' or 'insurance' in its name, unless it has the appropriate permission from the Central Bank or the Minister for Enterprise, Trade and Employment.

A name would also be undesirable if it is the same or similar to an existing company's name or trademark. A new company should check the existing names on the Company Index in the Companies Registration Office. Taking a name that is the same as or similar to those listed is prohibited. A refusal to register a name can be appealed to court.

Under section 23, CA 1963 the Minister may compel a company to change its name within six months of incorporation if its name is too similar to an already registered name. This is to cover situations in which, through inadvertence, a name is registered that is similar to or the same as an existing company. For example, Kitty O Shea's Tavern (Cork) Ltd was recently directed by the Minister to change its name, following a complaint by Kitty O'Shea's Ltd, a Dublin pub. The company was prosecuted for failing to comply with directions under section 23, CA 1963 and fined £100 (€127). It subsequently changed it name.

3. Passing Off a Name

The new company's name must not attempt to *pass off* that of another business. 'Passing off' is a tort that occurs when a person or business uses a name so like that of an existing business that there is likely to be confusion in the minds of potential customers and a possible divergence of trade from the plaintiff's business. Passing off can be restrained by an injunction.

> *Ewing v Buttercup Margarine Co Ltd* (1917)
> The plaintiff sold margarine as a sole trader under the name 'The Buttercup Dairy Co' and had 150 shops in the North of England and Scotland. The defendant registered a company with the name 'Buttercup Margarine Co Ltd' and sold margarine wholesale. The court granted an injunction to restrain the defendant from using that name, as there could be confusion between the two businesses.

> *Muckross Park Hotel v Randles* (1995) Ire
> In this case, the High Court granted an injunction to prevent a new hotel called the 'Muckross Court Hotel' from using the word 'Muckross' in its name, as an older hotel two miles away, the 'Muckross Park Hotel', had the sole right to use the word 'Muckross' in its title.

> *Guinness Ltd, Smithwick and Sons of Kilkenny v Kilkenny Brewing Co Ltd* (1999) Ire
> The defendant microbrewery was ordered to change its company name following legal action, because of the likelihood of confusion with 'Kilkenny Irish Beer' which is brewed by the plaintiffs. The court held that the plaintiffs had established good will in the word 'Kilkenny' when used in conjunction with 'beer'.

Damages are payable where a plaintiff can prove that its business suffered as a result of passing off. An action for passing off can be taken within six years of the first occurrence. One practical limitation in this area, however, is that there is no legal ownership of ordinary words such as 'hotel' or 'taxi' or place names such as Kilkenny. However, ordinary words in combination with other words can be protected.

4. Changing a Company Name

A company may change its name by special resolution (seventy-five per cent) of the shareholders along with the consent of the Minister. The Minister approves name changes for between one and two thousand companies each year.

As seen above, the Minister may order a company to change its name within six months of incorporation.

A company may also be ordered to change its name by a court order, following a successful action for passing off. It is important to notice that an action for passing off may be brought more than six months after a company has been incorporated.

5. Display of a Company Name

Section 114, CA 1963 states that a company must display its name at its office or place of business, on all business letters and notices, cheques, invoices and receipts. As explained in Chapter 9, failure to properly display its name may lead to the lifting of the corporate veil in a company and the fining of its officers. A company shall also have a company seal engraved with its name in legible characters.

6. Registration of Business Names

Any business, whether a sole trader, a partnership or a corporate body, may trade under a name other than its own name. Such a name is known as the 'business name' and must be registered under the Registration of Business Names Act 1963. An example would be when a company called 'Alpha Ltd' is purchased off the shelf. If I felt that this name was not suitable, I might register a business name of 'Eavan Murphy Gourmet Food Ltd', which is more reflective of my business. (Alternatively of course, I could simply change the name of the company by special resolution.)

To avoid confusion, the Registration of Business Names Act 1963 also provides that the corporate or company name and those of the directors must also be stated on all business letters and documents, and the business name must be conspicuously displayed in the registered office. Registration of a business name under this Act does not protect it from duplication nor does it not imply that the name will subsequently be accepted as a company name.

7. Domain Names

An emerging issue relevant to company names is Internet domain names. The registration of domain names under the top-level domain IE is administered by the Irish IE Domain Registry, at *www.domainregistry.ie*. A company may register an IE domain name provided it is derived from the full legal name of the company, subject to certain rules. Words such as 'Limited' and 'plc' may be omitted from the domain name. A company may also register a registered business name as a domain name. The registry will seek proof of the company's legal status and its connection to Ireland.

Objects Clause

The objects of a company are the company's aims, i.e. what it was set up to do. Each company in Ireland will have slightly different objects. For example, a pizza take-away restaurant will have the sale and delivery of hot and cold food as its basic object. A bicycle shop will have the sale, repair and rental of bicycles as its main object. Both companies will also have other objects to support the main one and to allow for future development.

A company can have any legal activity as its objects. Objects clauses are limited to an extent to protect shareholders and creditors who need to know the type of business in which the company is involved. However, in practice, many companies have objects clauses that are so wide and vague that it is hard to determine in what kind of business the company is involved.

A company is not permitted to go beyond its objects (by the *ultra vires* rule). Thus, historically, companies listed very long objects clauses to allow themselves scope for future developments. It is quite common to see companies set up in the 1990s list building railways and waterways among their objects, although they are highly unlikely to actually do so.

Another ploy companies use to achieve the same effect is to state that all objects listed are to be construed independently. For example, the object of renting bicycles in the bicycle company could be seen as separate from their sale and repair.

Yet another ploy that is still very common in objects clauses is to include what are sometimes known as 'Bell House clauses', which would have a phrase like 'to carry on any trade or business whatsoever' as an object. This effectively gives the company an object of doing anything that is lawful.

As you can see, any of these approaches would mean that a person who consults a company's memorandum will find it very difficult to know exactly the type of business in which the company is involved.

Powers

In addition to objects, a company will also have powers. Powers are ways of achieving the objects. Most companies have similar powers—both the pizza restaurant and the bicycle shop will have such powers as to buy supplies, sell goods, hire and fire employees, open bank accounts, write cheques and borrow money. A company's powers may be expressed in the objects clause, but they may also be implied. For example, a trading company will have a wide range of implied powers to do what is normal in the circumstances, including the power to borrow.

It is very important to grasp that a company's powers can only be used to achieve its objects. Thus the pizza company has the power to borrow money, but only to further the objects of selling food. The pizza company cannot use its power to borrow to enable a director to get money for a holiday or to branch out into producing sportswear. This is clearly illustrated in the following case.

> *Re German Date Coffee Co* (1882)
> In this case a company was incorporated with its main object being to make coffee from dates. It also had the usual powers to trade. The company failed to get a patent to make coffee from dates, so it began to make coffee from coffee beans instead. A shareholder objected on the grounds that this was not the object in which he had invested his money. The court held that the company could only exercise its powers to trade in furtherance of its object of making coffee from dates, so the company had exceeded its powers. (The making of the coffee from coffee beans was also *ultra vires*.)

(See also *Introductions Ltd v National Provincial Bank* (1970) disscussed in the next section in which a company used its power to borrow for a purpose that was outside its objects.)

E. The *Ultra Vires* Rule

If a company contracts to do something outside its objects, this is known as *ultra vires* or 'beyond the powers' of the company. Any such contracts are void.

This can be a difficult area to study. The keys things to be aware of are the pre-1963 law, the legislative changes in section 8(1) of the Companies Act 1963, Article 6 of the EC (Companies) Regulations 1973, the effects of an *ultra vires* contract and the position in relation to *ultra vires* gifts.

1. The Pre-1963 Position

The old approach to *ultra vires* held that if a company entered into a contract beyond its powers, the third parties who dealt with the company were presumed to know that the company was acting outside its objects because the third parties were assumed to know what the company's memorandum said. This is known as having 'constructive knowledge' of the objects clause in the memorandum. (Constructive knowledge in which the third party's knowledge is constructed or assumed is the opposite of actual knowledge in which the third party would have read the objects clause.)

For example, in pre-1963 days, if I supplied food to a pizza company, it would be assumed that I knew the contents of the memorandum of association. Therefore I could not complain if the pizza company later argued that it was in fact incorporated as a hardware shop, and the contract was outside its powers, or *ultra vires*. This operated very unfairly in practice, especially for small suppliers who were unlikely to consult the memorandum of a company that had ordered a small quantity of goods from them. The following two examples illustrate the unfairness of the old approach.

Re Jon Beauforte (London) Ltd (1953)
In this case a company had been incorporated with objects authorising them to manufacture gowns and costumes. The company diversified into manufacturing veneer wood panels, which was totally outside its objects clause. The company ordered fuel from a third party to be used in manufacturing the veneer. The notepaper on which the order was made stated that the company manufactured veneer panels. After the third party supplied the fuel, the company went into liquidation without paying its bill. The court held that the third party was not entitled to payment by the liquidator. This was because the contract was *ultra vires*, and the third party was taken to be constructively aware of this fact, as it could have consulted the company's memorandum. The fact that it did not consult the memorandum was immaterial.

Introductions Ltd v National Provincial Bank Ltd (1970)
In this case the plaintiff company's main object was to provide entertainment and accommodation for foreign visitors to England. As usual, the company had the power to borrow. The company diversified into pig breeding and borrowed money from the defendant for that purpose. The court held that pig breeding was *ultra vires* the company, as was the borrowing, so the loan could not be enforced.

(This case can be classed as a pre-1963 case for Irish purposes, as it occurred before the equivalent change in English law.)

2. The 1963 Act Changes

Section 8 of the Companies Act 1963 introduces a reform whereby a third party must have actual knowledge of the *ultra vires* activity. Section 8, CA 1963 states that:

> any thing or act done by a company which, if the company had been empowered to do the same, would have been lawfully and effectively done, shall, notwithstanding that the company has no power to do such act or thing, be effective in favour of any person relying on such an act or thing, who is not shown to have been *actually aware*, at the time when he or she so relied thereon, that such act or thing was not within the powers of the company, but any director or officer of the company who was responsible for the doing by the company of any such act or thing shall be liable to the company for any loss or damage suffered by the company in consequence thereof.

The effect of this section is that an act that is *ultra vires* a company is now enforceable against the company. A third party is no longer presumed to have constructive knowledge of a company's objects. Instead the third party must be *actually aware* that the company lacked power before the contract will be unenforceable. To illustrate this, if the *Beauforte* case was to occur today, the third party who supplied the fuel would be able to recover the money due because he or she was not actually aware that the company lacked power. Similarly, if *Introductions Ltd v National Provincial Bank* occurred today, the defendant bank would be able to recover its loan for the same reason.

However, a person who reads a company's memorandum and misunderstands it is not protected by section 8 of the 1963 Act. This unusual situation is clear from the following Irish case.

> *Northern Bank Finance Corporation Ltd v Quinn and Achates Investment Co* (1979) Ire
> Quinn borrowed £145,000 from Northern Bank Finance Corporation Ltd. The loan was guaranteed by Achates Investment Company. Quinn defaulted on the repayments, and the bank sought to recover the money from both defendants. The court established that the bank's solicitor had read the memorandum of association of Achates Investment Co prior to accepting it as guarantor. Achates did not actually have authority to guarantee loans. The High Court held that the bank could not rely on section 8 as the bank did not come within the scope of someone who was 'not . . . actually aware' of the objects of Achates Investment Co. Thus the guarantee was *ultra vires* and unenforceable.

This case creates the unusual situation that a third party who does not read a company's memorandum is in a better legal position than a person who reads and misunderstands the memorandum. Another example of such a situation appears in the following recent case on *ultra vires*.

> *In Re Frederick Inns Ltd (in Liquidation)* (1994) Ire
> Three companies operated pubs that were wholly owned subsidiaries of a fourth company. All four companies were put into liquidation, and the liquidator discovered that prior to his appointment, the holding company had paid £1.2 (€1.5) million to the Revenue Commissioners. The payment related to the tax liabilities of the four companies and also six other companies within the group. The liquidator challenged the payment of tax for the other six companies, as being *ultra vires* the holding company. The Supreme Court held that the payment of tax for a subsidiary company was *ultra vires* because there was nothing in the memorandum of association of the holding company to allow it. The Revenue Commissioners were not actually aware under section 8, CA 1963 that the company lacked power to pay the tax. However, the Revenue Commissioners could not rely on the protection of section 8, because the payment of another company's tax liabilities could not have been 'lawfully and effectively' done within section 8 as it was in total disregard of the company's creditors. The Revenue Commissioners

had to repay the tax paid for the six other companies to the liquidator. (The money was deemed to be held on a 'constructive trust' by the Revenue Commissioners, i.e. not an actual trust, but one that is constructive or assumed.)

3. EC Regulations 1973

Part of the reason that the law on *ultra vires* can be confusing is that there is a second piece of statutory regulation on the area. As a result of Ireland's membership in the European Communities in 1973, Article 6 of the EC (Companies) Regulations 1973 was added. It states that:

> in favour of any person dealing with a company in *good faith*, any transaction entered into by any organ of the company, being its board of directors or any other person registered under these regulations as a person authorised to bind a company, shall be deemed to be within the capacity of the company, and any limitation of the powers of that board or company, whether imposed by the memorandum or articles of association or otherwise, may not be relied upon as against any person so dealing with the company. Any such person is presumed to be acting in good faith unless the contrary is proved.

It is debatable whether this regulation was needed, as the area is already covered by section 8 of the Companies Act 1963. However, there are some differences between the two provisions.

- Article 6, ECR 1973 introduces a second alternative test of the 'good faith' of an outsider dealing with a company. Good faith is presumed unless the opposite can be proved. It is arguable that the solicitor for the Northern Bank Finance Corporation Ltd, who read and misunderstood the memorandum, acted in good faith and could have been covered by this regulation.
- Article 6 is limited to contracts entered into by the board of directors.
- Article 6 can only be used in relation to actions by limited companies. This is probably why it was not argued in Northern Bank Finance Corporation Ltd, as the second defendant was not a limited company.

4. The Effects of an *Ultra Vires* Contract

There are three primary results when a contract is held to be *ultra vires*.

(i) The contract is void and unenforceable by the company.
(ii) The third party may enforce the contract under section 8, CA 1963 and Article 6, EC Regulations 1973, as explained above.
(iii) Directors may be restrained by an injunction from making an *ultra vires* contract and may have to compensate the company for any such contract (see *Parke v Daily News* below).

5. *Ultra Vires* Gifts

The *ultra vires* issue is also relevant in relation to gifts made by companies. If a company decides to donate money to charity or to give gifts to its employees, it could be argued that the gift is beyond the company's powers. Commonly such arguments would be made by an aggrieved shareholder, who would rather see the money paid to him or her in dividends.

The rules in relation to *ultra vires* gifts can be stated as follows:

(i) An object or power to make gifts will be valid if it is expressed in the memorandum. Such a clause in the memorandum is quite common.

(ii) In addition, an object or power to make gifts can be implied in the memorandum, but it must be for the benefit of company as a whole. This can be difficult to show. The courts have taken the view that there must be a direct benefit to the company, as illustrated in the following cases.

> *Parke v Daily News* (1961)
> The business of the *Daily News* was sold for £2 million. A general meeting approved the distribution of £1.5 million among the employees. The plaintiff shareholder objected to the gift. The court held that the gift was *ultra vires* the company, as it did not benefit the company, i.e. the shareholders, as a whole.

> *Evans v Brunner Mond Ltd* (1921)
> In this case a chemical company made gifts to universities for scientific research. The court held that the gifts did benefit the company and were *intra vires*.

> Re *Lee Behrens & Co* (1932)
> A company paid a pension to the widow of a former director. When the company went into liquidation, the widow claimed as a creditor for the capital value of the pension. The court held that the gift was *ultra vires* as there was no benefit to the company but only to the widow.

> *Simmonds v Heffer* (1982)
> In this case a league against cruel sports gave a gift to the English labour party, £30,000 of which was to promote relevant anti-bloodsports legislation and an additional £50,000 for the party's election fund. This was challenged by a league member. The court held that the gift of £30,000 was a valid *intra vires* gift as it was in the best interests of the league, but the gift of £50,000 was *ultra vires* as it was not for the benefit of the league, in that the money could have been used for any purpose.

Section 52 of the Companies Act 1990 states that the directors of a company should have regard to the interest of the company's employees in general as well as the interests of shareholders in the performance of their duties. Arguably this gives a company a relevant new consideration in relation to gifts.

Additional Obligatory Clauses

Having considered the name and objects clauses, we will now consider the remaining obligatory clauses of a memorandum of association.

1. Limited Liability Clause

The limited liability clause is simply a statement that 'the liability of the members is limited'. (It is obviously not necessary in an unlimited company.)

2. Capital Clause

In a company limited by shares, a capital clause must state the amount of the nominal capital and the number, division and amount of each share. This will be discussed in greater detail in Chapter 11.

3. Association Clause

The last clause in the memorandum is a clause in which the subscribers (first shareholders) express their wish to form a company and their agreement to take shares. The name, address and occupation of each subscriber is set out along with the number of shares taken. The memorandum is also signed by the first subscriber or subscribers, and the first directors are named.

Altering the Memorandum

The memorandum of a company can be altered to take account of changes in the company. The name clause can be altered by special resolution and consent of the Minister, as explained above. The objects clause can be altered by special resolution. However, ffiteen per cent of the shareholders can object to the alteration in court, within twenty-one days, provided that they did not agree with the alteration at the initial vote. The capital clause can be altered under rules that vary with the type of alteration being made. This will be explained in greater detail in Chapter 11. The limited liability clause can be altered to change the company from being a limited to unlimited status by the written consent of *all* the members.

F. The Articles of Association

The articles of association are the rules and regulations of the company. In comparison with the memorandum, the articles are said to be for internal use because outsiders will rarely have any interest in them, as the articles in all Irish companies are very similar. The rules and regulations of the articles deal with such things as share capital, company meetings and directors. If the company has different classes of shares, this will be treated in the articles.

There is a standard set of articles for a company limited by shares, which is called 'Table A' in the first schedule to the Companies Act 1963. If a company does not register articles of association, it will receive Table A by default. In practice, most companies adopt Table A with whatever alterations they wish. Typically, a set of articles would start with a statement that Table A applies with the following amendments or that Table A does not apply.

Table A of the Companies Act 1963 is reproduced for your convenience at the back of this text and should be consulted when there is a reference made to an article from Table A.

The articles of association must be signed by the subscribers and are registered along with the other documentation. Once the articles are registered, they are deemed to create a legally binding contract. Section 25, CA 1963 states that on registration, the memorandum and articles bind the company and its members as if they had been signed and sealed by everyone. Effectively this means that the articles create a contract between the company and its members. This is very useful in relation to minority protection (see Chapter 15) because, for example, a shareholder who is denied a right to vote can claim this is in breach of his or her contract with the company.

However, this is not the only use of the articles as a contract. The articles can be enforced as a contract:

- by the members against the company;
- by the company against the members;
- by the members against each other.

> *Pender v Lushington* (1877)
> In this case a company's articles gave one vote per ten shares, subject to a one hundred vote maximum for any one shareholder. Prior to an important vote, one shareholder who was at the maximum votes transferred some of his shares to the plaintiff with the intention of increasing their combined voting power. The company rejected the plaintiff's votes at the general meeting. The court held that the plaintiff's votes were his property and that the articles protected this and could be used to enforce the right.

In a case of conflict, where the memorandum says one thing and the articles say another, the memorandum prevails, as the more important document.

Alteration of the Articles

The articles of association can be altered or increased by a special resolution of the members, subject to the provisions of the Act and the memorandum, by section 15, CA 1963. However, there are a number of limitations on this freedom of alteration. An alteration:

- cannot overrule the Companies Acts;
- cannot overrule the memorandum;
- cannot overrule the general law of the State.

In addition, a company cannot bind itself not to alter its articles at a later date, although to do so may lead to breach of contract.

Although the law allows alterations of a company's articles, there is a strict requirement from case-law that the alteration must be *bona fide* (or genuinely) in the best interests of company as a whole. This is a subjective test and very much depends on the facts of each case.

> *Greenhalgh v Arderne Cinemas Ltd* (1951)
> The shares in a cinema company were held between a family group and one outsider. After a clash between the two, the family group proposed an alteration to the articles that would enable the shareholders to sell their shares without first offering them to existing shareholders. When this was challenged by the non-family-member, the court held that the alteration was in the best interests of the company as a whole, as it applied to all members equally, whether family members or not.

The courts are particularly suspicious of an alteration that has the effect of expelling a member from the company, as occurred in the following case.

> *Sidebotham v Kershaw, Leese & Co Ltd* (1920)
> The articles of association of the defendant company were altered to allow the purchase at a fair price of the shares of any shareholder who competed with the business of the company. The minority against whom this alteration was aimed challenged its validity. The court held that such an 'expulsion' was acceptable if it was *bona fide* (or genuinely) in the interests of the company as a whole, and this alteration was *bona fide* on the facts.

> *Shuttleworth v Cox Bros & Co* (1927)
> The company's articles provided that the plaintiff was to be a director for life and could only be removed on one of six specified grounds. A special resolution was passed to amend the articles and allow for a seventh ground for dismissal of a director when requested by all other directors in writing. The court held that such an alteration was acceptable if the alteration was done in the best interests of the company as a whole. In the circumstances, the removal of a director who had continually failed to account for moneys he had received was in the best interests of the company.

The removal of a member may give rise to action under section 205, CA 1963 for oppression (see Chapter 15).

CHAPTER 11

The Capital and Finances of a Company

Summary of chapter

In this chapter we will explain the various types of capital a company may have. We will consider the practical issues involved that arise when a company allots new shares. We will consider the workings of the four rules of capital maintenance. The second part of the chapter will deal with classes of shares, class rights and share transfers, and dividends

In the previous chapter, we considered how a new company can been established, and we have seen that the capital clause in the memorandum of association outlines the company's capital. We will now consider the issue of company capital in detail.

A company's capital is the money it has available with which it can operate, i.e. the basic funding of the company. Capital can take two different forms: share capital and loan capital. Share capital, which we will be considering in this chapter, is the money invested by shareholders to run the company. Loan capital, which we will be considering in detail in Chapter 12, is the money the company borrows to undertake its business objectives. Both types of capital are subject to company law rules, but we will firstly consider shares and share capital.

A. Share Capital

There are various ways a company can raise capital, such as borrowing (whether from the companies own shareholders, personal investors or financial institutions), a rights issue, gearing or state aids and grants. As seen in the previous chapter, a company needs an object or the power to borrow and will usually also need security.

Types of Capital

There are different types of share capital: nominal or authorised, issued or allotted, call-up or paid-up and reserve.

1. Nominal or Authorised Share Capital

Nominal or authorised share capital is the total amount of shares the company has authority to issue. It is common in Ireland for a private company to have a relatively large authorised capital, for example, €10,000.

2. Issued or Allotted Capital

Issued or allotted capital is the nominal value of shares the company has actually issued.

A company is not obliged to allot all of its share capital, and very often there is a difference between the nominal/authorised share capital a company is allowed to issue and the issued/allotted share capital it has actually issued. Very often, a company with a large authorised capital will have a very small issued share capital. (Typically, a private company might have an authorised capital of €10,000 but an issued capital of only €1,000.) The rest of the capital is called the 'unissued capital'.

3. Called-up or Paid-up Capital

Called-up or paid-up capital is the value of shares that members have been called on to pay to the company. For example, a company may issue 100 shares with a nominal value of €1 of which 50c has been called-up or paid-up. Thus the called-up or paid-up share capital of the company is €50. The remaining 50c per share that each shareholder owes the company is known as the 'uncalled capital'. (In practice most shares are fully paid for on purchase, so there is rarely any uncalled capital.)

4. Reserve Capital

Reserve capital is an amount of uncalled capital reserved for a special purpose. Under section 67, CA 1963, when a company has uncalled capital, it may pass a special resolution stating that some or all of the uncalled capital may only be called up when the company is being woundup. (This puts the company in a position similar to that of a company limited by guarantee.)

Alteration of the Capital Clause

According to section 68, CA 1963, a limited company, if authorised by its articles, may in a general meeting make various alterations to its capital clause.

1. Increase Share Capital

For example, a company might increase its share capital from €1,000 to €2,000 by creating 1,000 new €1 shares.

2. Consolidate Existing Shares

A company may consolidate its existing shares into shares of larger nominal value. For example, two 50c shares might be consolidated into one €1 share.

3. Divide Existing Shares

A company may divide its existing shares into shares of smaller nominal value. For example, one €5 share might be divided into five €1 shares.

4. Conversion/Reconversion

A company may convert shares into stock, and reconvert that stock into paid-up shares.

5. Reduce the Authorised Capital

A company may cancel unissued shares and reduce the authorised share capital. For example, a company might have an authorised share capital of €10,000 in €1 shares of which €7,000 is issued. The company could then cancel up to €3,000 in unissued shares and reduce its authorised share capital to €7,000. (Note that if a company wishes to reduce its issued/allotted share capital, it must go through the reduction of capital procedure explained below under 'Capital Maintenance'.)

Table A, Article 44 provides that a company may make these alterations by way of an ordinary resolution. Section 69, CA 1963 requires that a company must inform the Registrar of Companies within one month of altering its share capital.

Allotment of Shares

The original allotment in a company is specified when the company is formed, and the subscribers agree in the memorandum to take shares. Subsequently, when a company decides to allot shares, it is creating and selling new shares for the first time. (Do not confuse this with the transfer of shares that have already been created.) The allotment of shares is an increase in the company's capital.

The allotment of shares is a binding contract between the company and the new subscriber. Once the new subscriber is entered onto the register of members, he or she will be legally a member of the company. In technical terms, the *allotment* of shares occurs when the new subscriber acquires the right to be entered in the register of members. The *issue* of shares, which is not a legislative term, is taken to occur when the subscriber receives his or her share certificate. In other words, the issuing of shares follows naturally from the allotment.

Shares may be allotted at a premium, i.e. above their par value. The excess must be paid into the share premium account. For example, a well-established company may be able to sell new €1 shares for €1.20, and the 20c is the share premium. This premium is not part of the trading profits of the company, and according to section 62, CA 1963, it can only be used for:

- paying up unissued shares for use in a bonus issue (a gift of shares to existing shareholders);
- writing off preliminary expenses of the company;
- paying any premium due on redemption of redeemable preference shares (see below).

Shares may not be allotted at a discount. Thus a €1 share may not be allotted for 80c. This was first prohibited at common law by the following case.

> *Ooregum Gold Mining Co of India v Roper* (1892)
> In this case, preference shares with a par value of £1 were issued with 75p credited as paid as a way of getting public investment in a company whose shares were being traded below par value. In an action by the ordinary shareholders, the court held that the company could not validly issue shares at a discount. The court also held that an allottee must repay any discount to the company plus five per cent interest.

This prohibition was first given statutory effect in section 27, Companies (Amendment) Act 1983 (C(A)A 1983), which simply states that 'shares of a company shall not be allotted at a discount'. However, there are exceptions to this in practice.

1. Overvalue of Assets

A private company allotting shares for noncash consideration may 'honestly and reasonably' overvalue assets. This was established in the following case.

> *Re Wragg Ltd* (1897)
> In this case two men formed a company to acquire a business run by them. The purchase price was paid partly in cash and partly by the allotment to them of fully paid shares. When the company went into liquidation, the liquidator argued that the purchase price had been overstated. The court held that a company may purchase property at any price they wish and pay for it in fully paid up shares.

2. Payment of Commission

If shares are allotted through an issuing house, commission may lawfully be paid on the sale. To pay commission, there must be authority in the company's articles, the payment must be disclosed in the prospectus and not more than ten per cent commission may be paid.

Restrictions on Allotment

The Companies (Amendment) Act 1983 introduced a number of restrictions on a company's ability to allot new shares. In summary, the directors must have authority to allot the shares, and they must offer the existing shareholders the right to buy shares, known as a 'rights issue', or 'pre-emption'. In addition, there are rules in relation to the payment that may be accepted for shares.

1. Directors' Authority to Allot

The decision to allot new shares in a company is not a decision for the directors alone. Section 20, C(A)A 1983 states that directors must have the authority to allot, which is given by the company in a general meeting or the articles of the company. Section 20 also provides that the authority must state the maximum amount of shares that may be allotted and the term of the allotment, which must not exceed five years.

There are also exceptions in the section for shares taken by original subscribers and shares taken under employee share schemes.

If directors allot shares without authority, the allotment is valid but the directors can be fined €3,197 for knowingly breaching the regulations.

Another obvious restriction on the directors' authority to allot shares is that a private company or its officers may not offer shares or debentures in a private company to the public.

2. Pre-emption

Section 23, C(A)A 1983 creates statutory pre-emption rights, also known as a 'rights issue'. The details of section 23 provide that a company may not allot equity securities (defined as ordinary shares issued for cash) without first offering them to the holders of relevant shares (defined as excluding preference shares and employee share schemes) in similar proportions to their existing shareholdings. The purpose of this rule is to allow existing shareholders to buy more shares to keep their levels of shareholding constant. This is their right, hence the name 'rights issue'.

A shareholder must be given notice in writing of his or her pre-emption right, which is the same notice as for a general meeting, and the offer must be irrevocable for twenty-one days. A shareholder can receive compensation for failure by the company to offer pre-emption.

The right of pre-emption may be disapplied by the company. This may occur in a number of ways. In a private company, the right of pre-emption may be permanently excluded by either the memorandum or articles of association. In a private company or public company, a special resolution may be used to disapply the right for one occasion. This resolution may be combined with a grant of authority to the directors to allot shares under section 20. This disapplication is then limited to a five-year maximum. In this case, the directors, who are asking shareholders to forego their right of first refusal, must explain the reasons for the request and the price at which the shares are to be offered to a nonmember.

3. Allotment of Shares for Noncash Consideration in Public Limited Companies

Historically, shares could be issued for other than cash. However, for public limited companies, the C(A)A 1983 introduced strict rules on when shares in a public company could be purchased for a noncash consideration, that is for a noncash purchase price. The rules are given in sections 26, 29 and 30, C(A)A 1983.

Section 26, C(A)A 1983: A plc shall not accept as payment for its shares an undertaking that work or services will be performed for the company. In other words, if the consideration for the shares is work or services, the work or services must be performed *before* allotment. The obvious reason for this restriction is the fear that work or services might not be forthcoming after the shares had been allotted. However, goodwill and expertise are both acceptable consideration.

Section 29, C(A)A 1983: If the consideration is an undertaking or promise to perform an act, that undertaking must be performed within five years. This is in the interests of certainty.

Section 30, C(A)A 1983: If the consideration is a noncash asset, the asset must be valued by an independent valuer. The independent valuation must take place within six months prior to the allotment, and the valuation must be done by someone who is qualified to be an auditor.

If any of these sections are breached, the allottee may be personally liable to the company, and an officer of the company who is in default of the above provisions shall be guilty of an offence. If a company contravenes sections 26 or 29, the allottee must pay the company the nominal value of the shares plus any premium.

Note that these rules apply only in public limited companies. Private limited companies may accept noncash consideration in payment for shares, even when the consideration had been 'honestly and reasonably' overvalued, according to *Re Wragg Ltd* (1897), on page 202.

Allotment of Shares by a Public Company

It has already been stated that a public company must have a minimum paid-up share capital of €38,092. In addition, there is a requirement that a share may not be allotted unless it is at least twenty-five per cent paid up, according to section 28, C(A)A 1983. (This section does not apply to shares taken under an employee share scheme.) There are also three major limitations on the power of a public company to allot shares.

1. Minimum Subscription

Under section 53, CA 1963 there must have been a minimum response to the public invitation to subscribe for shares. In making an offer to the public, the directors must state the minimum amount that must be raised by the pubic subscription. This is to ensure that the company has satisfied the public that it has sufficient investment before proceeding with the public flotation. If the minimum subscription is not raised within forty days of the issue of the prospectus, any moneys received for shares must be repaid.

Section 22, C(A)A 1983 further provides that a plc may not allot shares unless the capital is subscribed in full or the offer states that should the capital not be subscribed in full, the amount of the capital subscribed may be allotted in any event or in the event of specified conditions being satisfied.

If an allotment is made contrary to either section, the directors may be made personally liable to repay any money received plus five per cent interest.

2. No Allotment until a Specified Period after Issuance of Prospectus

Section 56, CA 1963 provides that no allotment can be made until the fourth day after the issuance of the prospectus. The prospectus itself may fix a longer period. The purpose is to allow potential investors time to consider investing.

3. Permission from the Stock Exchange

Under section 57, CA 1963 if a company states that permission has or will be sought to deal shares on the stock exchange, then permission must be sought within three days of the issuance of the prospectus, or any allotment of shares will be void. Equally, any allotment will be void if permission has not been granted within six months of the closing of the subscription lists.

Capital Maintenance

The theory of capital maintenance is that the capital the company gets from shareholders must be maintained to provide a 'creditor's buffer', i.e. a fund to which creditors can look if the company is unable to pay its debts. However, in practice the invested capital may not be of much help to the creditors because it may have been diminished by trading losses. Also, the invested capital may only be a small amount, and thus the detailed rules of maintenance are largely irrelevant. For example, a company may be incorporated with an issued share capital of €100, which is hardly a substantial fund on which creditors can fall back in times of financial crisis.

The issues involved in capital maintenance are:

(1) a company increasing its capital through allotment of new shares;
(2) a company reducing its capital;
(3) a company purchasing its own shares;
(4) a company providing finance for the purchase of its shares.

We will consider these in turn.

1. Increase of Capital

A company increases its capital when it allots new shares. This can be done by an ordinary resolution, as explained above.

2. Reduction of Capital

As explained above, a company may cancel its unissued shares, which reduces the authorised share capital, but this does not alter the company's overall financial position.

A company may cancel its unissued shares, which reduces the authorised share capital, but this does not alter the company's overall financial position. Under section 72, CA 1963, if a company wishes to reduce its issued share capital, it may do so provided:

(1) it has authority to do so in its articles of association;
(2) it passes a special resolution; and
(3) it obtains court approval for the reduction.

The first two points do not give rise to any difficulty in practice. (Remember that if a company does not have authority in its articles, this may be altered by special resolution.) The court's role in the reduction is to ensure creditors are not prejudiced.

The acceptable types of reductions are explained in section 72, CA 1963.

3. Restrictions on a Company Purchasing Its Own Shares

The prohibition that a company may not purchase its own shares was seen as an essential part of maintaining the creditor's buffer. The purpose was to avoid the company manipulating its share price and possibly eroding the rights of shareholders by purchasing its own shares. The prohibition has its origin in *Trevor v Whitworth* (1887) but was not specifically prohibited by legislation until section 41, C(A)A 1983, as amended by section 232, CA 1990. Although the prohibition still continues in theory, in practice a company can purchase its own shares in a wide variety of cases.

Section 41, C(A)A 1983 provides that 'no company limited by shares or by guarantee shall acquire its own shares whether by purchase or otherwise'. However, a number of exceptions are specified:

(a) the redemption of redeemable preference shares in pursuance of Part XI, CA 1990;
(b) the acquisition of shares as part of a reduction of capital;
(c) the purchase of shares under a court order under section 10 or 205, CA 1963 or section 15, C(A)A 1983;
(d) the forfeiture or surrender of shares for failure to pay any sums outstanding.

> *Irish Press plc v Ingersoll Irish Publications Ltd* (1994) Ire
> In this case the High Court ordered the defendant to sell its shares in a company to the plaintiff under section 205, CA 1963. (This case is covered in detail in Chapter 15.)

Further exceptions to the general prohibition were introduced by the 1990 Act, under which a company can purchase its own shares either on or off market.

According to section 212, CA 1990 a 'market purchase' occurs when the shares in a public company are purchased on a recognised stock exchange and are subject to a marketing agreement. A 'marketing agreement' means that a company is either listed on the stock exchange or has been granted unconditional share dealing facilities on the exchange.

Under section 215, CA 1990 a company may make a market purchase if authorised by an ordinary resolution at a general meeting. This can be a general authority to cover many on-market purchases, unlike the individual authority needed for each off-market purchase. Here, an 'off-market purchase' means shares are purchased other than on a recognised stock exchange or are purchased on a recognised stock exchange but are not subject to a marketing agreement on that exchange. In practice this means a purchase by a private company or a public company not listed on the stock exchange.

Under section 213, CA 1990 a company may make an off-market purchase if authorised by a special resolution dealing with one specific transaction, and the seller does not vote on the resolution.

4. Restrictions on a Company Giving Financial Assistance to Purchase Its Shares

Sometimes a company may wish to sell shares to a person who does not have the cash to purchase them, and the company might seek to loan that person the money to buy the shares. The idea that a company might give financial assistance to a third party to purchase shares in the company was first prohibited by section 60, CA 1963. Due to the many forms that such assistance could take, section 60 prohibits the giving, 'whether directly or indirectly, and whether by means of a loan, guarantee, provision of security or otherwise, of any financial assistance for purpose of or in connection with a purchase or subscription of or for any shares held in the company'.

There are, however, exceptions to this prohibition. In a private company, under section 60, CA 1963, the company may pass a special resolution at a general meeting to authorise the assistance, which must be accompanied by a statutory declaration of solvency. This statutory declaration must be registered in the Companies Registration Office. As an example, a company may wish to appoint a new director who is required to own shares but does not have the means to purchase them. The private company may vote to allow assistance to such a person.

The special resolution must have taken place within the twelve months prior to the assistance. The statutory declaration must be made by a majority of the directors in advance of the general meeting. The statutory declaration must detail the form of assistance, the recipient, the purpose of the assistance and the fact that the company will be able to pay its debts after giving such assistance. Then, ten per cent of the company's shareholders can apply to court within twenty-eight days to cancel the resolution, provided they did not originally vote in its favour.

If a company gives financial assistance to a person by means of an unlawful loan, the loan contract is illegal, and the money cannot be recovered. However, if the company suffers a loss as a result, its directors can be sued as constructive trustees of the loan money, i.e. as if they held the money the company lost on trust for the company.

In all companies, private or public, section 60, CA 1963 does not prohibit assistance in the form of:

(a) lending money in the ordinary course of business;

(b) loans to *bona fide* nondirector employees;

(c) employee share schemes.

If the prohibition on providing finance in section 60 is breached, the transaction is voidable by the company against a person who had actual notice of the breach.

Meeting re Serious Loss of Capital

Under section 40, C(A)A 1983, if the net assets of a company are half or less of the company's called-up share capital, the directors must convene a meeting of the company to discuss this serious loss of capital. This is known as a capital haemorrhage and will be discussed in Chapter 15 on meetings.

B. Shares

In this section we will consider the classes of shares a company can have and the rights of these classes of shares. We will also consider the transfer of shares and the directors' role in this transfer.

'Shares' were defined in *Borland's Trustee v Steel Bros & Co Ltd* (1901) as 'the interest of a shareholder in a company measured by a sum of money, for the purposes of liability in the first place, and of interest in the second'. As well as this, as we have seen above, shares are a contract between a company and its shareholders, consisting of a series of rights and obligations.

Types of Shares

If a company simply refers to 'shares', it is presumed that all shares are the same type. If not, a company's memorandum may attach special rights to its shares, which then give rise to a number of different classes of shares.

1. Preference Shares

A 'preference share' usually has one or both of two main rights: firstly, a prior right to receive a fixed dividend, for example, at ten per cent, and the right to participate in the winding up of a company in priority to other shareholders.

The fixed dividend makes the preference share an attractively safe investment option in comparison with ordinary shares in which the rate of dividend will fluctuate. A number of points must be noted about preference shares.

In the first place, the payment of the dividend is presumed to be cumulative. This means that if a dividend is not paid in one year, the arrears will be paid as soon as profits allow.

Secondly, dividends do not bring any right to payment above the fixed rate. For example, if the rate of interest is ten per cent, a preference shareholder cannot demand payment above that rate in a year in which the company makes very high profits and pays a twenty per cent dividend to its ordinary shareholders. However, a preference shareholder may participate above the fixed rate if this is specified in the articles of association.

In addition, a shareholder cannot compel a company to pay a dividend. The case of *Bond v Barrow Haematite Steel* (1902) held that this is a management decision.

Fourthly, holders of preference shares rarely have the right to vote at general meetings.

Finally, if a company with an unpaid cumulative dividend goes into liquidation, the preference shareholders are not entitled to a dividend unless provision was made in the articles of association or the dividend had been declared but not paid when the company went into liquidation. Dividends are dealt with in more detail on page 214.

2. Redeemable Preference Shares

Redeemable preference shares are a type of preference share the company issues with the intention of redeeming them (or buying them back) at a later date. As such, redeemable preference shares constitute an exception to the rule that a company may not purchase its own shares. Under section 207, CA 1990 the rules on redeemable preference shares are as follows.

(a) At least one-tenth of the company's issued share capital are nonredeemable.

(b) Redeemable preference shares may only be redeemed when they are fully paid.

(c) Redeemable preference shares may only be redeemed out of profits that are available for distribution (so that when the share capital is reduced on cancellation of the shares, the corresponding assets are still intact).

(d) However, if a company intends to cancel shares on redemption, it may redeem the shares out of a fresh issue of shares. (In this way the share capital remains the same.)

(e) If a company pays a shareholder a premium on redemption of redeemable preference shares, the premium must be paid out of profits available for distribution. The one exception to this is if the shares were originally *issued* at a premium and are to be redeemed out of proceeds of a fresh issue of shares. Then the premium is to be paid out of a share premium account.

(f) If shares are cancelled on redemption, the company's issued share capital can be reduced by the nominal value of the redeemed shares, but an equivalent amount must be transferred to the 'Capital Redemption Reserve Fund', which is treated as capital (and subject to the same rules on reduction). However, if shares are not cancelled, they must be retained as 'Treasury Shares'. These shares keep the capital the same but are effectively frozen as they have no rights to vote or dividends. These shares can later be reissued. Only ten per cent of shares may be treasury.

3. Ordinary Shares

Ordinary shares are all other shares. Ordinary shares are by far the most common in Irish companies.

Shareholders' Rights

The rights of shareholders depend on the class, or type, of share held. Class rights are those attaching to a particular class. If a company has different classes, they may be varied as set out in section 38, C(A)A 1983. The variation depends on whether the right is stated in the memorandum or articles and whether there is a procedure provided.

Section 38, C(A)A 1983 provides that when the right is in the company's memorandum or articles, a variation procedure is stated and the variation concerns the directors' authority to allot shares under section 20, CA 1963 or a reduction of capital under section 72, CA 1963, then the agreement of seventy-five per cent of the company is required. The holders of ten per cent of the shares may object to the court within twenty-eight days, provided they did not previously vote for the variation.

Section 38 also provides that if the right is in the memorandum and no procedure is stated, the agreement of all members of the company is needed. However, if the right is in the articles and no procedure is stated, the agreement of seventy-five per cent of the company is needed (subject to the right of ten per cent to object to the court within twenty-one days).

In all cases under section 38, agreement can be by consent in writing or by special resolution.

Transmission and Transfer of Shares

If a shareholder wishes to assign his or her shares to another person, it is not enough to give that second person the shares. The new owner must also be registered as a member of the company.

Such an assignment may be voluntary, known as 'transfer', or involuntary, known as 'transmission'.

'Transmission' is an involuntary process. When a shareholder dies or becomes bankrupt, the right to deal with his or her shares is legally transmitted to the shareholder's personal representatives in the case of death or to his or her assignees in the case of bankruptcy. This person may then become a member if the shares are registered in his or her name under section 81, CA 1963, or this personal representative or assignee may see that the shares are transferred to another person.

The transfer of shares is the more normal process, under which a shareholder decides to sell or make a gift of all or part of his or her shares to another person. To legally transfer shares, a proper instrument of transfer must be used and stamp duty must be paid.

A transfer can be by one of two methods:

(1) a simple transfer, when the owner is transferring all of his or her shares together;
(2) a certified transfer, when the owner transfers part of his or her shareholding.

1. Restrictions on Transferability of Shares

Remember that shares are said to be freely transferable. However, this is subject to the limit that in a private company the directors will usually have the discretion to refuse to register a transfer. (This may be done in a public limited company but is very unlikely.) Alternatively, a company's articles may specify when the directors may refuse a transfer, but this is less common.

The power to refuse a transfer is a fiduciary power of the directors and must be exercised in good faith, acting in the best interests of the company as a whole. A number of cases illustrate how the courts approach this discretion of directors.

> *Re Hackney Pavillion Ltd* (1924)
> When considering the transfer of shares of a deceased director–shareholder, the two remaining directors disagreed, and no decision was made regarding the registration of the transfer. The company secretary wrote to the deceased's executors informing them that the transfer had been refused. The court held that this was untrue, as an actual act of refusal is necessary.

> *Re Smith & Fawcett Ltd* (1942)
> Two directors of a company held fifty per cent of the shares each. When one died, his son, acting as executor, sought to transfer the shares to himself. The directors refused by exercising their 'absolute and uncontrolled discretion' but offered to transfer twenty-five per cent of the shares to the son if the remaining twenty-five per cent was transferred to the remaining shareholder–director. The son objected,

but the court held that this was justified to keep continued management control, which was in the best interests of the company.

Re Hafner, Olhausen v Powderly (1943) Ire
The plaintiff inherited shares in his uncle's business, but the transfer was refused by the directors, exercising their 'absolute and uncontrolled discretion without assigning reasons'. The plaintiff alleged that the refusal was because the company's director–shareholders voted themselves excessive pay, which he could have challenged. The court said that although the company was entitled to refuse without giving reasons, the court was entitled to draw conclusions from failure to give reasons. In this case the court concluded that the plaintiff's fears were justified. The discretion to refuse the transfer was not exercised in good faith for the benefit of the company as a whole.

2. Incorrect Transfers

The buyer becomes the legal owner of the shares when his or her name is entered onto the register of members. A share certificate is prima facie evidence of membership, and a company may be estopped from stating that the information on the share certificate is correct. As we have seen in earlier chapters, an estoppel is a rule of evidence that originates from the system of equity. An estoppel operates as follows: when a person makes a statement knowing that there will be reliance on it, then that person is 'estopped,' or stopped, from denying the truth of the statement when that reliance occurs.

Bloomenthal v Ford (1897)
A company issued a share certificate that incorrectly stated that a person's shares were fully paid up. The company were estopped from stating that this statement was untrue and calling for the unpaid amounts.

3. Forged Transfers

The issue of forged share transfers is slightly more complicated. It is important to remember that a forgery is a nullity in law, and a person who relies on a forgery may be held to be personally liable on it, even though he or she is completely innocent of the forgery. For example, a person who unknowingly hands a forged bank note into a shop will find that if the forgery is discovered, the shop will refuse to honour the note, and the owner of the note will be held personally liable.

If a person suffers as a result of an incorrect share certificate, the company will be liable in damages, as it is estopped from denying that the share certificate is correct. If a forged transfer is used, the company will be liable to the person who purchases the shares on the faith of the transfer.

Re Bahia and San Francisco Railway Co (1868)
T was the registered owner of shares and had deposited her share certificate with her broker. Her signature was forged on a transfer in favour of S and forwarded to the company with her share certificate. A new share certificate was issued to S, who then sold the shares to X who was registered as the owner. When the fraud was discovered, T's name was restored to the register. The court held that the company should compensate X for the value of the shares. The certificate issued by the company to S was a statement that S was entitled to the shares, which the company were estopped from denying as X had suffered loss as a result of it.

To prevent forged transfers companies often write to a shareholder from whom they have received a request to transfer, requesting the shareholder to inform them immediately if he or she does not wish the transfer to proceed. However, if the shareholder fails to respond to such a letter, he or she may still claim that the transfer was a forgery.

A company will not be liable if the share certificate itself is a forgery, issued by a person who had no authority to do so, as in *Ruben v Great Fingall Consolidated Co* (1906). If the transferee is aware that the share certificate is incorrect, the company will not be liable.

Other Issues in Relation to Shares

1. Shares as Security

Shares are often used as security for borrowing, and commonly, shares will be mortgaged as a way of raising finance.

The mortgage of shares is the same as a domestic mortgage of a house. A house mortgage can be a legal mortgage, in which the title of the house is transferred to the lender, and if the borrower defaults on his or her payments, the lender can sell the house. Alternatively, an equitable mortgage could be created in which the title deeds of the house are simply deposited with the lender, who can obtain a court order to sell the house in the event of the borrower being unable to repay.

Similarly, shares may be the subject of a legal mortgage in which the mortgagee, or lender, becomes the registered holder of the shares, with a separate agreement to retransfer ownership on repayment of the loan. Due to the complications involved in this, such as the payment of dividends, it is rarely done in practice.

An equitable mortgage involves the deposit of the share certificate with the lender, but ownership remains with the borrower. A signed instrument of transfer is usually deposited with the share certificate, and if the borrower defaults, the lender simply fills in the transfer and sells the shares. Due to its simplicity, the equitable mortgage is much more common in practice.

2. Share Warrants

A share warrant is a document stating that the bearer is the owner of the shares. By section 88, CA 1963 a company limited by shares with authority in its articles may issue warrants for fully paid up shares. The company must remove the name of the holder from the register of members and record the fact that a warrant has been issued for the shares. Once a share warrant is delivered to another person, that other person becomes the legal owner of the shares. Due to the obvious difficulties created by theft and loss, share warrants are very rare in Ireland.

3. Lien, Surrender and Forfeiture

The company can also exercise a lien over its members' shares for money owed to the company if the articles allow it. This is simply a provision that gives the company first claim on the shares if the shareholder is in debt to the company. The right to use a lien must be stated in the company's articles.

A shareholder who has unpaid amounts on his or her shares may decide to surrender them to the company rather than to pay the outstanding amounts. Similarly, a company's articles may provide for forfeiture of shares by the company if the shareholder cannot pay the outstanding amounts on his or her shares. However, because most shares in Ireland are fully paid up when issued, neither surrender or forfeiture arises much in practice.

Dividends

A shareholder normally invests in a company in the hope of making a profit at a later date. There are two main ways of making such a profit—selling the shares at a profit, or earning dividends on the shares.

A shareholder generally has the right to earn dividends, i.e. periodic payments of money which represent the company's profits. The payment of dividends is regulated by the company's memorandum and articles, and legal rules.

Declaration of Dividend

A company has an implied right to declare a dividend, but it is usually dealt with in the articles of association. Under Table A:

(1) A dividend must be declared by the company in general meeting. This declaration cannot exceed the amount recommended by the directors.

(2) The directors may also declare an interim dividend as they see fit.

(3) A shareholder is not entitled to a dividend unless it has been declared according to the articles and the date for payment has arrived. Thus preference shareholders are only entitled to their dividend when their specified date of payment arrives.

(4) The directors, before paying dividends, may set aside profits to be used for other purposes. This is a management decision, i.e. a company does not have to pay a dividend and cannot be compelled to do so according to *Bond v Barrow Haematite Steel Co* (1902).

(5) Dividends are declared as payable on paid-up amounts of shares only, i.e. if shares are only fifty per cent partly paid, then fifty per cent of the full dividend will be paid.

(6) Dividends are paid in cash only, unless the company provides otherwise. Dividends paid other than in cash are known as paid in specie.

(7) Dividends shall only be paid in accordance with Part IV of the Companies (Amendment) Act 1983.

Part IV of the Companies (Amendment) Act 1983: The key rule is section 45, C(A)A 1983 which states that:

(1) Dividends must be paid out of the profits available for the distribution. In other words, dividends cannot be paid out of a company's capital, as this would be an unauthorised reduction of capital.

According to section 45, the profits available for distribution are: 'a company's accumulated realised profits, so far as not previously utilised by distribution or capitalisation, less its accumulated realised losses, so far as not previously written off in a reduction or reorganisation of capital duly made'.

(2) A company must be solvent, that is in a position to pay its debts as they fall due, before a dividend can be paid.

(3) Section 46, C(A)A 1983 provides the rule for a public limited company— 'a dividend can only be paid if its net assets are not less than the aggregate of the called up share capital and undistributable reserves, and the distribution does not reduce the amount of those assets to less than the aggregate amount'.

'Undistributable reserves' include:

- the share premium account;
- the capital redemption reserve fund;
- any surplus of accumulated unrealised profits over accumulated unrealised losses;
- any reserve which the company's memorandum or articles prohibit it from distributing.

Additional Points

Special rules apply to investment companies under section 47, C(A)A 1983 and to assurance companies under section 48, C(A)A 1983. The onus is on a company's accountant to determine whether a dividend should be paid, by consulting properly prepared relevant accounts. Failure to do so may give rise to liability in negligence. If an unlawful distribution is made by a company to a member who has reasonable grounds to believe it was unlawful, the company may recover the money.

Company with an Unpaid Cumulative Dividend

If a company with an unpaid cumulative dividend goes into liquidation, the preference shareholders are not entitled to a dividend, unless this is provided for in the articles of association, or the dividend has been declared but not paid when the company goes into liquidation.

CHAPTER 12

Company Borrowing—Debentures and Charges

Summary of chapter

In this chapter we will look at the way companies borrow money through debentures. We will differentiate between fixed and floating charges and among the hybrid of fixed charges over book debts. We will then consider the order of priority in which charges are paid in the event of a receivership or liquidation and when charges will be invalid.

Every company will need to borrow at some time in its business life. Companies have an implied power to borrow, but they will usually also have an expressed power to borrow, as financial institutions and lenders prefer an expressed power. (These issues have been dealt with in Chapter 10. Note that there is an overlap between company borrowing and the issues of *ultra vires* borrowing and director's authority to borrow.)

Companies borrow by way of debentures, i.e. by issuing a document known as a debenture to a lender, detailing the amount the company owes that lender.

If a company wishes to raise capital, it may do so in the form of share capital or loan capital. 'Loan capital' is the term used for all moneys the company has borrowed by way of debenture. If a company issues more shares, the power of the existing shareholders will be diluted, unless pre-emption is applied, so a company may decide to raise money by borrowing instead. A number of essential legal differences are involved in the company's decision as to which form of security to issue:

(1) A shareholder is an *owner* of the company, whereas a debenture holder is a *creditor*.

(2) On liquidation, debts to debenture holders are repaid in advance of debts to shareholders.

(3) The interest that a company pays on a debenture is tax deductable, which makes it attractive to a company.

(4) A company may purchase its own debentures (unless the debenture provides otherwise). Redeemed debentures may be reissued.

A. Debentures

Companies may borrow from various sources: shareholders, personal investors, financial institutions. Most loans are by way of debentures.

There is no statutory definition of a debenture. The usual definition is that a 'debenture' is a document acknowledging a debt by a company. For example, if a financial institution lends €10,000 to a company, the company will issue a debenture to the lender, which details the loan, the rate of repayment and any security to which the loan attaches. If a lender has a secured debenture and the loan is not repaid, the lender can appoint a receiver to sell the security to pay the debt. This is the main remedy of a secured debenture holder and will be explained in detail in Chapter 13. Security may be by way of a fixed or floating charge, and of course debentures may be unsecured.

Types of Debentures

Debentures may take three forms: single, series and stock debentures.

1. A Single Debenture

A single debenture is the most common type of debenture in Ireland. It is an individual loan made to a company.

2. A Series of Debentures

A series of debenture is a group of separate loans issued on standard conditions. The key condition is that all the debentures rank equally (or *pari passu*), although the loans may be created on different dates. This is done to raise a total amount, usually from a company's members or directors.

3. Debenture Stock

'Debenture Stock' refers to a large group of lenders who subscribe for debentures. In this case the loan is treated as part of an overall stock figure. It is used by public companies to raise finance from the public at large, and for convenience all the loans are treated as part of a fictional overall figure. Each loan may be split into amounts, e.g. €10, and is transferable.

Debenture Trust Deed

A debenture trust deed may be used with a series of debentures and debenture stock. It is a legal document appointing a trustee to act on behalf of all the debenture holders to enforce the security and appoint the receiver. The contents of a debenture trust deed would usually be as follows:

(a) The name and address of the trustee. (This person is appointed by the company in the first place and thereafter by the shareholders if there is a change in trustee. The trustee is usually a financial institution, insurance company or an individual.)

(b) Provision for the payment of the trustee.

(c) A statement that the trustee represents the interests of the debenture holder.

(d) An undertaking by the company to repay the loan and interest at specified times.

(e) The creation of a legal mortgage on the company's assets to form the security.

(f) A statement of when these securities may be enforced.

(g) The authorisation of the trustee to enforce the security and appoint a receiver in case of default.

(h) An undertaking by the company to maintain and insure the charged property.

(i) Detailed provisions dealing with a register of debenture stockholders, meeting of debenture holders, issue of certificates, transfer of stock and other specific issues.

The advantages of a debenture trust deed are speed, in that the trustee can act quicker than a group of individual debenture holders, and convenience, in that individual debenture holders do not have to liase with each other or supervise their investment. However, the debenture trust deed is an additional cost to the debenture holder.

Registration and Transferability

1. Register of Debenture Holders

The company must keep a register of debenture holders under section 91, CA 1963. The register must contain the names and addresses of the debenture holders and the amount of debentures held by each. The register must be kept at the company's registered office or at another place of which the Registrar of Companies has notice.

2. Transferability of Debentures

A debenture is transferable according to the terms of the debenture itself. There are also *bearer debentures*, which are payable to the bearer and are transferred by delivery, in the same way as share warrants (see Chapter 11). These are negotiable instruments, and the individual to whom the debentures are delivered or given takes all legal rights to them.

Convertible Debentures

Convertible debentures, are those that may be converted into shares in the company at a specified rate of exchange. This is a device used when investors might be slow to buy shares in a company that may not make profits for some time to come (for example, while a business is being developed) but when, ultimately, there is a possibility of a high return. A company may decide to raise capital in the form of debentures that may be converted into shares in the company at a specified date in the future, when the company anticipates that it will be in profit. It is important to understand that there is no ban on a company issuing debentures at a discount, so that a company may issue a €1,000 debenture for €750, redeemable at par value in three years' time. The investor receives interest on the sum of €1,000, which is €250 more than he or she invested, and also has a capital growth of €250 over three years.

B. Company Charges

Debentures may be unsecured (or naked) but are usually secured by charges. A 'charge' is security for a debt. The purpose of the charge is to give the secured creditor a charge over the company's assets with which to enforce prior payment of the debts. As mentioned above, the main remedy of the secured debenture holder is the right to appoint a receiver to dispose of the secured asset to pay the debt secured. There are two main types of charges: fixed and floating. There is also a hybrid clause, which is a fixed charge over book debts.

Types of Charges

1. A Fixed Charge

A fixed charge attaches to a specific asset, and the borrowing company cannot deal with the charged assets without the consent of the chargeholder. A fixed charge would normally attach to such assets as property, plant and machinery and vehicles. A fixed charge can be by way of a legal or equitable mortgage over an asset. A domestic house mortgage would be an example of a fixed charge. In the event of the householder defaulting on the loan repayments, the lender may sell the asset to repay the debt. The big advantage of the fixed charge is that it ranks in priority to a floating charge when it comes to repayment (see below).

2. A Floating Charge

A floating charge is one that does not attach to specific assets until crystallisation. It is an equitable charge. Floating charges were defined in *Re Yorkshire Woolcombers' Association* (1903) as having three features:

(a) a charge on a class of assets of a company present and future;

(b) which class is, in the ordinarily course of the company business, changing from time to time; and

(c) until the holder enforces the charge, the company may carry on business and deal with the charged assets.

Figure 12.1 **Floating charge over stock. (a) During the course of the floating charge, the charge floats over the secured asset. (b) On the occurrence of a crystallising event, the floating charge attaches to whatever part of the asset is available at that time.**

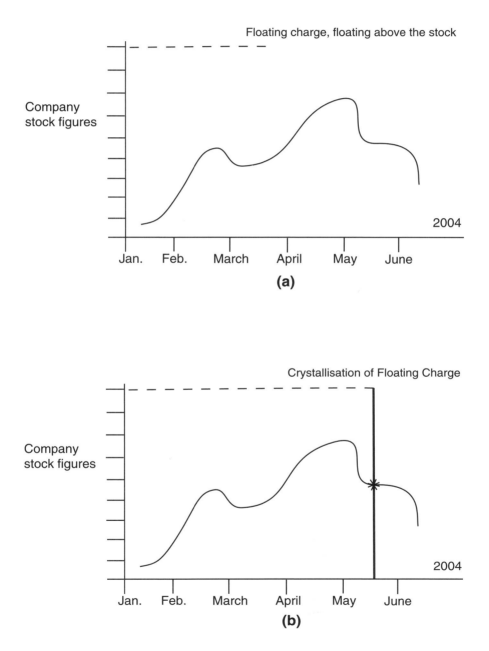

However, the court also made it clear that a charge could still be a floating charge if it did not have all three characteristics. An example of this is seen in the following case.

> *Welch v Bowmaker (Ireland) Ltd and the Bank of Ireland* (1980) Ire
> In this case a floating charge was created over land, which is not an asset that would change from time to time. The Supreme Court accepted that this could still be a valid floating charge.

A floating charge would typically be created over stock, which is a class of changing assets with which the company carries on business. A floating charge may also be created over book debts, which is considered at the end of the chapter. Floating charges are usually created by companies that have already created fixed charges on all suitable assets or by companies that do not have any assets suitable for the creation of fixed charges.

As the name suggest, a floating charge 'floats' over the class of assets, such as stock, without affixing to any specific part of the asset to security. If the debt that a floating charge secures is paid, the charge simply ceases to exist. However, if the security has to be enforced, the floating charge is said to 'crystallise', at which point it affixes to whatever part of the asset is available at that time. For example, with a floating charge over stock, if the charge crystallises on 28 March, it attaches to whatever is in the stockroom at that date. (If there is insufficent stock to meet the charge, the borrower ranks as an unsecured creditor for the balance.) A floating charge crystallises:

- on the liquidation of a company;
- on the appointment of a receiver to the company;
- when the parties stipulate (although some academic debate surrounds this point);
- on the cessation of the company's business which includes the sale of a company's business.

> *Re The Real Meat Co Ltd* (1995) Ire
> A company created a floating charge in favour of a creditor. Subsequently, the company sold its business. The debenture did not provide for crystallisation in such a case or for an automatic crystallisation clause. The court held that the sale of the business was a cessation of business, which caused the floating charge to crystallise automatically.

A floating charge that crystallises on the appointment of a receiver becomes a floating charge again on the appointment of an examiner. This was established in *Re Holidair Ltd* (1994) Ire.

Floating charges have a number of disadvantages.

(a) They rank third in priority for payment, after fixed charges and preferential debts.

(b) The precise value of the security is uncertain until crystallisation occurs.

(c) They cannot take effect over goods the company does not yet own, such as goods under a retention of title clause or on hire purchase.

(d) A receiver can invalidate a floating charge in a number of ways:

- if a charge is not registered under section 99, CA 1963;
- if a charge is a fraudulent preference under section 286, CA 1963;
- if a charge is created within one year of a company going into insolvent liquidation under section 288, CA 1963 (see below).

Fixed Charges versus Floating Charges: Many investors prefer fixed charges because they rank in priority over other debts when it comes to repayment. Some investors prefer floating charges over stock because stock is often more disposable by the receiver than assets subject to a fixed charge, such as premises.

In addition, a floating charge may be the only option open to a company which has no uncharged fixed assets, or they are all already subject charges.

3. Fixed Charge over Book Debts

A fixed charge over book debts is a hybrid charge. It is quite permissible to create a floating charge over book debts, but of course such a charge would lose out to fixed charges and preferential debts. If a charge over book debts could be created as a fixed charge, its main advantage would be that it would take priority over preferential debts. As a result, in the 1980s, banks preferred to create such charges as fixed charges. However, the Revenue Commissioners objected to such charges because they took priority over debts to the Revenue Commissioners, which ranked second as preferential debts. Such schemes usually provided that the borrower was to collect the debts and keep them in a special bank. These are sometimes know as *Siebe Gorman* clauses, after the English case which established them (*Siebe Gorman v Barclays Bank Ltd* (1977)). They were accepted in Ireland by the Supreme Court in *Re Keenan Brothers Ltd* (1985) Ire, which held that the charge could only attach to uncollected debts, as collected debts would no longer be debts.

Since the Finance Act 1986, section 115, the holder of a fixed charge over book debts is liable to pay the borrowing company's debts to the Revenue Commissioners if the borrowing company fails to pay. Thus, the Revenue Commissioners have priority over fixed charges over book debts, so they are rarely created any more. However, this provision led to difficulties for small companies seeking to borrow from banks. As a result, section 174, Finance Act 1995 provides that section 115 does not apply when 'within twenty-one days of the creation of the fixed charge, the holder of the charge furnishes the Revenue Commissioners with a copy of the charge to be registered under section 99, CA 1963'.

Re Holidair Ltd (1994) Ire

Holidair Ltd sought the protection of the appointment of an examiner for itself and eighteen related companies, known as the Kentz Group. Under the Companies Act 1990, the examiner was given power to borrow on behalf of the company. However, a bank claimed that Holidair Ltd had created a fixed charge over book debts in its favour in 1984, and thus the examiner could not borrow without its consent. The Supreme Court held that the charge over book debts (dating from 1984) was a floating charge, as it was a class of assets that changed from time to time, and the companies were free to draw moneys from these bank accounts. The court also held that a floating charge that had crystallised on the appointment of a receiver would begin to float again on the appoinment of an examiner.

Registration of Charges

Section 99, CA 1963 provides that a company must register charges with the Registrar of Companies within twenty-one days of creation. Nine types of charges must be registered, which cover almost every type of asset.

If a charge is not registered, the charge is void, and the debt it secures is repayable immediately. This means that the lender should be repaid its money at once without interest, which is unlikely to be possible as the borrower will already have put the money to a particular purpose. For this reason, the lender should ensure that the charge is registered as required, although the lender is not obliged to do this.

The company is not required to keep a register of charges, unlike in English company law. However, the company must keep copies of every instrument of charge requiring registration at its offices. There is an important difference here: because the list of charges to be registered under section 99 is not exhaustive, it is possible that a charge that defeats a later lender may not be registered or recorded, and the later lender would thus be unaware of it.

When the Registrar issues a certificate of registration, that is conclusive evidence that there has been compliance with the requirements of company law.

Late Registration

Charges must be registered within twenty-one days, but an extension of time may be given by the court under section 106, CA 1963. The extension may be given if the delay was 'accidental or due to inadvertence' and the extension is not prejudicial to any party, such as the creditors, shareholders or company. Where an extension of time is granted, it is usually subject to a proviso that registration is not to affect the rights of parties who acquired rights before the actual time of registration.

Re Telford Motors Ltd (1978) Ire

A debenture holder sought to register his charge under section 106, CA 1963 when he became aware that the company was considering winding up. As the delay was due to inadvertence, the High Court granted the extension for registration. The debenture holder gave an undertaking that if the company was wound up within twenty-one days, then the liquidator could apply to the court to discharge the order and the debenture holder would abide by any order the court might make to remove him from the register at that time. The company was wound up and the liquidator sought to set aside the later registration of the charge. The court agreed on the basis that the unsecured creditors had acquired rights after the winding up and were entitled to protection by the undertaking.

Priority of Charges

The basic order of priority for the payment of debts is:

(1) fixed charges—rank in order of creation, i.e. oldest charges first;
(2) preferential debts—all rank equally;
(3) floating charges—rank in order of creation, i.e. oldest charges first.

Preferential charges under section 285, CA 1963 are:

- all local rates within the last twelve months;
- all assessed taxes not exceeding one year's assessment;
- all PRSI within the last year;
- all wages and salary within the last four months;
- all accrued holiday pay.

However, in some cases it may be more complicated than this. In trying to decide the order of priorities of charges, you must consider the type of charge, i.e. fixed or floating, with fixed charges taking priority, and the date on which the charge was created, i.e. within each category charges rank according to the date on which they were created, with the oldest charges being the first to be paid.

For example, suppose a company has the following charges:

- a fixed charge created on 1/3/2000;
- a floating charge created on 1/10/2000;
- a fixed charge created on 1/1/2003;
- a floating charge created on 1/8/2004.

These would rank as follows:

(1) the fixed charge created on 1/3/2000;
(2) the fixed charge created on 1/1/2003;
(3) the floating charge created on 1/10/2000;
(4) the floating charge created on 1/8/2004.

However, the order of priorities is sometimes more complicated than this. Consideration may also need to be given to other issues in deciding the priorities of charges.

(1) Fixed charges take priority over floating charges created over the same asset.

(2) Legal charges take priority over equitable charges. Charges can be created legally or equitably, in the same way as mortgages over shares are created, as explained in Chapter 11. A 'legal charge' would occur when the debenture holder becomes the legal owner of the security, and an 'equitable charge' would occur when the borrower remains the owner of the asset.

(3) Floating charges rank in the order in which they were created, but a charge over a specific class of assets takes priority over an earlier charge over all the assets.

(4) A company cannot create a second floating charge on the same assets ranking in priority to or equally with an existing floating charge.

(5) A negative pledge clause is only valid if the holder of the subsequent charge has actual notice of the restriction (see below).

(6) A floating charge may be invalid under section 288, CA 1963 if it was registered within twelve months of a liquidation and the company was not solvent at the date of its creation. The period is two years in relation to charges created in favour of a connected person (see below).

(7) Any charge may be invalid under section 286, CA 1963 as a fraudulent preference if it was created within six months of a liquidation. The period is two years in relation to charges created in favour of a connected person (see below).

Negative Pledge Clause

A negative pledge clause is usually a feature of a floating charge. It is a restriction on the borrowing company's ability to create subsequent charges ranking in priority to the current one. The aim is to avoid the fear that a floating charge would lose out to a later fixed charge.

A negative pledge clause binds both parties and also any subsequent secured creditors, provided they have *actual notice* of the clause. A subsequent charge holder will generally be aware of the previous charge because of the requirement of registration but may not be aware of the prohibition contained therein.

> *Welch v Bowmaker (Ireland) Ltd and the Bank of Ireland* (1980) Ire
> A company gave Bowmaker a floating charge over its land. The floating charge contained a negative pledge clause. A month later the company gave the Bank of Ireland an equitable deposit of title deeds over the same property. The Bank of Ireland was aware of the earlier floating charge but did not know the details of its terms. When the company was wound up,

the question of priorities over the piece of land arose because there was insufficient money to pay both debts. Bowmaker argued that the Bank of Ireland, as subsequent charge holders, should have *constructive notice* of the negative pledge clause in the prior floating charge because such clauses were so common. The Supreme Court held that *actual notice* was required. Thus the second charge took priority as it was a fixed charge.

Invalidity of Charges

Very often when a company goes into liquidation, there will not be sufficient money to pay all a company's debts. In such circumstances, the liquidator has to decide which charges will be paid and which, if any, can be avoided.

1. A Floating Charge May Be Invalid

Under section 288, CA 1963 (as substituted by section 136, CA 1990), when a company is being wound up, any floating charge registered within twelve months of a liquidation will be void unless it is proved that the company was solvent immediately after the creation of the charge. 'Solvent' for the purposes of section 288 means 'an ability to pay one's debts as they fall due'.

If the floating charge was created in favour of a 'connected person,' any floating charge within the last two years will be void. A 'connected person' means:

- a director of the company;
- a shadow director of the company;
- a director's spouse, parent, brother, sister and child;
- a trustee of a trust, the principle beneficiary of which is a director, the director's spouse or children or any company the director controls;
- a partner of a director.

2. Fraudulent Preference

Section 286, CA 1963 provides that any act relating to property done by a company that is unable to pay its debts in favour of a creditor, with a view to giving such a creditor a preference over other creditors, shall be invalid if created within six months of a liquidation. In other words, when a company is in financial difficulty and does something in an attempt to fraudulently prefer one creditor over another, this will be invalid. Typically, when a company has a number of unsecured creditors, it might create a floating charge in favour of one creditor, with the result that the creditor is in a favourable position when the company is wound up. However, such a transaction will not be valid if it is within six months of the company being wound up, or within two years if the transaction was in favour of a connected person.

CHAPTER 13

The Remedies of a Debenture Holder

Summary of chapter

In this chapter we will focus on the main remedy available to a debenture holder who has loaned money to a company: the right to appoint a receiver. The role of the receiver will be explained, including qualifications, appointment, powers and duties.

As stated in the last chapter, debentures may be secured or unsecured. Unsecured debentures are rare because of their low position in the order of priorities for repayment. An unpaid, unsecured creditor may sue the company for the debts outstanding and may also seek to wind up the company on the grounds that it is unable to pay its debts. However, both of these are likely to be unsuccessful because the unsecured creditor ranks in such a low position.

A secured debenture holder can also sue for the debts and seek to wind up the company. However, the main remedy of the secured debenture holder is that he or she can appoint, or seek to appoint, a receiver who will sell the charged asset to pay the outstanding debt. This is the most important remedy of the secured debenture holder.

A. The Function of a Receiver

A receiver's function is exactly as it sounds: to receive the asset and sell it to pay the debt owing to the secured debenture holder. English law makes a distinction between a receiver and an administrative receiver who is appointed under a floating charge that covers all or the bulk of the company's property. There is no such distinction in Irish company law. There is, however, a receiver–manager, although this is not a legislative term. Where someone is appointed as a receiver–manager, it simply means that the receiver will manage the company's affairs. A receiver–manger is often appointed under a floating charge that covers most of the company's assets and, in this way, is somewhat similar to an administrative receiver.

Qualifications

There are no set qualifications for a receiver, but the position is normally filled by an accountant. However, section 315, CA 1963 as amended by section 170, CA 1990, disqualifies the following people from acting as receiver:

- a body corporate;
- an undischarged bankrupt;
- someone who has been an officer or servant of the company within the past twelve months;
- the partner or employee of an officer or servant of the company;
- a parent, spouse, brother, sister or child of an officer of the company.

B. The Appointment of a Receiver

How a receiver is appointed is very important in relation to the cost of the receivership and some of the effects of the appointment. A receiver may be appointed by the High Court or by the debenture holder or trustee out of court. Obviously, an application to the High Court will involve expense. When a receiver is appointed by the court, the receiver is an officer of the court. The most important consequence of the court's appointing a receiver is that the company's employees are automatically dismissed (see below).

The alternative is that the receiver can be appointed out of court under the terms of the debenture by the debenture holder or the debenture trustee. This is much more common. In these cases the receiver will be the agent of the company or the debenture holder, depending on what is stated in the terms of the debenture.

The grounds upon which a receiver can be appointed are usually expressed in general terms as when the moneys secured by the debenture become payable. It is usual to provide, in more detail, that the loan becomes payable:

- if repayment of the principal or interest is in arrears;
- if a receiver is appointed to the company by another party;
- if the company has begun to be wound up or if this appears likely;
- if the security attaching to the loan is in jeopardy.

The Registrar must be notified of the appointment, as must the company (who may or may not know that such an appointment is imminent) and the public by way of a notice in *Iris Oifigiúil* and one daily paper. After the appointment of a receiver, all company documents must state 'In receivership'.

The Effect of a Receiver's Appointment

One of the most important issues to understand is the effect of the receiver's appointment. The effect centers on issues of crystallisation, management, sale, representation and liability.

1. Crystallisation

All floating charges crystallise and become fixed to whatever property is available at that time. (It is important to remember that a crystallised floating charge is still a floating charge and not a fixed charge, so it ranks third in the order of priorities.)

2. Management

The director's management powers are suspended in relation to the charged assets. However, if a receiver–manager is appointed, he or she also manages all the company's affairs.

> *Lascomme Ltd v United Dominions Trust (Ireland) Ltd* (1993) Ire
> The plaintiff company, a hotel, borrowed money from the defendant bank and created a debenture in its favour. The plaintiff later instituted legal proceedings against the bank, claiming that it had agreed to lend them money but had failed to do so. A receiver was then appointed under the debenture by the defendants. The bank sought to stop the court case on the grounds that it had not been authorised by the receiver. The key point of their argument was that in the event of the action being dismissed with costs in favour of the bank, the bank's security would be endangered since it would be the only asset available to satisfy the order of costs.
>
> The court held that the plaintiff was entitled to proceed with the case. The appointment of a receiver did not terminate the powers vested in the company directors, including the power to institute and proceed with litigation in the company's name where it was in the best interests of the company.
>
> However, the director's powers could not be exercised to inhibit the receiver in the performance of his duties, or in a manner which would adversely affect the position of the debenture holder by threatening the value of the charged assets.
>
> The fact that the receiver could not recover the costs of a successful action was not a reason to halt proceedings because otherwise an insolvent company could not take a case against a debenture holder which it alleged had caused the insolvency.

3. Sale

The receiver can sell, or 'realise', the asset (subject to his or her duties, as explained below).

4. Contracts of Employment/Receiver as Agent

The issue of who the receiver represents is of particular importance in relation to whether the employees of the company are dismissed following the receiver's appointment. The distinction depends on whose agent the receiver is deemed to be. The situation can be explained as follows. If the receiver is the agent of the debenture holder, then employees are automatically dismissed. If the receiver is the agent or officer of the High Court, then the employees are automatically dismissed. If, however, the receiver is the agent of the company, then the employees are not automatically dismissed.

It follows that the receiver is most commonly appointed as the agent of the company, as this safeguards the jobs of the employees. This also has the advantage of protecting the debenture holder from personal liability for the acts or omissions of the receiver. If there is nothing specified in the debenture, the receiver will be the agent of the debenture holder.

5. Liability

A receiver is not liable on contracts made prior to his or her appointment, unless he or she specifically agrees to be. Under section 316, CA 1963 a receiver is liable on any contract entered into by him or her in the performance of his or her functions, unless the contract provides otherwise. It is usual for the receiver to be so indemnified.

> *Ardmore Studios (Ireland) Ltd v Lynch* (1965)
> A collective agreement between a trade union and a company did not bind a receiver–manager who was appointed after the agreement was concluded.

> *W & L Crowe Ltd and Another v ESB* (1984) Ire
> The ESB refused to enter into a new contract for a power supply with the receiver of a company unless the company's account was settled. The High Court upheld ESB's refusal and held that there was no entitlement to a new supply in such a case.

This decision has the effect of making a supplier a 'super-preferential creditor' of the company, i.e. someone who is entitled to be paid before the preferentail creditors in some circumstances.

C. The Powers of a Receiver

The powers of the receiver are partly specified in company law but largely result from case-law and common practice. The powers of a receiver are as follows.

1. Possession of Property

The receiver has the power to take possession of the property that is the subject of the charge.

2. Sell or Realise the Charged Asset

Section 316A, CA 1963, as inserted by section 172, CA 1990, places the receiver who is selling property under a duty to get the best price reasonably possible for the property at the time of the sale. This is to prevent the receiver selling the property substantially below its value. It is still unclear if a receiver has a duty to wait for the market to improve before selling an asset or whether the receiver can sell the asset at a bargain price. In such circumstances, the receiver could apply to the court for directions as to the best course of action.

3. Apply to the High Court for Directions

As a receiver is not usually legally qualified, section 316, CA 1963, as amended by section 171, CA 1990, provides that a receiver may apply to the High Court for directions in relation to any matter in connection with the performance of his or her functions.

4. To Appoint Assistants

The receiver has the power to appoint a solicitor, accountant or other professional to assist him or her.

In addition to the basic powers of a receiver, the receiver–manager has additional powers:

- to carry on the business of the company;
- to bring or defend legal actions in the company's name or on its behalf;
- to have any disputes arbitrated;
- to do acts in the company's name, including using the company seal.

D. The Duties of a Receiver

The receiver is under a fiduciary duty owed primarily to the debenture holder, regardless of the method by which he or she was appointed. The receiver owes a secondary duty to the company and to the preferential creditors, if he or she is appointed under a floating charge. The receiver has a range of duties that he or she is required to fulfil.

1. Notification

The receiver has a duty to notify the company and the public of his or her appointment, as explained above.

2. Best Price

The receiver's duty to the debenture holder is a fiduciary duty, i.e. a duty of good faith, to act in the best interests of the other party. (This applies even though the debenture usually makes the receiver the agent of the company.) The receiver's duty under section 316, CA 1963 and section 172, CA 1990 is to get the best price for the charged asset in the circumstances, as part of the overall fiduciary duty.

3. Skill and Care

A receiver may be liable to pay damages to the debenture holder if he or she runs the receivership in a negligent manner.

4. Reporting

The receiver is under a duty to report on the course of the receivership. The receiver is given an initial 'Statement of Affairs' within fourteen days of his or her appointment by the company directors and secretary (or other persons as the receiver may specify). The Statement of Affairs details the company's assets and liabilities, creditors and securities. Within two months, the receiver must send a copy of the Statement of Affairs and any comments to the Registrar and the company. Within seven months of appointment and within one month of ceasing to be a receiver, the receiver must send the Registrar detailed particulars of the realised assets and receipts.

5. Application of Assets in Correct Order

The receiver has a duty to apply the assets in his or her hands in the correct order as listed below.

(a) Expenses: the receiver's expenses, expenses of the debenture trust deed, expenses of selling property and the cost of any application to court.
(b) Fixed charges—rank in order of creation, i.e. oldest charges first.
(c) Preferential debts—all rank equally.
(d) Floating charges—rank in order of creation, i.e. oldest charges first.

> *Re Manning Furniture Ltd (in receivership)* (1995) Ire
> ICC bank appointed a receiver to Manning Furniture Ltd, under a mortgage debenture which included a floating charge and two chattel mortgages. Between the creation of the first and second chattel mortgages, the company created a mortgage over premises in favour of First National Building Society. This charge was not registered under section 99, CA 1963, and an order was made for late registration, subject to the usual proviso that the order was without prejudice to the rights of parties acquired prior to the time when the particulars would be registered. The receiver appointed by ICC sold the chattels and contracted to sell the premises and held a surplus of in excess of £150,000 (€190,460). The receiver sought directions from the High Court as to whether he should pay the company's preferential creditors or pay the balance to the First National Building Society.
> The High Court held that the receiver was bound to discharge the preferential debts out of the proceeds of the sale. Due to the late registration of First National's mortgage, he held that the effect of the attached standard proviso was that the preferential creditors were given priority.

Re City Car Sales Ltd (1994) Ire

The liquidator brought an application to the High Court arising out of a prior receivership in the company. In the receivership of City Car Sales Ltd, the receiver had retained £37,300 (€47,361) for himself out of the gross profits of assets realised by him. The liquidator argued that the receiver was entitled to only a five per cent commission as calculated in section 24, Conveyancing Act 1881, which amounted to not more than £15,493.81 (€19,673).

Section 24 provides that a receiver may only retain as payment five per cent of the gross money received, as specified in his appointment; and if no rate is specified in the receiver's appointment then the receiver is entitled to five per cent 'or such higher rate as the court thinks fit to allow'.

The High Court held that the debenture clearly intended that section 24, Conveyancing Act 1881 apply to it. A receiver who is not satisfied with the five per cent commission can apply to court to have a higher rate set, which is what the receiver had done in this case. Although the receivership had come to an end, the High Court had jurisdiction to pay a higher rate of commission under the Act. The judge did so, and allowed the receiver the sum of £37,300 (€47,361) claimed. This sum, according to the judge, had been calculated on a normal accountancy basis, and the receiver had acted totally bona fide at all times and did not realise the problem arising under the 1881 Act.

There is no general duty on a receiver or a receiver–manager to report or account to the company he or she is managing.

Irish Oil and Cake Mills Ltd and Another v Donnelly (1983) Ire

In this case the High Court refused to grant an injunction against a receiver to compel him to furnish a company with certain information. The court held that this was not a contractual duty, and failure to provide information was not a breach of duty. However, the court did state that a receiver may have a duty to account in some circumstances.

Vacation of Office

A court-appointed receiver may only resign with the permission of the court and on any terms laid down by the court. A receiver appointed under a debenture may resign by giving one month's notice in writing to the debenture holders and the company under section 177, CA 1990.

A receiver may be removed by the court if good grounds to do so are proven, and the court may then appoint another receiver under section 175, CA 1990. As a receivership often leads to the ultimate liquidation of a company, a receiver may be removed by the High Court to avoid duplication and additional expense according to section 176, CA 1990.

CHAPTER 14

The Management and Administration of a Company

Summary of chapter

As an artificial legal person, a company cannot manage itself but must delegate this power to the company directors. In this chapter, we will consider the role of the directors in company management. We will also consider the role of the company secretary and the company auditor.

In theory, the ownership and management of a company are separate functions to be performed by separate people. The company is owned by the shareholders and managed by the directors. However, as many Irish companies are small, family-run operations, this distinction is often more theoretical than practical, and the major shareholder will probably be a director of the company, an employee and perhaps also the company secretary. Since the introduction of one-person companies in Ireland in 1994, companies owned and managed by the same person have become even more common.

A. Directors

There is no comprehensive statutory definition of a director. The interpretation section of the 1963 Companies Act (CA 1963) states that a 'director' includes any person occupying the position of director, by whatever name called'. A director is usually defined as a person involved in the management of a company.

Under section 174, CA 1963 every company must have at least two directors. It is possible for a company's articles to provide that it shall have more than the statutory minimum. There is a slight inconsistency in the law here because under the EC (Single Member Private Companies) Regulations 1994, a company need have only one shareholder, but it still must have two directors.

Since the Companies (Amendment)(No. 2) Act 1999 (C(A)A (No. 2) 1999), a person shall not be a director of more than twenty-five companies at any one time. Section 43 C(A)A (No. 2) 1999 requires that at least one of a company's directors shall be resident in the State.

Types of Directors

There are a number of different types of directors (although most of these terms are not used in the Companies Acts).

1. Executive and Nonexecutive

An executive director is generally defined as someone who manages the company on a full-time basis. This director is often an employee or is under a contract for services. A nonexecutive director is someone who manages the company on a part-time basis. Such a person is often brought into a company to bring his or her expert knowledge to board meetings, especially in public companies.

2. Managing Director

A managing director is the person who carries on the day-to-day management of the company, as provided for in the articles of association. These articles also provide that the managing director has a second, or casting, vote in the event of a tied vote at board meetings. The managing director is the agent of the company and will have authority to bind the company to contracts.

3. Director for Life

A director for life is a type of director applicable only to a private company. It is a reward for the Mr or Ms Salomon-type person who sets up a company and contributes to society through job creation and the payment of tax. Such a title has no effect in a public company.

4. Alternate Director

Table A, Part II envisages the appointment of 'alternate', or 'substitute', directors to attend and vote at meetings when another director cannot. It is useful in cases of prolonged absences by a director, such as illness or travel. A fellow director may be appointed or an outsider may be. Such an appointment may be revoked by the board or the company in a general meeting.

5. Nominee Director

A nominee director is appointed to a company on the nomination of a powerful outsider such as a major creditor or a major shareholder. Such a person does not have a right to appoint a director, but a company may agree to his request. The nominee director must act in the best interests of the company, as well as his own interests or that of his nominator.

6. Shadow Director

According to section 27, CA 1990 a shadow director is someone in accordance with whose instructions the company acts. This person will be liable as a director in cases such as fraudulent trading. A professional advisor will not be treated as a shadow director. The category is aimed at a person who seeks to deliberately control a company while on paper remaining outside it. The extension of liability to shadow directors was seen as one of the most important developments of the 1990 Companies Act.

> *Re Vehicle Imports Ltd* (2001) Ire
> A company accountant was held liable as its shadow director, where he had overstepped his role, as evidenced by his being given excessive salary payments and blank cheques.

Appointment and Removal of Directors

1. Appointment

When a company is first registered, Form A1 is used to state the names of the first directors and secretary. In a private company, the names are often also stated in the articles. Under section 181, CA 1963 directors may only be appointed individually. This is to ensure that each director is elected on his or her own merit rather than on the strength of a fellow nominee. The procedure for appointing the directors is in the articles of association, as is the procedure for retirement.

2. Retirement

Retirement of directors is 'by rotation', according to article 92 of Table A. This procedure provides that each year one-third of the directors (or the nearest number) shall retire. This is interpreted to mean that the directors must offer to resign, and the shareholders may accept or refuse this offer. This provision does not apply to the managing director or a director for life in a private company. The aim of rotation is to ensure that the directors do not become too comfortable in their positions and that they realise that they hold their positions at the discretion of the shareholders.

3. Resignation

A director may resign by giving notice in writing to the company.

4. Casual Vacancy

A casual vacancy may arise in a company. This is a vacancy that arises between annual general meetings due, perhaps, to death or resignation. A casual vacancy may be filed by the remaining directors co-opting a person to sit on the board until the next election. The difference between an appointment for a casual vacancy and an alternate director is that a casual vacancy is filled for a period of time, and then a new director is appointed. An alternate director is appointed for a period, after which the original director returns to the company.

5. Validity of Appointment

Section 178, CA 1963 provides that the acts of a director shall be valid notwithstanding any defect that may afterwards be discovered in his or her appointment or qualification. The effect of this provision is that a director who is not validly appointed is still a director. This might occur where a private company fails to hold an annual general meeting, and thus the directors have not been validly appointed.

6. Removal

A director may be removed from a company by an ordinary resolution requiring extended notice of twenty eight days, according to section 182, CA 1963. The fact that only an ordinary resolution, i.e. a simple majority, is required is part of the division of power between shareholders and directors and shows that directors hold their positions at the discretion of the shareholders. The requirement for extended notice is to ensure that the director to be removed has sufficient time to canvass the shareholders and ask them not to support the proposed removal.

In theory a director for life in a private company cannot be removed. However, this is not always the case. It it is possible to remove a director for life in certain circumstances when he or she has breached a duty to the company.

> *Shuttleworth v Cox Bros & Co* (1927)
> A director for life had continually failed to account for moneys he received on behalf of the company and had failed to attend company meetings. He was successfully removed when the articles of association were altered to allow the removal of any director when requested by all the others.

7. Compensation for Removal

Section 182(7), CA 1963 provides that nothing in that section shall be taken as depriving a person so removed of compensation payable in respect of termination of any appointment. This means that a removed director may have the right to damages for breach of contract in wrongful dismissal or for unfair dismissal if he or she was an employee. Companies must also observe natural justice, or fairness, in the removal of directors.

> *Carvill v Irish Industrial Bank* (1968) Ire
> The plaintiff had no written contract for his position as managing director in the defendant bank. He was dismissed and claimed wrongful dismissal. The Supreme Court held that he had an implied contract which could be terminated by a year's notice. As such notice had not been given, the dismissal was wrongful, and damages of a year's salary were awarded.

See also *Glover v BLN Ltd* (1973) Ire (Chapter 8).

Section 28, CA 1990 limits directors' service contracts to a maximum of five years. This is to avoid companies making long service contracts with directors and then paying large payouts if these contracts are breached; i.e. so-called 'golden parachutes'.

Disqualification of Directors

A director may be forced to quit his or her office. The articles of association may provide for disqualification of certain directors, and the High Court can do so as well.

1. Ineligibility

The 1963 Companies Act prohibits the following people from acting as directors:

- undischarged bankrupts;
- a body corporate (only a human person may be a director);
- the auditor of the company or its holding company.

2. Disqualification under the Articles

Table A, Article 91 provides that a director must vacate his or her office if he or she:

(a) fails to acquire his or her share qualifications, as required by section 180, CA 1963;
(b) becomes bankrupt or makes an arrangement with his or her creditors;
(c) becomes prohibited from being a director by reason of any order made by the High Court under Part VII, CA 1990 in relation to disqualification and restriction of directors;
(d) becomes of unsound mind;
(e) resigns the office by notice in writing to the company;
(f) is convicted of any indictable offence (the other directors may waive this requirement);
(g) is absent without leave from board meetings for more than six months.

3. Disqualification by the Court

Under section 160, CA 1990, the following people may be disqualified from acting as director:

(1) a person convicted of an indictable offence relating to the company, fraud or dishonesty;
(2) a person who has been guilty of fraud while acting as a promoter, officer, auditor, receiver, liquidator or examiner of a company;

(3) a person guilty of reckless or fraudulent trading;

(4) a person unfit to be involved in the management of a company by reason of his or her conduct in the roles mentioned in (2) above;

(5) a person unfit to be involved in the management of a company following an inspector's report under the Companies Acts by reason of his or her conduct in the roles mentioned in (2) above;

(6) a person persistently in default in relation to the filing requirements of the Companies Acts;

(7) a person convicted of acting as promoter, officer, auditor, receiver, liquidator or examiner of a company while an undischarged bankrupt under section 169, CA 1990.

The High Court also has discretion to disqualify in other cases. Only one director has been disqualified since the introduction of section 160, CA 1990.

In the report of the Company Law Review Group in 1994, it was recommended that the disqualification provisions under section 160, CA 1990 should be strengthened. Specifically, it was recommended that a special unit should be set up within the Department of Enterprise, Trade and Employment to apply for the disqualification of directors of companies in insolvent liquidation or receivership. An application for a disqualification order can now be made by the Director of Public Prosecutions, the Registrar of Companies or the Director of Corporate Enforcement. Section 56 of the Company Law Enforcement Act 2001 (CLEA 2001) provides that a liquidator of an insolvent company must apply to the court to restrict the directors under section 150, CA 1990.

If the court judges that disqualification is not justified, it may make a restriction order under section 150, CA 1990.

Restrictions on Directors

Section 150, CA 1990, as amended by section 41, CLEA 2001, restricts a director of an insolvent company from being a director of another company for five years. This is to avoid an abuse of separate legal personality and limited liability whereby a person winds up an insolvent company owing large debts and shortly afterwards starts up another company without ever having to make good the debts of the first company. This is known as 'phoenix trading', where the phoenix of the new company rises from the ashes of the old.

Under this section a person who was a director, including a shadow director, of a company, within twelve months of its going into insolvent liquidation, will be restricted for a period of five years from acting as director or secretary of or in forming of another company. This is a controversial provision and has been criticised as being too harsh. However, the legislation does provide for a number of limited exceptions to restriction:

(a) if the director acted honestly and responsibly, and there is no other reason why it would be just and equitable to restrict him or her;

(b) if the person was a director solely as the nominee of a financial institution lending to the company and that institution had not obtained any personal guarantee of repayment from a director;

(c) if the person was a director solely as a nominee of a venture capital company.

Both (b) and (c) are also subject to the requirement that the person must have acted honestly and responsibly.

A restricted director may act for a highly capitalised company, which is one with an allotted share capital of at least €63,487 in a private company and €317,435 in a public company, fully paid up in cash. If such a company takes on a restricted director, it loses the benefit of certain provisions on capital maintenance. Section 155, CA 1990 provides that such a company may not provide any assistance for the purchase of its own shares, purchase a noncash asset from any connected person or make any loan to a director.

It is also a criminal offence to act for a company while restricted, and doing so leads to automatic disqualification. If a restricted director acts as director of another company that goes into liquidation, the restricted director can be made personally liable without limit for the debts of the second company if he or she was a director within twelve months of the insolvent liquidation. This is the main civil sanction against acting as a director while restricted.

Relief from restriction can be sought under section 152, CA 1990. A director may apply for relief to the court within one year of restriction and the court may grant whatever relief it sees fit.

When this legislation was introduced, it was much criticised as being draconian. The worst case scenario envisaged was that honest directors of companies which become insolvent would be unfairly penalised. In fact the number of directors being restricted was quite low.

The low number of restrictions was because of a considerable gap in the legislation; it does not impose a duty on anyone to bring a case before the High Court so that the court can exercise its mandatory duty to restrict. In a creditor's voluntary liquidation (the most common in Ireland) the creditors as liquidators did not bother seeking to restrict a director when they were not obliged to do so. Thus the doomsday scenario of restriction being a common occurrence under the CA did not happen.

However, this changed under section 56, CLEA 2001, which made it mandatory for the liquidator of a company to apply for restriction of the directors. An application for restriction of a director under section 150 may be made by a receiver, a liquidator or the Director of Corporate Enforcement. The court may order a director to bear the cost of such an application.

Re Costello Doors Ltd (1995) Ire

This case concerned an application by directors of an insolvent company for an exemption from the provisions of the Companies Act 1990 in relation to the restriction of directors. The directors were three employees of the company and Mr and Ms Costello, who were also the only shareholders. The company employed two full-time bookkeepers and retained a firm of accountants, but there were some defects in the company's control system. The court held that none of the directors had acted dishonestly or irresponsibly and did not make an order restricting them.

Business Communications Ltd v Baxter and Parsons (1995) Ire

The defendants were the main shareholder and directors in Business Communications Ltd. The company's finances came under pressure, followed by a breakdown among the directors. The company was insolvent, and a decision to wind up was made. The company continued to trade for six months until it went into voluntary liquidation. The court held that a 'suitable degree' of honesty was required before a director could avail of the exemption in section 150, CA 1963. This would ordinarily require compliance with the Companies Acts and the maintenance of the required records to enable the directors to make reasonable commercial transactions. The conduct of the company's business in its last six months did not comply with this. Therefore the directors were restricted, and an exemption was not granted.

Moselle Clothing Ltd v Soualhi (1998) Ire

Soualhi was a director and ninety-nine per cent shareholder of Moselle Clothing Ltd. Soualhi was restricted because the company had traded while insolvent. The court held that the test to determine whether a director was acting responsibly must consider:

- the extent of compliance with the Companies Acts;
- whether the director's conduct was so incompetent as to be irresponsible;
- the extent of the director's responsibility for the insolvency;
- the extent of the director's responsibility for the net deficiency in assets at winding up;
- the extent to which the director displayed a lack of commercial probity or want of proper standards.

This test was approved by the Supreme Court in *Re Squash (Ireland) Ltd* (2001) Ire.

In the report of the Company Law Review Group in 1994, it was stated that restriction of directors is not a sufficient sanction, and that disqualification of directors under section 160, CA 1990 would be more appropriate to deal with such cases. A similar statement was made by the judge in *Re Business Communication Ltd* who said that he regarded restriction as 'a far lesser penalty than that which may be imposed by disqualification or the reckless and fraudulent trading provisions'.

The big difference between the two is that a restricted person cannot be a director or secretary, but a disqualified director is prohibited from a much wider range of activities—from being director, secretary, auditor, receiver, liquidator or examiner or 'be in any way, whether directly or indirectly, concerned or take part in the promotion, formation or management of any company'.

Even though disqualification lasts for the same basic length of time as restriction, i.e. five years, disqualification is seen as more appropriate to prevent unsuitable people from having anything to do with companies.

The provisions on restriction of directors also apply to 'shadow directors'. Under section 27, CA 1990 a shadow director is someone in accordance with whose instructions the company acts. A recent English case has stated that such a director can also be disqualified under the equivalent English law.

Duties of Directors

Article 80 of Table A deals with the powers and duties of the directors. Article 80 states: 'The business of the company shall be managed by the directors', and the directors 'may exercise all such powers of the company as are not, by the Companies Acts . . . , required to be exercised by the company in general meeting'. Again, this highlights the balance of power in a company, with the directors only having residual power, in theory. However, in practice, directors in larger companies will only be reporting to shareholders once a year, so they will have considerable discretion in the management of the company.

Directors owe three main duties to a company: fiduciary duties, the duty of skill and care and statutory duties. Before we look at these in detail, it is worth highlighting a relevant judicial statement in relation to the duties of directors. It is very common in Ireland that the directors of a small private company would be those who set it up and some people close to them, such as a spouse or family members.

> *Re Costello Doors Ltd* (1995) Ire
> This case concerned an application by directors of an insolvent company for an exemption from the provisions of the Companies Act 1990 in relation to the restriction of directors. The directors were Mr and Ms Costello, who were also the only shareholders, and three employees of the company. The High Court stated that it 'could not accept that anyone who agrees to act as director of a company can be excused from acting responsibly merely because he or she is a friend, relative or spouse of the proprietor of the company and accepts the

office to facilitate the proprietor of the company without being prepared to involve himself or herself in any aspect of the management
of the company'.

Thus the director's duties apply to all directors.

1. Fiduciary duties

A 'fiduciary duty' is a duty to act in the best interests of another person. It
is a relationship based on trust and confidence. The duty is owed to the
shareholders at large, rather than individually, although an individual
shareholder can claim the remedy of oppression under section 205, CA
1963, as explained in Chapter 15.

Case law in this area has further defined the concept of fiduciary duties,
and the following specific duties can be seen with regard to directors: to act
in good faith, to exercise power properly and to avoid conflicts of interest.

To Act in Good Faith in the Best Interests of the Company as a Whole

Re Lee Behrens & Co (1932)
A company paid a pension to the widow of a former director. When
the company went into liquidation, the widow claimed as a creditor for
the capital value of the pension. The court held that the gift was *ultra
vires* as there was no benefit to the company.

Parke v Daily News (1961)
A newspaper company was sold, and the owners decided to pay the
bulk of the purchase price to the employees who were to be made
redundant. The plaintiff shareholder objected on the grounds that the
distribution deprived shareholders of dividends. The court held that
the distribution was not in the best interests of the company as a
whole.

Crindle Investments v Wymes (1998) Ire
The plaintiffs and defendants bought land rich in ore and formed two
companies to exploit it, the second and third defendants. The parties
became involved in litigation with other parties and a serious dispute
arose about how the litigation was to be conducted. The plaintiffs
claimed that the defendants were acting oppressively under section
205, CA 1963, and were in breach of their fiduciary duties as directors
of the companies. The Supreme Court held that company directors do
not, merely by virtue of their office, owe a fiduciary duty to individual
shareholders, although they may do so in exceptional circumstances.
Directors' duties are owed to the company as a whole.

It is arguable that case law, such as *Re Frederick Inns* (1994) Ire and *Jones
v Gunn* (1997) Ire, has extended this director's duty to creditors, but this
has not yet been clearly established.

Section 52, CA 1990 provides that directors of a company must have regard to the interests of the employees as well as the members in the performance of their duties.

To Exercise Powers for the Purposes for Which They Were Conferred

If there is more than one purpose, the courts look at the 'substantial purpose'.

- In the case of illegal acts, the directors may be liable to the company for such. Illegal acts cannot be ratified by a company, even unanimously, but shareholders can absolve directors from liability to compensate the company for such acts.
- In the case of *ultra vires* acts, these cannot be ratified by the shareholders. Section 8, CA 1963 allows third parties to enforce *ultra vires* contracts against the company. Shareholders can seek to stop *ultra vires* acts by use of an injunction (see Chapter 10).
- Difficulties may arise where directors allot new shares in the company to themselves. (This is now subject to C(A)A 1983 whereby directors must get prior approval from shareholders for allotment of new shares, see Chapter 11).

In a private company, directors usually have discretion to refuse to register a transfer of existing shares to a new shareholder. Difficulties arise where they refuse to transfer; see *Re Hafner, Olhausen v Powderly* (1943) Ire, in Chapter 11.

Howard Smith Ltd v Ampol Petroleum Ltd and Another (1974)
Two shareholders held fifty-five per cent of the shares in a company between them. They were opposed to a forthcoming takeover bid for the company. The directors honestly believed that the takeover was in the best interest of the company, so they allotted new shares to the takeover bidder so that the bid would succeed. The court held that the directors' power to allot shares was used for an improper purpose, i.e. to dilute the power of the majority.

Nash v Lancegaye (Ireland) Ltd (1958) Ire
The plaintiff was a director and shareholder in the defendant company. Differences arose between himself and another major shareholder director, the second defendant X. The directors who supported X allotted new shares to give a clear majority to X and his supporters. The plaintiff sought to set aside the allotment. The court held that the allotment had been made to ensure that X's family controlled the company and was not in good faith in the best interest of the company as a whole.

To Avoid Any Conflicts of Interest

A conflict usually takes one of two forms:

(a) diverting a business opportunity from the company

> *Cook v Deeks* (1916)
> Directors of a railway company were offered a construction contract on behalf of the company. Instead, they took the contract for themselves, and used their votes as shareholders to endorse their action. The court held that this was in breach of their duties to the company, and consequently a fraud on the minority.

> *Industrial Development Consultants Ltd v Cooley* (1972)
> Cooley was a director in the plaintiff company. He bid for a contract with a gas board on the company's behalf, but the bid failed. However, he was then approached by the gas board who offered the work to him personally, making it clear that the board would not deal with the plaintiff. Cooley pretended that he had a serious illness and was released from his service contract with IDC. He then took on the contract work with the gas board. The court held that this was a conflict of interest. Cooley had to account to IDC for the profit he made on the contract, even though IDC could not have made the contract itself.

This case illustrates that in cases of a conflict of interest, any profits made are held in trust for the company. This legal fiction is known as a 'constructive trust' and was also seen in *Guinness plc v Saunders* (1988) below.

(b) a concealed interest in another business

> *Aberdeen Rly Co v Blaikie Bros* (1854)
> A railway company made a contract to purchase goods from a firm in which one of the directors was a partner. The court held that the contract was voidable at the option of the company, i.e. it is valid until the company sets it aside due to the conflict of interest.

Section 194, CA 1963 now requires directors to disclose their interest in contracts made by the company. The disclosure should be made at the meeting at which the contract is considered or at the first meeting after the director becomes interested. Disclosure to part of the board is insufficient.

> *Guinness plc v Saunders* (1988)
> The second defendant Ward was a director of Guinness when it launched a takeover bid for Distillers plc. A company controlled by Ward was paid £5.2 million by Guinness for services in connection with the take-over. Ward had disclosed his interest to a committee of the board of directors but not to the full board. On discovery of the facts, Guinness sought to recover the £5.2 million. The court held that this was not sufficient disclosure, in that disclosure must be to a properly

convened meeting of the entire board. The court also held that Ward held the money on 'constructive trust' for Guinness and must repay it.

In Re Frederick Inns Ltd (in Liquidation) (1994) Ire

Three companies operated pubs, which were wholly owned subsidiaries of a fourth company. All four companies were put into liquidation, and the liquidator discovered that prior to his appointment, the holding company had paid £1.2 (€1.5) million to the Revenue Commissioners relating to the tax liabilities of the four companies and also of six other companies within the group. The liquidator challenged the payment of tax for the other six companies as being *ultra vires* the holding company. The Supreme Court held that the *ultra vires* payment of tax was a misapplication of funds by the directors and was in breach of their fiduciary duties to the company.

See also *Crindle Investments v Wynes* (1998) Ire above.

2. Duty of Skill and Care

Directors owe a duty to the company to exercise all due skill and care. This is a very general principle, especially as there is no set qualification for a director against which the duty could be measured. The standard of care owed has been established from case law, mainly from the case of *Re City Equitable Fire Insurance Co Ltd* (1925). The facts of *City Equitable* are no longer important, but the three principles it developed are crucial.

The Subjective Test: The duty of skill and care is a subjective test, based on the knowledge and experience of the particular director. Thus a director need only act as a reasonable person would have acted in those circumstances.

Re PMPA Garages Ltd (1992) Ire

Various companies in the PMPA group were garage proprietors. One of the garage companies executed a guarantee in favour of the PMPS on behalf of the other thirty-four companies. All the companies had the same directors and worked closely together. In the liquidation of PMPS it was argued that the decision of the board of directors of the various garage companies to execute the guarantees was an abuse of their powers.

The High Court held that the execution of the guarantees was within the powers of the company and within the directors' fiduciary duties. (This is because the guarantees allowed each company to borrow, which was in furtherance of its objects.)

When a director of a company within a group is exercising his powers, he is entitled to consider the interests of the group as a whole.

The directors faced a dilemma as directors of both the parent and subsidiary companies. Thus the court held that the manner in which the directors fulfilled their duties as directors of the subsidiary companies was one which had to be judged in the circumstances.

Hindsight is not to be applied when judging the behaviour of directors; thus failure to address problems with the subsidiaries which only came to light at a later date did not amount to a breach of a fiduciary duty.

Delegation: Directors can leave the routine business of the company to the management. Directors have this discretion, provided it is normal business practice and there are no suspicious circumstances that should put the directors on notice to look further into the issue.

Duty at Meetings Only: A director's duty of care to the company is owed at board meetings only. This is clear in the case of nonexecutive directors whose input into a company is usually limited to board meetings. However, even an executive director, such as a financial controller, will be acting as a director for only a small part of the time while working for the company and the rest of the time will be acting as financial controller. In addition, directors need only attend board meetings 'regularly' to comply with their duties, according to case law. (Remember that a director can be removed from a company only after being absent *without leave* from board meetings for six months.)

The articles of the company in the *City Equitable* case provided that the directors were not legally liable, except in case of wilful neglect or default. In response to criticisms of this, section 200, CA 1963 provides that any provision in the articles of a company exempting any officer, or auditor, of a company from liability attaching from any negligence, default, breach of duty or breach of trust shall be void. However, section 200 also provides that a company may indemnify any officer or auditor from any liability in defending civil or criminal proceedings in which judgement is given in his or her favour or in which he or she is acquitted.

In addition, section 391, CA 1963 provides that there can be proceedings against any officer or auditor in negligence, default, breach of duty or breach of trust, but an officer or auditor may be granted relief by the court if it sees fit.

The result of these provisions is that an officer cannot be given a blanket exclusion from liability, but an indemnity may be given in limited circumstances if the question of liability has already arisen.

Cases on directors' negligence are rare because of the subjective nature of the test in *Re City Equitable*. An English case provides the following tests:

Dorchester Finance Ltd v Stebbings (1977)
The defendants were three directors of the plaintiff finance company. Stebbings had wide business experience, and the other two directors were chartered accountants. The two chartered accountants were nonexecutive directors who rarely visited the company, and signed blank cheques for Stebbings to use. Stebbings mismanaged the company, and the company claimed against all three directors in

negligence. The court held that the directors were liable in negligence, as the standard of care owed by them was judged from their professional experience and qualifications. Specifically, the court stated that:

- a director must use a degree of skill as would reasonably be expected from a person with his or her knowledge and experience;
- a director should take such care in the performance of his or her duties as an ordinary person might take on his or her own behalf;
- a director must exercise his or her powers honestly, in good faith and in the best interests of company as a whole, i.e. the test in *Re City Equitable Fire Insurance Co Ltd* (1925).

3. Statutory Duties

The Companies Act 1990 introduced new duties on directors requiring them to disclose certain transactions and prohibiting others as a means of making directors more accountable for their actions.

Loans to Directors: The 1963 Act did not contain any restrictions on a company making loans to its directors. As a result of this, some directors used the company as a personal bank by borrowing money from it. In some cases this led the company into financial difficulties.

Section 31, CA 1990 now prohibits a company from making loans to its directors, although there are a number of exceptions to this prohibition. Section 31 prohibits:

(a) making a loan or quasi-loan to a director of a company or its holding company;
(b) making a loan or quasi-loan to a person connected with a director;
(c) entering into a credit transaction as creditor for a director or connected person;
(d) entering into a guarantee or providing security for a loan, quasi-loan or credit transaction made by a director or connected person.

A 'quasi-loan' is a transaction in which one person pays money to another or reimburses expenditures incurred by another. A 'connected person' is the spouse, parent, brother, sister or child of a director, a partner of the director or the trustee of a trust that benefits a director, his or her children or any company he or she controls. There is a rebuttable presumption that a sole member of a single-member private limited company is a person connected to the director of that company.

There are exceptions to the ban on loans in the 1990 Act. Under section 31, CA 1990 a company may loan money to its director or connected person if the loan is less than ten per cent of the value of the company's assets or the advancing of money to a director for reasonable expenses.

The penalties for breach of section 31 are:

(a) the director or connected person must account to the company for any gains made as a result of the transaction;

(b) the prohibited transaction is voidable at the company's option;

(c) if the company is subsequently wound up and the court considers that a transaction prohibited by section 31 'contributed materially' to its insolvency or 'substantially impeded the orderly winding up', the court may declare any person who benefited from such a prohibited loan personally liable for the company's debts, with or without limit.

The CLEA 2001 introduced new rules for companies guaranteeing or securing loans by another person to the director, or connected person, of a holding company. The company must approve the guarantee by special resolution and statutory declaration.

Directors' Interests in Contracts: Section 29, CA 1990 requires that directors must obtain approval from the company before they enter into certain substantial property transactions. Section 29 provides that where a director or connected person is to acquire a noncash asset from the company or where the company is to acquire a noncash asset from a director or connected person and the value of the asset exceeds €63,487 or ten per cent of the company's assets, the transaction must first be approved by a resolution in a general meeting.

There are also related provisions to enforce these requirements in that the director or connected person must account to the company for any gain. However, breach of section 29 is not a criminal offence.

Directors' Interests in Shares: Section 30, CA 1990 prohibits directors from buying options to buy or sell shares of the company or its associated companies. Section 53, CA 1990 provides that directors must also disclose their dealings or interests in shares or debentures in the company or its associated companies. Under Section 47, CA 1990 a director must disclose his interest or dealings in shares.

(**Note:** The area of directors' duties overlaps with the issue of minority protection which is dealt with in Chapter 15, and an exam problem may mix the two issues.)

Political Donations by Companies: Under section 26 of the Electoral Act 1997, all donations for political purposes exceeding €5,079 must be included in the Director's Report under section 158, CA 1963 and in the Annual Report under sections 125 and 126, CA 1963. This includes all donations for political purposes, for members or candidates for the Dáil, Seanad, or European Parliament. A donation is any money, property, or goods supplied at less than commercial rates, any use of property or goods without payment, or supply of services without payment.

Legal Action against Directors

Section 55, CLEA 2001 provides that the High Court may order a director or other officer not to remove his or her assets outside the jurisdiction. The company, a director, member, receiver, liquidator, creditor or the Director of Corporate Enforcement may apply, and the court may make the order where it is satisfied that:

- the applicant has a substantive civil action or claim for damages; and
- there are grounds for believing that the respondent may remove or dispose of his or her or the company's assets with a view to frustrating a court order.

Personal Liability of Directors

We have already discussed many cases in which directors can be declared to be personally liable for the debts of the company. In summary, these cases occur:

(1) when the corporate veil is lifted;

(2) when a company is unlimited;

(3) when there is fraudulent trading under section 297, CA 1963, as inserted by section 137, CA 1990;

(4) when there is reckless trading under section 297A, CA 1963, as inserted by section 138, CA 1990;

(5) when a director has made a false declaration of solvency in a voluntary member's liquidation;

(6) when a director has made a false declaration of solvency to a company giving financial assistance for the purchase of the company's shares

(7) when a director acts while restricted;

(8) when any officer acts on the instructions of a restricted director;

(9) when the company fails to keep proper books of account, which contributes to the company going into insolvent liquidation;

(10) when the company makes a prohibited loan to a director that materially contributes to the company's going into insolvent liquidation;

(11) when a director is disqualified and the company is liquidated within twelve months of the disqualification.

A shadow director can be made liable for acting in any of the above circumstances.

B. The Company Secretary

In comparison with directors, very little is said in the Companies Acts about the role of the company secretary. Every company must have a secretary, according to section 172, CA 1963. Section 175, CA 1963 also provides that the secretary may be one of the directors. If the secretary is also a director, then anything required to be done by a director and secretary cannot be done by the same person acting in a dual capacity as director and secretary according to section 177, CA 1963. (In practice this is not a problem, as a company must have two directors.)

Appointment

The first company secretary may be named in the memorandum or articles of association. The appointment of the secretary is a decision for the directors or the shareholders. The secretary must be named in Form A1, which is part of the company's registration documentation.

A company secretary can be a body corporate (unlike the rule prohibiting bodies corporate from being directors of a company).

Qualification

There are no qualifications or disqualifications specified in the companies legislation for the secretary of a private company. Since 1990 there are qualifications for the secretary of a public company, but these are very broad.

Section 236, CA 1990 provides that it is the duty of the directors of a public company to ensure that the secretary of the company has the necessary knowledge and experience. They must also ensure that the secretary has the appropriate qualification by reason of being:

- a secretary of the company on the commencement of the section in 1990;
- a secretary of a company for three out of the five years prior to his or her appointment;
- a person who appears to the directors to be capable of discharging the functions based on experience or professional membership;
- a member of a relevant professional body recognised by the Minister for Enterprise and Employment.

To date, the professional bodies recognised by the Minister are the Institute of Chartered Secretaries and Administrators and the Institute of Secretaries and Administrators (which merged with the Institute of Chartered Secretaries and Administrators in 1997).

Duties

A secretary's duties are not defined in legislation and will vary from company to company. However, it is clear that his or her duties are administrative rather than managerial. In summary a secretary's duties are to ensure that the company complies with the Companies Acts. The specific duties are:

- to keep charge of the statutory registers;
- to make the annual return to the Registrar of Companies;
- to give members due notice of meetings;
- to keep minutes of general meetings and board meetings;
- to file details of all charges with the Registrar of Companies.

Clearly, a secretary may be given express authority to act on behalf of a company. It has been established by case law that the secretary may have implied authority to act on behalf of the company, that the secretary may have usual authority to act as agent and that the secretary also has apparent authority.

> *Panorama Developments (Guildford) Ltd v Fidelis Furnishing Fabrics Ltd* (1971)
> The secretary of the defendant company hired cars in the name of the company. This was apparently done for the convenience of the company's customers, but in fact he was using the cars for his own purposes. The court held that the company was liable to pay the hire costs because a secretary had apparent authority to make such contracts. This decision recognises that the secretary can have wide general duties.

Where reference is made to the 'officers of a company', this includes a director and secretary, according to section 2, CA 1963.

C. The Auditor

Certain companies must have an auditor, whose duty is to analyse the company accounts on an annual basis and ensure that a true and fair account of the company's affairs is given. The publication of this information is one of the prices a company pays for limited liability.

Under section 160, CA 1963, every company must appoint an auditor at a general meeting. However, this rule was modified by section 32, C(A)A (No. 2) 1999 which allows for the removal of the statutory audit for small companies. If a private company's turnover does not exceed €317,435, balance sheet total does not exceed €1,904,607 and the average number of employees does not exceed fifty, the directors can decide to avail of the exemption from having accounts audited.

Under section 35, C(A)A (No. 2) 1999 a company must appoint an auditor as soon as possible after it becomes clear that any of the conditions necessary for availing of the exemption from an audit no longer apply.

An auditor must be suitably qualified, registered and independent and must not have been disqualified.

Qualifications

Section 187, CA 1990, as amended by the Companies (Auditing and Accounting) Act 2003 (C(AA)A 2003), sets out the acceptable qualifications of an auditor, which are:

(1) membership in the following accounting bodies recognised by the Irish Auditing and Accounting Supervisory Authority:
   - ACA, the Institute of Chartered Accountants in Ireland, England and Wales and Scotland,
   - ACCA, the Chartered Association of Certified Accountants,
   - CPA, the Institute of Certified Public Accountants in Ireland,
   - IIPA, the Institute of Incorporated Public Accountants in Ireland;

(2) professional or practical training with any of the recognised accounting bodies;

(3) authorisation by the Minister as practising members of accountancy bodies recognised under the Companies Act 1963;

(4) authorisation by the Minister as practising members of accountancy bodies recognised under the law of another country.

Section 72 of the Company Law Enforcement Act 2001 amends section 178, CA 1990 by providing that the Director may demand that a purported auditor produce of evidence of his or her qualifications, and that failure to do so is an offence.

Registered auditor

The holder of such an auditing qualification must also be a registered auditor under section 198, CA 1990, as amended by C(AA)A 2003. This section obliges the Registrar of Companies to maintain a register of the names and addresses of persons who he or she has been informed are qualified for appointment as an auditor.

Disqualification

The following are disqualified from acting as an auditor under section 187 CA 1990 as amended by C(AA)A 2003:

(1) an officer or servant of the company;

(2) an ex-officer or ex-servant of the company within a period in respect of which accounts would be audited by him or her if appointed auditor;

(3) a parent, spouse, brother, sister or child of an officer of the company;

(4) a partner or employee of an officer of the company;

(5) a person disqualified from being an auditor of the company's holding company or subsidiary;

(6) a body corporate. (This is to ensure that accountants do not form companies, but remain trading in partnerships.)

Appointment and Re-appointment

The first auditor of a company may be appointed by the directors at any time before the first annual general meeting according to section 160, CA 1963. Such an auditor holds office until the company's first annual general meeting, and thereafter the auditor holds his or her office until the next annual general meeting.

Section 160, as amended by section 183, CA 1990, also provides that at an annual general meeting, a retiring auditor will be re-appointed without any resolution being passed unless the auditor is not qualified for reappointment, a resolution has been passed at that meeting appointing another person as auditor or expressly providing that the auditor shall not be reappointed or the auditor has given the company notice in writing of his or her unwillingness to be reappointed. This section also provides that the directors may fill a casual vacancy arising during the year (for example, due to death or disqualification) and that the remuneration of the auditor is to be fixed by the directors.

Removal

An auditor may be removed from office by an ordinary resolution passed by the shareholders under section 183, CA 1990. A copy of the resolution must be sent to the Registrar of Companies within fourteen days and to the auditor whose removal is intended. Extended notice of twenty-eight days must be given for:

(1) a resolution at an annual general meeting proposing the appointment of someone other than the retiring auditor or providing that a resigning auditor shall not be re-appointed;
(2) a resolution at an annual general meeting removing an auditor before the expiration of his or her term;
(3) a resolution at an annual general meeting filling a casual vacancy in the office of auditor.

An auditor who is being removed has certain rights. He or she may make representations in writing to the company and request notification to the shareholders. However, if the High Court decides that such written representations are 'needless publicity for defamatory matter', they need not be made.

An auditor who is being removed also has the right to attend the annual general meeting of the company at which his or her term of office would have expired, but for the removal, and also the annual general meeting at which it is proposed to fill the vacancy created by the removal according to section 161, CA 1963, as amended by section 184, CA 1990. The purpose is to guard against a company removing an auditor who has uncovered information that the directors would prefer to see kept from the shareholders.

Retirement

Since the passing of section 185, CA 1990, an auditor can resign during his or her term of office. (Prior to this, an auditor had to wait until his or her reappointment and then refuse, without giving reasons for the resignation.) Section 185 gives an auditor the power to resign and to either state that there are no circumstances connected with the company or state any circumstances that should be brought to the attention of the members or creditors of the company. If there are circumstances to be brought to the attention of the members or creditors, the company must notify every person entitled to receive a copy of the accounts and the Registrar of Companies, subject to the above proviso about 'needless publicity for defamatory matter'. An auditor who resigns in such circumstances may request a general meeting to consider the auditor's account and explanation of his or her resignation under section 163, CA 1963.

Duties

To carry out their duties, auditors need certain powers. Under section 193, CA 1990 an auditor has the power to access all written information and ask questions of the company's employees and officers. Most of the duties of an auditor derive from statute.

1. Duty to Report to Members

Section 163, CA 1963 states that the auditor shall report to the members on the accounts examined by them and on every balance sheet, profit and loss account and all group accounts laid before the company in general meeting during his or her term of office. The auditor must state that in his or her opinion, the accounts reflect the company's true financial position.

2. Duty to Investigate and Report

The general duty of an auditor to exercise skill and care in investigating a company was expressed in the famous case of *Re Kingston Cotton Mill Co (No. 2)* (1896), where it was stated that the law treats an auditor as 'a watchdog, not a bloodhound'. This means that the auditor must take care to ensure that the accounts are correct, but he or she is not a detective who is expected to sniff out dishonesty.

An auditor's report must state that he or she obtained all the necessary information, and in his or her opinion, proper books of account were kept, proper returns were received and the balance sheet and profit and loss account are in agreement with the accounts and returns. Overall, the accounts must give the information required by the Companies Acts and give a true and fair view. An auditor must give a qualified opinion if there are circumstances that require information to be drawn to the attention of the company.

3. Duty to Act with Professional Integrity

Section 193, CA 1990 states that an auditor shall be under a general duty to carry out the audit with professional integrity. This is just a statutory form of a duty that already existed under the codes of practice of the professional accountancy bodies.

4. Duty of Skill and Care

The legal liability of an auditor is a contentious area. If an auditor fails to perform his or her duties with reasonable care and skill, he or she may be liable to the company. An auditor has a duty to the company in contract and a potential duty to third parties in tort. The duty to the company in contract is straightforward. The potential duty in tort is more complicated.

> *Hedley Byrne & Co v Heller and Partners* (1964)
> The plaintiff was an advertising agency that was approached by a new client called Easipower. Hedley Byrne made enquires about Easipower's credit worthiness to the defendant, which was Easipower's bank. The bank gave the plaintiff two positive credit references, which an exemption clause stated to be 'without responsibility'. Hedley Byrne relied on these references and lost £17,000 when Easipower went into liquidation. Hedley Byrne sued Heller and Partners for a tort known as negligent misstatement, i.e. to negligently provide information knowing there will be reliance on it by the party to whom the information was supplied. The English House of Lords established the principle of legal liability in negligent misstatement for a person who gives information to another, knowing that there will be reliance on the information. However, the court held that because of the exemption clause, the defendant bank was not liable on the facts.

The *obiter dictum* in this case was quickly established as setting a precedent that auditors could be liable to persons who they could foresee relying on the annual accounts they had audited, based on the tort of negligent misstatement. However, this precedent has been changed in recent years in England.

> *Caparo Industries plc v Dickman* (1990)
> The plaintiff owned shares in Company X, which was audited by the defendant. The plaintiff mounted a successful takeover bid of Company X, based on the audited accounts. The accounts had been negligently audited, and Caparo lost a substantial amount of money,

which they sought to recover from the auditors, based on the precedent of *Hedley Byrne*. The House of Lords stated that an audit was done to comply with the Companies Acts, not to provide information to the public or potential investors. Thus the court held that an auditor did not owe a duty of care to potential takeover bidders, as the auditors did not know that the information was going to be used for such a purpose. In addition, the court held that the auditors had no liability to existing shareholders on an individual basis but only as a group, and the shareholders as a group had not complained of any wrongdoing.

The precedent of *Caparo* has not yet been followed in Ireland.

5. Duties under the Finance Act 1995

The Finance Act 1995 imposes duties on an auditor in relation to the commission of certain tax offences. Section 172 of the Finance Act 1995 provides that when an auditor of a company becomes aware that a company has committed or is committing an offence in relation to taxation, he or she shall communicate the offence to the company and request the company to take action to rectify the matter or notify an officer of the Revenue Commissioners.

Unless the auditor is satisfied that the company has done this, the auditor shall cease to act as auditor for three years or until he or she is are satisfied that the necessary notification has taken place.

6. Duties under the Company Law Enforcement Act 2001

If the auditor believes that the company has failed to keep proper books of account, the auditor shall notify the company and the Registrar, who in turn will notify the Director of Corporate Enforcement.

Section 194(4) CA 1990, as inserted by section 74, CLEA 2001, provides that where an auditor comes to the opinion that a company or its officers or agents has committed an indictable offence under the Companies Acts, it shall notify the Director of Corporate Enforcement, providing details. Compliance with this section is not regarded as a contravention of an auditor's professional or legal duties.

7. Duties under the Companies (Auditing and Accounting) Act 2003

The Companies (Auditing and Accounting) Act 2003 created the Irish Auditing and Accounting Supervisory Authority. The Supervisory Authority consists of members from the accounting bodies, designated bodies such as IBEC, ICTU, the Revenue Commissioners, and the Director of Corporate Enforcement.

Some of the functions of the Supervisory Authority are:

(1) to grant recognition to accountancy bodies under section 187, CA 1990;

(2) to attach terms and conditions to the recognition of accountancy bodies;

(3) to require and approve changes to internal regulations of accountancy bodies;

(4) to conduct enquiries into accountancy bodies and impose sanctions if necessary;

(5) to monitor the Companies Acts in relation to the independence of auditors;

(6) to supervise certain aspects of the functioning of accountancy bodies.

The overall function of the Act is to strengthen the regulation of auditors.

CHAPTER 15

Company Meetings and Shareholders' Rights

Summary of chapter

In this chapter we deal first with the ordinary shareholder's major right, which is to attend and vote at company meetings. Then we discuss a shareholder's right to challenge decisions of the company on the ground that they treat the minority shareholders unfairly. This right arose at common law in the rule in *Foss v Harbottle* (1843) and also under the Companies Acts.

We have already considered the division of power between the shareholders and the board of directors. Both bodies act collectively through meetings. Before looking at company meetings, we will look briefly at meetings of the board of directors.

A. Meetings of the Board of Directors

In comparison with shareholders, the directors of a company usually meet frequently, with the result that their meetings are usually far less formal than the general company meetings. The same basic rules apply to board meetings as for general meetings, in that board meetings must be properly convened by notice, have a quorum and chairperson and follow proper proceedings. However, because board meetings may need to be convened in a hurry, Article 101, Table A states that the directors may meet together for the dispatch of business, adjourn and otherwise regulate their meetings as they see fit. Article 101 also provides that any director may convene a meeting at any time.

Article 110, Table A provides that the directors may appoint one of themselves to be managing director. The managing director has a second, or casting, vote in the event of an equal vote at board meetings.

The Rule in Turquand's Case

The 'indoor management rule', or the rule in *Turquand's Case*, provides that outside third parties are entitled to presume that things done within a company were done according to correct procedures as required by the articles of association. In other words, an outsider is entitled to assume that issues of internal management have been done correctly.

Royal British Bank v Turquand (1856)

Under a company's documentation, the directors were only entitled to borrow above a certain sum of money if they were authorised by an ordinary resolution of a company meeting. The directors borrowed in excess of the authorised amount without the approval of the shareholders. The company then argued that the loan from the Royal British Bank was invalid. The court held that although the borrowing was beyond the powers of the directors in the circumstances, the bank could enforce it against the company. Borrowing was within the company's general powers, and the bank had no way of checking if an ordinary resolution had been passed in this case. Thus the bank, as an outsider, was entitled to assume that issues of internal policy, such as the taking of votes, had been done properly. The loan was valid and had to be repaid.

Note: If an outsider has been told that a special resolution was passed, he or she would be able to check this, as it should be registered in the Companies Registration Office.

To give another example, suppose Simon was offered the job of financial controller in a company by one of its directors. The director contacted Simon a week later and told him that his appointment was invalid because one of the directors had not been notified of the meeting that approved his appointment. In these circumstances Simon would have no way of checking the validity of this statement. Simon would be entitled to rely on the internal management rule that internal procedures within the company were properly followed. Thus Simon would be entitled to the job, and the company could not use the lack of a procedural requirement to defeat his contract.

The indoor management rule does not apply in cases where the facts should make the outsider enquire further. If, for example, there are suspicious circumstances, the outsider should enquire further.

Underwood v Bank of Liverpool (1924)

Mr Underwood had a personal account with the defendant bank. He also ran a company under the name AL Underwood Ltd, in which he was the major shareholder and the only director. Mr Underwood paid company cheques into his personal account. When AL Underwood Ltd went into receivership, it sued the bank for the money lodged to Mr Underwood's personal account. The bank argued that it was entitled to assume that the account into which the cheques were paid was an internal issue for the company. The court held that the lodging of company cheques into a personal account was so unusual that the bank should have made further enquiries. Thus the bank was not able to rely on the rule in *Turquand's Case*.

The effect of the indoor management rule is to give some protection to outsiders dealing with a company by providing that the outsider can presume that all acts of internal management were properly performed. Outsiders dealing with a company are also protected by the *ultra vires* rule, as explained in Chapter 10.

B. Company Meetings

Shareholders in the company that they own have the right to attend and vote at general meetings. Thus the rules of meetings are very important, as they guarantee the right of involvement of the shareholders. Note that where a company's articles of association refer to the 'members' of a company, these are the shareholders.

One-Person Company

Since the EC (Single Member Private Limited Companies) Regulations 1994, a company can be formed with only one shareholder. Obviously, it would be ridiculous if this one shareholder was required by law to hold meetings with himself or herself as the only person in attendance. As a result, section 8 of the 1994 regulations enables the sole member of a one-person company to dispense with the holding of an annual general meeting, and if he or she does so, section 131, CA 1963 shall not apply. The requirements of laying accounts and reports before a general meeting are satisfied when such information is sent to the single member. However, section 8 provides that a single member may not exercise the power to remove an auditor without calling the requisite meeting as required by section 160, CA 1963. Any decision required to be taken by a company can be the decisions of the single member and must be forwarded to the company in writing. A quorum is a single member present in person or by proxy, according to section 10 of the regulations.

Types of Meetings

1. Annual General Meetings (AGMs)

The AGM of a company is the main forum in which shareholders are informed about the company and get to express their opinions. Even though the business is often routine, the meeting forms a useful opportunity for members to have a say in the company management. However, as stated in Chapter 10, in a small, owner-run company, the AGM is a largely unnecessary formality.

In circumstances other than a single-member company, section 131, CA 1963 applies. This states that every company must hold an annual general meeting every calendar year (in addition to any other meetings held in that year). The maximum time allowed between annual general meetings is fifteen months. An exception is made in the case of a company's first AGM;

section 131 states that if the first AGM takes place within eighteen months of incorporation, there need not be another general meeting in the company's first two years. A company's AGM must be held in the State, unless the articles provide otherwise (section 140, CA 1963).

If the company directors fail to call an AGM, any member may apply to the Director of Corporate Enforcement (DCE) to call or direct the calling of a general meeting under section 131, CA 1963. The DCE may give any ancillary directions as he or she sees fit. (For example, the DCE may set the quorum of a meeting at one present or by proxy, which is very useful in a two-shareholder company in which those shareholders have had a falling out, and both refuse to attend meetings with the other.) A company may be prosecuted for failure to hold an AGM, as in *Re Muckross Park Hotel Ltd* (2001) Ire.

The main business of an AGM is for the directors to lay before the meeting the profit and loss account, the balance sheet, the auditor's report and the directors' report. A company's articles of association usually provide that the ordinary business to be conducted at an AGM is:

- the declaration of a dividend;
- the consideration of the accounts;
- the election of directors;
- the re-appointment of the auditors.

Special business is anything else, and appropriate notice must be given.

Note: An easy way to remember the ordinary business of a company is that it creates the mnemonic of DADA: dividends, accounts, directors, auditor.

2. Extraordinary General Meetings (EGMs)

An extraordinary general meeting is any meeting that is not an annual general meeting. Many companies will go through their entire business lives without having an EGM. All business at an EGM is special business.

There are various specific regulations for convening an EGM.

Article 50, Table A: Article 50 provides that an EGM may be convened by the company directors as they think fit. This gives the directors considerable discretion and is the most common way to call an EGM.

Section 132, CA 1963: Section 132 states that the directors shall, on the requisition of members holding not less than ten per cent of the paid-up share capital, convene an EGM. Such a requisition must state the reason for the meeting and be signed by the parties seeking the meeting. If the directors fail to call such a meeting within twenty-one days, the requisitioners may themselves convene a meeting within three months. (Note that any one shareholder can seek to call an AGM, as it is a right of membership, whereas it requires ten per cent to call an EGM. This is to avoid cranks and time wasters calling unnecessary meetings.)

Section 135, CA 1963: Section 135 states that if for any reason it is impracticable to call or conduct a meeting in the manner provided for by the articles or act, the High Court may order a meeting to be called and conducted as the court sees fit. The court may call such a meeting itself or on the application of any director or on the application of any member who would be entitled to vote at the meeting. The court can set the quorum for such a meeting as one person present or by proxy.

Other Specific Instances of Extraordinary General Meetings: There are certain other circumstances in which EGMs are called.

Section 40, C(A)A 1983 deals with the so-called 'capital haemorrhage' explained in Chapter 11. If the value of the net assets falls below half or less of the value of the called-up share capital, the directors shall convene a general meeting. Such a meeting must consider what, if any, measures must be taken to deal with the situation. This is a rather toothless provision, as it does not require any specific action to be taken.

Section 186, CA 1990 provides that a resigning auditor may call a general meeting to explain the circumstances connected to his or her resignation. The directors must convene such a meeting within twenty-eight days.

Section 251, CA 1963 provides that a company may be wound up voluntarily after the members pass a special resolution. Such a resolution is usually passed at an EGM.

Notice

For a meeting to be valid, the appropriate length of notice must be given. The length of notice depends on the type of meeting, the type of company and the type of resolution.

The *minimum* lengths of notice are as follows:

- an annual general meeting in a private or public company requires twenty-one days' written notice under section 133, CA 1963;
- an extraordinary general meeting in a public company requires fourteen days' written notice under section 133, CA 1963;
- an extraordinary general meeting in a private company requires seven days' written notice under section 133, CA 1963.

Any provision of a company's articles that provides for the calling of a meeting by shorter notice than the above shall be void under section 133, CA 1963.

In addition:

- if a special resolution is proposed, twenty-one days' written notice must be given, regardless of the type of meeting under section 141, CA 1963;
- if an ordinary resolution requiring extended notice is proposed, twenty-eight days' written notice must be given under section 142 CA 1963. (Examples would be resolutions to remove a director or auditor.)

Short Notice

It is obviously inconvenient for many small companies to observe these periods whenever a meeting is called. Therefore, section 133, CA 1963 provides for the calling of a meeting by 'short notice'. Consent to short notice must be given by all members entitled to attend and vote at a meeting and the auditor. (This is a useful provision for small companies that can contact all their shareholders easily, but it is not of much practical significance in larger companies.) In the case of a meeting to consider a special resolution, short notice can be given by shareholders holding ninety per cent of the votes (see below).

Notice Procedure

The articles of association normally set out the notice procedures. Article 51, Table A provides that:

- all notice be 'clear', i.e. exclusive of the day the notice was served and the day of the meeting;
- the notice shall specify the place, the day and the hour of the meeting and the general nature of any special business;
- the accidental omission to give notice of a meeting to or the nonreceipt of notice of a meeting by any person entitled does not invalidate the procedures at the meeting.

Resolutions

The decisions that a company makes at a meeting are known as 'resolutions'. Resolutions must be formally proposed in advance by a person authorised to do so. There are two forms: ordinary and special resolutions.

1. Ordinary Resolutions

Ordinary resolutions may be proposed in advance of or at a general meeting and are passed by a simple majority of the votes cast. When the Companies Acts provide for a matter to be dealt with in general meeting but the type of resolution to be used is not specified, an ordinary resolution will be sufficient.

Some ordinary resolutions require extended notice of twenty-eight days. These are ordinary resolutions because they can be passed by a simple majority, but a longer than usual period of notice is given because of the need for members to consider their stance on the resolution. Extended notice is required:

- to remove a director under section 182, CA 1963 or to appoint someone in place of a director so removed;
- to remove an auditor before the expiration of his or her term or to appoint an auditor other than the retiring auditor under section 161, CA 1963.

A company must give notice of the extended notice resolutions at the same time and in the same way as it gives notice of the meeting to consider the resolution.

2. Special Resolutions

Special resolutions must be proposed twenty-one days in advance and are passed by a three-quarters' majority. Less than twenty-one days' written notice may be given if not less than ninety per cent of the members entitled to attend and vote agree to do so according to section 141, CA 1963.

Special resolutions are used for major changes in a company such as:

- changing the company's name;
- altering the company's memorandum or articles;
- altering the company's objects clause;
- reducing the company's share capital;
- re-registering the private company as a public company or vice versa;
- permitting an off-market purchase of the company's own shares;
- winding up the company.

All special resolutions must be registered in the Companies Registration Office (as must some specified ordinary ones).

Amending a Resolution

An amendment to an ordinary resolution is allowed if it is within the scope of the notice. However, an amendment to the substance of a special resolution is not allowed, i.e. the special resolution voted upon must be the one circulated in advance of the meeting, except for minor changes of expression and style.

Proceedings at Meetings

A meeting is generally said to consist of two or more people. However, there can be one-person meetings, as in the case of a one-shareholder company as explained above. A class meeting can have only one person attending, if there is only one shareholder for that class. Under section 131, CA 1963, the Minister for Enterprise and Employment may convene an AGM giving any directions he or she sees fit, such as setting a quorum at one. This can be useful in cases of a deadlock between two shareholder–directors, as explained above.

A decision of a meeting is binding only if certain conditions apply. The meeting must have been properly convened by notice (as previously discussed), a chairperson must preside, the requisite quorum must be present and all proceedings including voting must be properly conducted.

1. Chairperson

Section 134, CA 1963 provides that the members present at a meeting may appoint any member as chairperson. However, a company's articles may provide otherwise and, in fact, normally do so. Article 104 provides that the directors may elect a chairperson for their meetings, and Article 56 then provides that the chairperson of the board of directors shall preside as chairperson at *every* general meeting.

The chairperson's function is to ensure that the meeting is properly conducted. Article 58 provides that the chairperson may adjourn a meeting with the consent of the meeting. The chairperson also has a common-law power to adjourn a meeting if it becomes disorderly, as seen in *Byng v London Life Assurance Ltd* (1987).

No business shall be conducted at the adjourned meeting except the unfinished business from the original meeting. If a meeting is adjourned for thirty days or more, notice must be given for the adjourned meeting, as would be done for an original meeting. If a meeting is improperly adjourned, the members may appoint a new chairperson and continue.

> *Byng v London Life Assurance Ltd* (1987)
> A company held an extraordinary general meeting in a cinema in London. Due to the large number of shareholders who attended, several screening rooms were used, and these were linked by audiovisual technology. During the meeting, the audiovisual links failed, and the bulk of the shareholders could not see or hear the proceedings. The chairperson adjourned the meeting. He reconvened a meeting for later that afternoon in a restaurant, and the validity of a resolution passed at the reconvened meeting was challenged by a shareholder. The court held that in the circumstances the adjournment was unreasonable, as many of the shareholders may not have been able to attend that afternoon and would be unable to lodge proxy votes. The fact that the chairperson acted in good faith was irrelevant. The resolution passed at the second meeting was declared to be invalid.

2. Quorum

The quorum is the minimum attendance required for a meeting. If there is no quorum, there can be no meeting. Unless the articles provide otherwise, the quorum will be as follows:

- In a private company, two members personally present will constitute a quorum under section 134, CA 1963. However, Article 54, Table A provides that in a private company three members 'present in person' shall be the quorum.

- In a public company, three members personally present will constitute a quorum under section 134, CA 1963.

- In a single-member private company, one member present or by proxy will constitute a quorum under section 10, EC (Single Member Private Limited Companies) Regulations 1994. (It seems strange that the quorum for a single-member meeting is one person present or by proxy. It is unlikely that a single shareholder would wish or need to send someone else to a meeting, which is only necessary in one situation, i.e. to remove an auditor.)

Article 55 provides that if a quorum is not present within half an hour of the time of the meeting, the meeting shall be adjourned to the same time, place and day of the next week, or any such time, place and day of the week as the directors may determine. If there is no quorum at the adjourned meeting, the members present shall constitute a quorum. (This is designed to ease a situation in which shareholders attempt to frustrate the holding of a meeting by refusing to attend.)

In some companies, the articles may provide that the quorum must be present only at the beginning of meeting.

> *Re Hartley Baird* (1955)
> The company's articles provided for a quorum of 'more than two' to be present 'when the meeting proceeds to business'. At a meeting of three members, one withdrew before the vote, and the remaining two members passed the resolution. The court held that the articles simply required that the meeting have a quorum when it began, not when the vote was taken. The resolution was valid.

3. Proper Voting Proceedings

The main proceedings of the meeting are the voting procedures. There are two methods of voting at company meetings: a show of hands and a poll.

Show of Hands: Unless the articles provide otherwise, all issues at a meeting are to be decided in the first place by a show of hands. Article 63 provides that each person present and every proxy has one vote.

However, voting members cannot vote on proxies for another shareholder (for the simple reason that they cannot raise more than two hands, should they be voting for more than one other person).

It is the chairperson's duty to count the hands, and his or her declaration of the result is conclusive, unless it was fraudulent or obviously wrong.

As a show of hands only allows one vote per person, regardless of the level of shareholding, it is not always acceptable to members. As a result, members can insist on a vote by a poll.

Poll: Section 137, CA 1963 provides that a poll may be demanded after a show of hands. This right to a poll cannot be excluded by the company's articles. A poll overrides a vote on a show of hands (for obvious reasons of fairness). Each share carries one vote. As a result, polls are usually called for on any important or contentious issue.

Under section 137, a poll can be demanded by five shareholders who have the right to vote or by shareholders holding ten per cent of the voting rights.

Article 59, Table A further provides that a poll can be demanded by the chairperson, by at least three members present in person or by proxy and by shareholders holding ten per cent of the voting rights in person or by proxy.

The right to a poll can be excluded when it concerns the electing of a chairperson or the adjourning of a meeting.

4. Proxies

An important part of the voting proceedings is the procedures relating to proxies. The word 'proxy' can be used for the substitute person who attends meetings and also for the written document appointing that person, which is also known as the'proxy form'.

Section 136, CA 1963 provides that any member of a company entitled to attend and vote at a meeting shall be entitled to appoint another person to attend and vote instead of him or her. This fundamental right cannot be excluded, and the notice of the meeting must state that members have the right to appoint a proxy. The proxy is entitled to speak at meetings as well as to vote.

A member appointing a proxy can direct the proxy how to vote or give them discretion in the circumstances. The latter is known as a 'two-way proxy' and is more usual in public companies.

Section 136, CA 1963 provides that a company's article cannot require a proxy form to be received by the company more than forty-eight hours before a meeting.

5. 'Meeting' by Written Resolution

Section 141, CA 1963 provides that if a company's articles allow it, a written resolution signed by all members entitled to attend and vote at a meeting shall be valid and effective for all purposes, as if the resolution had been passed at a general meeting duly convened and held. This effectively means that a company can dispense with a meeting if all members agree in writing to a resolution. This is not common in practice.

Common law provides that in the case of a private company, if a meeting is not properly convened or conducted but the decision is unanimous, the decision will be treated as binding and the irregularities overlooked.

6. Minutes

Section 145, CA 1963 provides that every company shall keep minutes of all general meetings, entered in special books and kept at the registered office for inspection by the members of the company. Once the minutes are signed by the chairperson of the meeting, they become *prima facie* evidence of what happened at the meeting. Minutes of directors' meetings must also be kept, usually by the company secretary. Section 145, CA 1963, as amended by section 19, CLEA 2001, states that a company may be ordered to produce books of minutes for the inspection of the Director of Corporate Enforcement.

Majority Control and the Protection of Minority Shareholders

As we have already seen, the basic principle in company law is majority control. Ultimate decision-making power rests with the shareholders in general meeting, whether acting through a simple or qualified majority. If a minority of the shareholders is unhappy with a decision of the company, the rules of democracy require that the minority must simply put up with the situation. However, there are two legal provisions that protect the rights of minority shareholders: the common law rule in *Foss v Harbottle* (1843) and the statutory remedy of section 205, CA 1963 dealing with oppression of a minority shareholder.

1. The Rule in *Foss v Harbottle*

A basic principle in company law as illustrated in *Salomon v Salomon & Co Ltd* (1897) is that once a company is formed, it is a separate legal person in its own right. One result of this is the rule in *Foss v Harbottle* (1843).

> *Foss v Harbottle* (1843)
> The facts of this case are that two minority shareholders in a company brought an action against the company directors (who were also shareholders). They alleged that the directors had misapplied some company assets, and they sought an order compelling the return of the property or its value. The court held that the shareholders were not the proper plaintiffs to bring such a case. When a wrong is done to a company, the principle of separate legal personality dictates that the company itself is the proper plaintiff.

Thus the rule in *Foss v Harbottle* (1843) is that an individual or minority shareholder cannot sue to redress a wrong done to the company. The proper plaintiff is the company itself.

There are a number of reasons for the rule:

(a) it protects the principle of separate legal personality;

(b) it avoids the multiplicity of actions that would arise if individual shareholders could bring actions for wrongs done to the company;

(c) if the action complained of could have been sanctioned by the company in general meeting, bringing a legal action would be futile.

> *O'Neill v Ryan and Others* (1990) Ire
> The plaintiff was the chief executive officer of Ryanair Ltd and also a minority shareholder in the company. Following a dispute, he was removed from his position and began legal actions against the principal shareholder in Ryanair and the company itself. O'Neill alleged that the principal shareholder (Ryan) and Aer Lingus had contracted to contravene European Union competition regulations, which in turn adversely affected the value of his shareholding in Ryanair. In turn, Ryan and Aer Lingus claimed that any wrong was done to the company, and the action could not proceed due to the rule in *Foss v Harbottle*. The High Court held that this was 'a classic case to which the rule in *Foss v Harbottle* applies', and no exception applied. As a result, the plaintiff's action failed.

Exceptions to the Rule: Over the years a number of exceptions have developed to the rule, allowing the minority to bring a legal action. What these cases have in common is that the people who committed the wrong usually control the company, so the company will not take any action. In other words, the rule in *Foss v Harbottle* will not be allowed to result in unfairness or injustice.

The first exception is that the majority cannot sanction an act that is illegal or *ultra vires* the company. In such a case, the minority can always bring legal proceedings.

> *Parke v Daily News* (1961)
> A company ceasing to trade sought to pay £1.5 million pounds to its employees. The plaintiff shareholder objected to this *ultra vires* gift, and the court restrained the directors from paying it.

This is an obvious example in which the company itself would not take action as the company proposed and supported the gift.

A second exception is that the majority cannot approve a wrong when proper procedures are not followed.

> *Edwards v Halliwell* (1950)
> The rules of a trade union required a secret ballot to be taken, and instead an open vote was taken. In this case, the minority were entitled to have the improperly taken decision set aside.

This precedent applies in cases in which proper procedures were not followed within a company.

A third exception is that the majority cannot deprive a member of a personal or individual right of membership. For example, on buying shares, a shareholder enters into a contract with a company giving him or her individual rights. These cannot be removed or varied. The most obvious right is the right to vote in a general meeting.

> *Pender v Lushington* (1877)
> The articles of a company gave each member one vote per ten shares, subject to a maximum of one hundred votes per person. A company that was a large shareholder and had reached the maximum one hundred votes, transferred shares to the plaintiff, with the intention that he would vote with the company and thus increase the combined voting strength. The plaintiff's votes were rejected by the company chairperson, and the plainitff sued. The court held that the right to vote was a personal 'right of property' that the plaintiff was entitled to protect by taking a legal action against the company.

A fourth exception is that the majority cannot commit a wrong that would be a fraud on the minority. In this context 'fraud' need not be dishonesty or criminality; it may simply be the misuse of power. Thus *Parke v Daily News* (1961) could be seen as a fraud on the minority, as it involved the majority giving away the company's money, even though this was done with the best of intentions.

> *Balkanbank v Taher* (1992) Ire
> The plaintiff was one of two shareholders in Balkanbank, a joint venture company. Both shareholders nominated directors to the company. One shareholder alleged that the directors nominated by the other share-holder opened bank accounts and made drawings and disbursments that amounted to fraud. The High Court held that these transactions were done with the knowledge and consent of the director nominated by the plaintiff, so this did not amount to fraud (although it may have been breach of duty). This action was treated as a derivative action (see below).

Many of the cases on breach of directors' duties are also examples of fraud on the minority, such as *Cook v Deeks* (1916) in which the director–shareholders of a railway company took for themselves a contract that should have gone to the company.

There is also a possible fifth exception to the rule in *Foss v Harbottle*, as suggested by the court in the following case.

> *Moylan v Irish Whiting Manufacturers Ltd and Others* (1980)
> In this case the judge stated *obiter dictum* that 'having regard to the provisions of Bunreacht na hÉireann, I am satisfied that an exception

to the rule [in *Foss*] must be made when the justice of the case demands it'.

This exception would be extremely useful, as it is less rigid than the other categories. However, it remains to be seen if the courts will embrace it further in the future.

It has been established in *Balkanbank v Taher* (1992) Ire that a fifty per cent shareholding may be a minority for the purposes of the rule in *Foss v Harbottle* (1843), when two shareholders are deadlocked.

Form of a Shareholder's Action: When a shareholder brings a minority action, it may take one of three forms. A plaintiff may bring a representative action on behalf of other affected shareholders or a personal action for himself or herself or a derivative action, which is an action on behalf of the company. In *Balkanbank v Taher* (1992) Ire the Supreme Court decided that the High Court judge should not have treated the case as a derivative action, and thus any order made by the trial judge should be set aside.

2. The Statutory Remedy for Oppression

In addition to the common-law action for minority protection under the rule in *Foss v Harbottle*, there is also a statutory remedy provided for under the principal Companies Act. Until 1963 the principle remedy available to shareholders who were dissatisfied with the way in which the company was being run was either to sell their shares (if there was an available market) or to petition the company to be wound up. It was thought that there should be some other remedy available that would have the effect of allowing the court to make whatever order it thought fair to grant relief in the matter. This remedy is now to be found in section 205, CA 1963 dealing with 'oppression' of a minority shareholder.

Grounds for the Action under Section 205: Any member of a company may apply to the court under section 205 on the grounds that the affairs of the company are being conducted or the powers of the directors are being exercised in a manner oppressive to a member or in disregard of the member's interests.

In such circumstance the court can make such order as it sees fit, including:

- directing or prohibiting any act;
- cancelling or varying any transaction;
- regulating the conduct of the company's affairs in the future;
- requiring the purchase of any member's shares by other members or the company.

The court cannot make an award of compensation except in very limited circumstances, as in the following case.

Irish Press plc v Ingersoll Irish Publications Ltd (1995) Ire
The plaintiff and defendant companies formed two companies to run the Irish Press newspaper titles in which the plaintiff and defendant held equal shareholdings. The relationship deteriorated, and Irish Press plc instituted proceedings for oppression under section 205. The plaintiff alleged that the defendant ceased to provide management services but insisted on the continuance of the management agreement and that the defendant acted in its own interests and contrary to the interests of the subject companies. The High Court held that there had been oppression and ordered the defendant to sell its shares to the plaintiff at a price to be set by the Court and to pay damages of £6 (€7.6) million. On appeal to the Supreme Court, it was held that section 205 did not empower the High Court to award damages in cases of oppression, rather it only permitted the Court to make such order as it thinks fit 'with a view to bringing to an end the matters complained of'. The award of £6 (€7.6) million in damages was not made with such a view but with the aim of compensating the plaintiff rather than ending the oppression. The Supreme Court ordered that the defendant's shares be transferred to the plaintiff at a nominal consideration.

Because the court has such wide powers under section 205, a claim for oppression is often added to another legal claim, such as an action for breach of director's duties.

Oppression: There is no statutory definition of oppression, but the definition of conduct that is 'burdensome, harsh and wrongful' from *Scottish Co-operative Wholesale Ltd v Meyer* (1959) has been accepted in Ireland. It is important to understand that oppressive conduct need not be illegal. (Although of course illegal conduct would, in fact, be oppressive, but there may be actions other than section 205 available in the case of illegal conduct.) The best way to understand the meaning of oppression is to look at examples.
Oppressive conduct need not be ongoing; it can be an isolated act.

Re Westwinds Holdings Ltd (1974) Ire
A company sold land to the controlling shareholder–director at a very cheap price. A minority shareholder claimed that this was unfair to him. The court held this to be oppression under section 205, CA 1963.

Some examples illustrate the diversity of what may be considered oppression:

Re Greenore Trading Co Ltd (1980) Ire
The court held that oppression occurred where a majority shareholder bought out another shareholder with a cheque drawn on the

company's account, where the plaintiff was not told of this or other transactions.

Re Clubman Shirts Ltd (1983) Ire

Directors had not held AGMs or prepared accounts or reports for several years. When liquidation seemed likely, directors transferred business to another company and shareholders received no payment or information. The court held that this was oppression under section 205, CA 1963.

Re Williams (Tullamore) Group Ltd (1986) Ire

The articles of association of a company provided that the ordinary shareholders did not have the right to attend and vote at general meetings. The ordinary shareholders sought relief under section 205 when the company attempted to create a new category of preference shareholders who would then obtain £133,000 (€168.874) in dividends which otherwise would have been distributed to the ordinary shareholders. The court held that the act proposed was oppressive as it disregarded the interests of the ordinary shareholders, and the fact that it was an isolated act was irrelevant.

Irish Press plc v Ingersoll Irish Publications Ltd (1995) Ire

The High Court held that there had been oppression when the defendant ceased to provide management services but insisted on the continuance of the management agreement and that the defendant acted in its own interests and contrary to the interests of the company.

Crindle Investments v Wymes (1998) Ire

In addition to the previous abridgment (see Chapter 14), the plaintiffs claimed that the defendants were in breach of the rule in *Foss v Harbottle*. The High Court granted relief for oppression because the defendants, as controlling shareholders, had failed to act reasonably in dealing with offers to settle the litigation. The court ordered that the plaintiff should be in control of any settlements negotiations.

The Supreme Court held that the plaintiffs' claim under the rule in *Foss* failed because it did not come within any of the exceptions to the rule.

Section 205 provides that the court may permit part or all of a petition hearing to be held *in camera*, i.e. in private, if the hearing would involve disclosure of information the publication of which would be seriously prejudical to the interest of the company. In *Re Irish Press Newspapers Ltd and Irish Press Publications Ltd* (1993) Ire, the Supreme Court held that there were no such interests and ordered the hearing to take place in public in the ordinary manner.

Winding Up a Company for Oppression: Allied to the relief in section 205 is that in section 213(f), CA 1963 whereby a company may be wound up if the court is of the opinion that it would be just and equitable to do so. In addition, Section 213(g), CA 1963 provides that winding up can be on the basis of oppression or disregard for the interests of a member. However, the court may dismiss a petition under section 213(g) if it feels proceedings under section 205 would be more appropriate.

Re Murph's Restaurant Ltd (1979) Ire
Three shareholder–directors ran a restaurant together. They had years of experience of running restaurants and working together prior to forming the company. The company was run on a very informal basis. Two of the shareholder– directors fell out with the third and removed him from the company. The third shareholder then sought to have the company wound up on the grounds that he had been treated oppressively or unfairly. The court held that the removal of the shareholder–director repudiated the relationship that was based on mutual trust and confidence and was more like a partnership than a company. As a result of this analysis, the court determined that it was just and equitable to lift the corporate veil and wind up the company under section 213(f).

CHAPTER 16

Examinerships and Liquidations

Summary of chapter

The Companies (Amendment) Act 1990 (C(A)A 1990) introduced the concept of the examiner into Irish company law. It is a one issue Act—its thirty-seven sections all deal with the introduction of examinerships into Irish law. The Act was originally intended to be part of the later Companies Act 1990, but was passed at special sittings of the Seanad during the summer of 1990. Further changes were made by the Companies (Amendment) (No. 2) Act 1999 (C(A)A (No. 2) 1999).

The aim of the legislation is to prevent companies from being wound up, by putting them into court protection for ninety days. At the end of that time, the company may return to normal business, or it may go into liquidation.

The second part of the chapter looks at the workings of liquidations, compulsory and voluntary, and the role of the liquidator.

A. The Examiner

Appointment

The ground for appointment of an examiner is that a company is unable to pay its debts, or is unlikely to be able to pay its debts. The tests are whether the company can pay its debts as they fall due, or its assets are less than liabilities, or a debt of €1,270 is outstanding. The company must not already be in liquidation. However, the High Court shall not appoint an examiner unless it is satisfied that there is a reasonable prospect of the survival of the whole or part of the company as a going concern. (This replaced the C(A)A 1990 standard of 'some' prospect of survival).

An application can be made by:

- the company;
- the directors;
- a creditor, or contingent or prospective creditor (including an employee);
- a member with at least ten per cent of the votes.

In the case of an insurance company or bank, the application can be made only by the Minister for Enterprise Trade and Employment or the Central Bank.

Unsecured creditors favour examinerships, because if the company can be saved it may be able to pay unsecured debts. As explained below,

277

examinerships may actually be detrimental to the interest of secured creditors, who generally favour receiverships or liquidations.

On hearing the application to appoint, the High Court has discretion to appoint an examiner, refuse, adjourn the petition, make an interim order or make such order as it thinks fit. An examiner may also be appointed to a related company.

Independent Accountant's Report

Critics of the C(A)A 1990 believed that it was too easy to appoint an examiner and that in many cases it merely postponed the inevitable liquidation. Under section 7, C(A)A (No. 2) 1999, a report by an independent accountant will accompany the petition for examinership. This accountant should either be the auditor of the company, or someone qualified to be its examiner. According to *Re Tuskar Resources plc* (2001) Ire, the independent accountant may be appointed examiner, although this may be undesirable in some cases.

The report shall contain a statement of affairs of the company, detailing its assets and liabilities (including contingent and prospective liabilities), details of creditors and their securities.

The accountant's report will also state his or her opinion on whether the company or any part of it has a reasonable prospect of survival as a going concern, and whether formulation and acceptance of a compromise or scheme of arrangement would offer a reasonable prospect of survival. A draft compromise or scheme of arrangement may be included.

The accountant's report must detail the funding required to enable the company to continue trading during examinership, and the source of such funding; recommendations on which liabilities incurred before the presentation of the petition should be paid; and whether a creditors' committee is appropriate. The accountant may also include such other matters he or she thinks are relevant. (The accountant may express a view on proceedings under section 297, CA 1963, with regards to fraudulent or reckless trading.)

In exceptional cases, if the report of the independent accountant is not available in time to accompany the petition, the court may place a company under interim protection pending the report for a period of up to ten days. The prior appointment of a receiver to the company is not considered exceptional circumstances. If the report is not available at the end of the extended time, the company shall cease to be under court protection. The directors of a company must co-operate with the independent accountant.

Petition to Appoint an Examiner

Under section 10, C(A)A (No. 2) 1999, creditors now have the right to be heard during the court hearing to consider appointment of an examiner. Each creditor who indicates his or her desire to be heard by the court in an application to appoint an examiner shall be given an opportunity. A creditor may also apply in writing to the independent accountant for a copy of his or her report.

Under section 13, C(A)A (No. 2) 1999, the petitioner and the independent accountant have a duty to disclose any information which is material to the exercise of the court's powers, and must act in good faith. Failure to do so will result in the court's declining to hear the petition. (In effect, this applied before 1999, as a result of *Re Wogans (Drogheda) Ltd (No. 2)* (1992) Ire, where the judge was very critical of a company director who had not disclosed large sums owing to the Revenue during the petition to appoint an examiner.)

Section 21, C(A)A (No. 2) 1999, provides that the court may hold a hearing to consider evidence of substantial disappearance of company property which is not adequately accounted for, or other serious irregularities.

Powers and Duties of the Examiner

Like a liquidator, an examiner is not required to have any professional qualification, but is usually an accountant. An examiner receives pay and expenses in a similar way to a liquidator, i.e. determined by the court. The examiner has powers similar to an auditor in relation to accessing information and convening meetings. The examiner can apply to the High Court for directions on any question. The examiner may take over management powers within a company in exceptional cases.

The examiner's duty is to conduct 'an examination of the affairs of a company' and report to the High Court within twenty-one days. At this point the examiner must report on whether he or she thinks the company can survive as a going concern and what steps should be taken to ensure this. The examiner may take over the director's management powers if the court thinks it is just and equitable to do so.

Effect of the Examiner's Appointment

(1) No winding up or receivership can commence—effectively the company has a seventy-day period of protection from its creditors, particularly secured creditors.

(2) A receivership created within the last three days ceases to operate—in effect, an examiner can be appointed after a secured creditor has appointed a receiver. The holders of floating charges particularly dislike this provision, as it means that their security may be reduced during the period of examinership and if the company does then go into receivership or liquidation, there may not be enough security to repay the debt.

(3) No legal actions can be initiated against the company.

(4) Goods under retention of title clauses or hire purchase cannot be recovered by their owners.

(5) The examiner may take over the director's management powers if the court thinks it is just and equitable to do so.

(6) The appointment of an examiner must be advertised in *Iris Oifigiúil* and two daily papers, and the company must amend all its documentation to include 'in examination' after the company name.

In effect, the appointment of an examiner freezes the company from the date of appointment and nothing bad can happen to the company for the next seventy days.

Course of an Examinership

The company directors must give a statement of affairs to the examiner, within thirty-five days of appointment, setting out details of the company assets, debts and liabilities. The examiner must report to the High Court within thirty-five days. This statement of affairs must detail the company's assets, debts and liabilities at the date of appointment, a list of creditors and securities. It will also contain a list of any shadow directors.

If the examiner feels that a company is not viable, the court must hold a hearing which may result in a winding up order. If he or she feels that a company is viable, he or she must hold meetings of creditors and members. A creditors' committee may be formed to assist the examiner.

The examiner then makes a second report to court. This report states the opinion that the company is capable of survival as a going concern, the necessary conditions for survival and recommendations of action to be taken, including a compromise or scheme of arrangement. The examiner must formulate proposals for such a scheme if it is recommended. These must be accepted by a majority of the different classes which will be affected by the proposals. For example, if the examiner recommends that creditors accept 50c in the euro, the majority of creditors must agree to this.

The examiner's second report must be considered by the High Court. The court will approve the proposals if:

- they are accepted by one class of members and creditors whose interests are impaired by the implementation;
- they are fair and equitable to classes who have not accepted it and whose interests would be impaired; and
- they are not primarily for tax avoidance purposes.

Once approved, the proposals will be binding on everyone concerned. If the examiner cannot secure approval the company will be liquidated, if the court feels that it is just and equitable to do so.

Any member or creditor whose interests would be impaired by implementation of the proposals can object to the court on a number of specified grounds, but not if he or she voted for acceptance of the proposal.

When a company is in examinership, the court has power to make company officers liable for fraudulent and reckless trading, the same as in liquidation (see below).

Companies that have undergone the examinership process and are still trading include the Goodman Group, Gallagher's Boxty House and Xtravision. Companies that went into receivership or liquidation following examinership include United Meat Packers and Don Bluth Studios.

> *Re Holidair* (1994) Ire
> During the examinership of the Kentz Group in Clonmel, the Supreme Court decided the following points:

- An examiner can be appointed after the appointment of a receiver. (The act provides that an examiner can be appointed within three days of a receiver, but it had not previously been tested in the Courts.)
- The examiner can borrow without the consent of the secured creditors. This has been much criticised by creditors and financial institutions.
- A floating charge which crystallised on the appointment of a receiver became a floating charge once again on the appointment of an examiner.
- A charge over book debts which was described as fixed, was in fact a floating charge because the class of assets changed from time to time and there was no restriction on the companies drawing monies from these accounts.

Priority of Costs in an Examinership

A criticism of the 1990 Act, as highlighted in *Re Holidair* was the examiner's ability to secure new company borrowings ahead of the existing secured creditors. Section 28, C(A)A (No. 2) 1999, now provides that the pay, costs and expenses of an examiner which have been sanctioned by the court shall be paid in full before any other claim secured or unsecured in any receivership or liquidation. Liabilities incurred by the company to which an examiner has been appointed are treated as expenses of the examiner and shall be paid before any other claim including a floating charge, but after a mortgage, charge, lien or encumbrance of a fixed charge, in any receivership or liquidation.

In effect, the order of priorities in an examinership is now:

(1) examiner's fees and expenses;

(2) fixed charges;

(3) liabilities certified by examiner (e.g. borrowing);

(4) preferential debts;

(5) floating charges.

B. Liquidations

A liquidation is the permanent dissolution of a company, also known as a 'winding up'. A liquidator will liquidate or sell all of a company's assets and then pay the company's debts in the order of priority. (There are many similarities between receiverships and liquidations—a receivership is like a temporary blip in a company's health, from which it may recover, but a liquidation is the death of the company.)

There are two categories of liquidations:

(1) compulsory liquidation (also known as Court liquidation);
(2) voluntary liquidation, which can be either a
   (a) member's voluntary winding up, or
   (b) creditor's voluntary winding up.

Compulsory Liquidation

A compulsory liquidation occurs where the decision to wind-up is forced upon the company and ordered by the High Court.

Grounds for Compulsory Liquidation

There are three grounds for seeking a liquidation:
(1) A company is unable to pay its debts. This is the most commonly used ground. 'Unable to pay its debts' may be decided according to the balance sheet test, i.e. where assets are less than liabilities, or the solvency test, i.e. where a company is unable to pay its debts as they fall due. A debt of €1,270 can also lead to liquidation.
(2) A company's affairs are being managed in an oppressive way under section 205, CA 1963, requiring a liquidation under Section 213 (f), CA 1963.

> *Re Murph's Restaurant Ltd* (1979) Ire
> Two shareholder-directors removed the third from the company after their personal relationships soured. In response, the third man sought to wind up the company on the grounds of oppression under section 205, CA 1963. The court held that it was just and equitable to lift the corporate veil and wind up the company, because the removal of the third man damaged a relationship based on 'mutual trust and confidence' which was more akin to a partnership than a company.

(3) Where it is just and equitable to do so.

> *Re Murph's Restaurant Ltd* is also an example of this category, but the two grounds are not the same. The just and equitable ground is wider.

> *Re German Date Coffee Co.* (1882)
> A company was formed with the object of making coffee from dates. When it failed to get a patent to do so, it began to make coffee from coffee beans. A shareholder objected to the change of business and sought to wind up the company. The court held that it was just and equitable to liquidate the company because it had exceeded its powers.

Seeking a Compulsory Liquidation

The petition to compulsorily liquidate a company may be entered in the High Court by:

- a creditor or creditors;
- the company itself;
- the Director of Corporate Enforcement;
- any shareholder under section 205, CA 1963;
- Any contributory, i.e. person liable to contribute to the company if it is wound up.

The procedure is that a petition is made in the High Court. If the High Court makes an appointment, the winding up order is backdated to the date of the petition. This is to prevent a company from attempting to dispose of its assets between the start of the liquidation process and the final order to liquidate, in an attempt to frustrate the creditors' interests. In addition, section 218, CA 1963 offers a basic protection for creditors of an insolvent company once a compulsory liquidation has started, as it prevents any disposal of property or transfer of shares without the consent of the court. This is to avoid abusive situations like a company selling its property cheaply between the start and end of a compulsory liquidation.

> *Re PMPA Coaches Ltd and McBirney & Co. Ltd* (1994) Ire
> The receiver and manager of both companies made payments to creditors of the company and another company of which he was also receiver. These payments were made after the presentation of an order to wind up both companies. The court held that section 218 applied in this case and the payments made were void. Money paid to creditors had to be repaid to the liquidator in full.

The court may appoint a Committee of Inspection (made up of creditors) to help the liquidator. A statement of affairs must be filed in the High Court within twenty-one days.

> *Re Dunleckney Ltd* (1999) Ire
> A company was put into compulsory liquidation. A director failed to file a statement of affairs and gave no explanation for his failure. The liquidator did not think that the statement would have revealed any information not readily available. The court held that failure to make a statutory statement of affairs was sufficient reason to restrict the director under section 150, CA 1990.

Voluntary Liquidation

All voluntary liquidations begin with a resolution of a general meeting to liquidate the company.

A Members' Voluntary Liquidation

A members' voluntary liquidation occurs where the company's members decide to wind up the company while solvent, e.g. the shareholders decide to divide the money and retire. A members' voluntary liquidation begins with a declaration of solvency, stating that the company will be able to pay all its debts within twelve months. This declaration is made by the directors and an accountant and, as a result, the company's creditors take no part in the winding up, i.e. there is no committee of inspection as they trust the company to pay the debts.

When the liquidator is appointed, the appointment is not backdated. The Registrar must be notified. In a members' voluntary liquidation there will usually be a surplus left after all the debts have been paid which will be distributed among the shareholders.

A voluntary liquidation is distinguished from a compulsory liquidation by the statutory declaration of solvency which the directors must create under section 256, CA 1963. This has the effect that the creditors do not take any direct part in the liquidation, as they have been guaranteed that all their debts will be paid within a year.

> *In re Favon Investment Co Ltd (in Liquidation)* (1993) Ire
> The liquidator of a company failed to file the declaration of solvency within the time limit and sought an extension of time and that the liquidation be allowed proceed as a members' voluntary liquidation. The court held that a creditors' voluntary liquidation became a members' voluntary liquidation automatically by operation of law, as the requirements of section 256 were mandatory. The court had no power to remedy the procedural defects which arose due to the liquidator's failure to comply with section 256.

A Creditors' Voluntary Liquidation

This is where the creditors of a company seek to liquidate it, with the assistance of the company. In this case there is no declaration of solvency, because the company is not solvent. There will be a creditors' meeting and a committee of inspection appointed to help the liquidator. A creditors' voluntary liquidation is used where the creditors believe that the company is unable to pay its debts as an alternative to compulsory liquidation. The creditors choose the liquidator, or leave it to the company. This is the most common type of liquidation.

A members' voluntary liquidation may be converted to a creditors' voluntary liquidation if the liquidator does not believe that the declaration of solvency is true, or if no declaration of solvency is made, as in *In re Favon Investment Co Ltd (in Liquidation)*. A director who makes a false declaration of solvency may be made personally liable without limit for the debts of the company.

Role of the Director of Corporate Enforcement in Voluntary Liquidations

Section 49, CLEA 2001 inserted a new section into section 282, CA 1963, which gives the court the power to order the Director of Corporate Enforcement to inspect the books of a company in voluntary liquidation. Officers must facilitate the Director. At the Director's request or on its own devices, the court may examine any person known or suspected to:

- have possession of company property; or
- who is indebted to the company; or
- who is capable of giving information about the promotion, formation, trade, dealings, affairs or property of the company.

Failure to attend examination is contempt of court and may lead to the arrest of the person to be examined.

The court may order a person indebted to the company to pay the debt to the liquidator, and order a person who possesses company documents and property to convey these to the liquidator. The court also has power to allow the Director or liquidator to enter and search the premises of such a person. Obstruction is a criminal offence. The court has the power to arrest an absconding officer or contributory.

Liquidator's Activities

Once appointed, the liquidator must notify the Registrar of Companies, who in turn will notify the Director of Corporate Enforcement. Regardless of the type of liquidation, a liquidator's duties are the same (and are very similar to the duties of a receiver). The duties are fiduciary.

The liquidator must sell the assets, pay the debts and distribute any surplus. The liquidator will pay:

(a) expenses—including liquidator's fees and expenses of selling property;

(b) fixed charges—rank in order of creation, i.e. oldest charges first;

(c) preferential debts—all rank equally;

(d) floating charges—rank in order of creation, i.e. oldest charges first;

(e) the unsecured creditors;

(f) any return to the shareholders.

Disclaim Unprofitable Contracts

The liquidator may disclaim unprofitable contracts under section 290, CA 1963 with the permission of the High Court. The court may require notice of the disclaimer to be given to any person interested and impose such conditions as it thinks just.

Fraudulent Preference

Any charge or transaction may be invalid under section 286, CA 1963 as a fraudulent preference if it was created within six months of a winding up. Section 286 prohibits 'any conveyance, mortgage, delivery of goods, payment, execution, or other act relating to property' done by an insolvent company which has the effect of preferring one creditor over another in the event of a liquidation. Such fraudulent preferences are invalid. If such a transaction or fraudulent preference is in favour of a director or connected person, the six-month period is extended to two years.

A connected person is a director, a shadow director, a director's spouse, parent, brother, sister or child, a partner of a director or the trustee of a trust which benefits a director, their spouse, child or a company which the director controls.

> *Re K M Kushler Ltd* (1943)
> The liquidator must prove an intention to prefer at the time the transaction was made. An inference may be draw from the facts if no other explanation is open to the liquidator.

> *Station Motors Ltd v AIB* (1985) Ire
> A company's overdraft with AIB was personally guaranteed by two directors. Three months later the company went into creditors' voluntary liquidation. Prior to the liquidation, almost half of the overdraft had been repaid. The liquidator argued that these payments were a fraudulent preference. The court held the pre-liquidation repayment of the overdraft was done to prefer AIB directly and the guarantors indirectly. The transaction was set aside by the liquidator and AIB had to repay the money to the company.

> *Business Communications Ltd v Baxter and Parsons* (1995) Ire
> Prior to the company going to insolvent liquidation, almost £30,000 (€38.092) was paid to AIB to reduce the company's overdraft, and thereby reduce the directors' personal liability as guarantors. This was a fraudulent preference.

Avoidance of Floating Charges

A liquidator may avoid floating charges under section 288, CA 1963 if it was registered within twelve months of a liquidation, and the company was not solvent at its creation. A floating charge created within two years of an insolvent liquidation may be avoided if the charge was in favour of a director or a connected person.

However, if money was advanced to a company by a creditor when the floating charge was created, section 288 does not apply as the company is deemed to be solvent. In other words, if a creditor advances fresh funds to the company when the floating charge is created, it is solvent at that time.

Re Daniel Murphy Ltd (1964) Ire
A company borrowed £15,000 from its bank in return for a floating charge. Two weeks after the delayed registration of the charge, the company went into liquidation. Between the creation of the floating charge and the liquidation the company had lodged cheques for £30,000 in its bank account and debited a similar amount. The court held the bank lent money to the company at the time of creation of the floating charge, thus the company was solvent at that time due to a fresh advance of funds.

Fraudulent Trading

Section 297, CA 1963 as amended by section 138 1990 states that 'any person knowingly a party to carrying on the business of a company with intent to defraud creditors of the company or for any fraudulent purpose shall be guilty of an offence'.

Fraudulent trading is usually prosecuted when a company is in liquidation (although this is not a condition). A person found guilty of fraudulent trading may be fined and/or imprisoned and made personally liable without limit for the debts of the company.

Any persons knowingly involved can be convicted of fraudulent trading, even though that person may have no connection on paper with the company.

Re Kelly's Carpetdrome Ltd (1983) Ire
A supermarket ceased trading and its stock was taken over by Kelly's Carpetdrome which had the same directors. All the supermarket's creditors were paid prior to it being liquidated except the Revenue Commissioners. Money was transferred from Carpetdrome to other companies controlled by the directors. When it became apparent that the Revenue Commissioners were about to seek monies owed to them, the stock of Carpetdrome was transferred to another company controlled by the same men, Kelly's Carpet Drive-in Ltd, and all Carpetdrome's debts were paid except the Revenue Commissioners. Carpetdrome Ltd went into liquidation owning large sums to the Revenue Commissioners. The liquidator discovered falsification and destruction of records within the company. The court held the directors had acted deliberately to defraud the Revenue Commissioners and were made personally liable for the debts of Carpetdrome.

Re Aluminium Fabricators Ltd (1983) Ire
Directors of a company siphoned off the assets for their own benefits and maintained two sets of accounts to conceal their actions from their auditors, creditors and the Revenue Commissioners. Company money had been used to buy cars and an aeroplane for the directors. The court held that the directors' actions constituted fraudulent trading and they were made personally liable without limit for all the debts of the company.

Re Synnott (1996) Ire

Mark Synnott (Life and Pensions) Brokers Ltd traded insolvently for fourteen years before the company went into insolvent liquidation with debts of £2 (€2.5) million. Synnott, one of the directors, was charged with fraudulent trading of £40,000 (€50,789), which he solicited as investments from customers when he knew the company was insolvent. The money was used as a down payment on a house and a stud farm. This was fraudulent trading, and the first conviction under the CA 1990.

Normally fraudulent trading is a continuous pattern, but a once-off transaction can also be fraudulent trading.

Re Hunting Lodges Ltd (1985) Ire

A company's main asset was a pub called 'Durty Nelly's' which was valued at £750,000. The company was insolvent and had debts to the Revenue Commissioners. The pub was sold for £480,000 and an additional £200,000 was paid in a secret transaction. The court held that an isolated transaction could, and did, constitute fraudulent trading in this case, and was done with intention to defraud creditors, i.e. the Revenue.

Reckless Trading

Reckless trading lacks the mental element of fraudulent trading, i.e. reckless trading is not pre-planned but is more like negligence or carelessness. Section 297, CA 1963, as amended by section 138, CA 1990, creates personal liability without limit for officers carrying on business in a reckless manner or when they ought to know it would cause loss to a company's creditors. The concept of reckless trading was introduced in 1990 to cover situations when the mental element or intention of fraud cannot be proven.

Re Hefferon Kearn Ltd (No. 2) (1993) Ire

The defendants were directors of a building company and held eighty-five per cent of the shares. The company was involved in three major contracts, two of which were for companies in which the directors held shares. The company got into financial difficulties and an examiner was appointed. The examiner sought to make the directors personally liable for the company's debts due to reckless trading. The High Court held that the directors had not traded recklessly, because they did not know of an obvious and serious risk of loss or damage to others, which they ignored or to which they were careless or indifferent.

The court stated the following important points:

- It is not necessary to prove fraud in an action for reckless trading.
- The reckless trading legislation does not impose collective responsibility on the board of directors. A case must be proven against each separate director based on his conduct.

- For a director to be 'knowingly' involved in reckless trading, he must have been a party to carrying on business in a manner which he knew very well involved a serious risk of loss or damage to others, and ignored that risk because he or she did not care whether such others suffered loss or damage or because his or her own selfish desire overode any concern which he or she ought to have for others.

- The law requires knowledge or imputed knowledge that a director's actions would cause loss to creditors; worry or uncertainty about the company's ability to pay is not sufficient to create liability.

Misfeasance Proceeding

Misfeasance under section 298, CA 1963 is an action for recovery of money misapplied by an officer of a company. This action has largely been superseded by the newer provisions on fraudulent and reckless trading.

Liquidation Following a Receivership

Very often, a company which has been in receivership will not recover but go into liquidation. In such a case, a preferential creditor may be able to claim twice.

> *Re H. Williams (Tallaght) Ltd (in receivership and liquidation)* (1996) Ire
> Section 98, CA 1963 provides that where a receiver is appointed by a debenture holder under a floating charge and the company is not in the course of a winding up, the preferential debts shall be paid by the receiver ahead of the floating charges.
> In 1987, a receiver was appointed to H. Williams (Tallaght) Ltd under a floating charge. The receiver sold the charged assets and paid preferential debts due to the Revenue Commissioners for PAYE and PRSI, and paid the floating charge holder. In 1991, the company went into liquidation. The Revenue Commissioners claimed to be preferential creditors under section 285, CA 1963 in respect of corporation tax owed by the company. The liquidator sought directions from the High Court, arguing that a preferential creditor could not claim in both a receivership and a liquidation. The court held that there was no restriction on a preferential creditor who was paid in a receivership making a subsequent claim in respect of preferential debts if the company goes into liquidation at a later date.

The Director of Corporate Enforcement

The Company Law Enforcement Act 2001 (CLEA 2001) gives a role to the Director of Corporate Enforcement in liquidations. Section 55, CLEA 2001 provides that within six months of appointment, the liquidator of an insolvent company must report to the Director on the conduct of the company directors. Section 56 provides that a liquidator of an insolvent company shall subsequently apply to the court to restrict the directors under section 150, CA 1990, see Chapter 14.

Section 57 gives the Director power to examine the liquidator's books. A member, creditor or contributory may request the Director to do so, or the Director may act alone. The Director can examine the books of an individual liquidation or all those carried out by the liquidator. Section 58 provides that if a professional body disciplinary committee makes a finding of misconduct by a member during a receivership or liquidation, the body shall report the matter to the Director.

Under section 243, CA 1963, as amended by section 43, CLEA 2001, the court may order the inspection of company documents by the Director, as well as creditors and contributories.

The liquidator or Director may get a court order to enter the dwelling of a person indebted to the company or possessing company documents, to search and seize company documents, property or money found on the premises. Obstruction of such a search is a criminal offence.

CHAPTER 17

The External Regulation of Companies

Summary of chapter

The purpose of this chapter is to briefly outline the important external regulatory bodies that affect the operation of companies.

A. The Department of Enterprise, Trade and Employment

The Department of Enterprise, Trade and Employment is responsible for the supervision and enforcement of many provisions of the Companies Acts, for example, the running of the Companies Registration Office, as explained in Chapter 10. Section 392, CA 1963 provides that the Minister for Enterprise, Trade and Employment shall present to the Oireachtas an annual general report on matters within the Companies Acts.

B. The Director of Corporate Enforcement

The role of the Director of Corporate Enforcement (DCE) was created by the Company Law Enforcement Act 2001 (CLEA 2001). The DCE is a corporation sole, appointed for a five-year term. The DCE is assisted by officers, including Gardaí, accountants and lawyers. The functions of the DCE are:

- to encourage compliance with the Companies Acts;
- to enforce the Companies Acts, including prosecution of offences;
- to investigate suspected offences under the Companies Acts;
- to refer cases to the DPP where appropriate;
- to supervise the activities of receivers and liquidators where appropriate;
- to perform other activities where appropriate;
- to apply to the High Court for restriction and disqualification of company directors (see Chapter 14).

Each year, the DCE must report to the Minister for Enterprise, Trade and Employment about the performance of the DCE's office for that year.

C. The Company Law Review Group

The Company Law review group was also formally created by the CLEA 2001. The function of the group is to act as an expert body to advise the Minister for Enterprise, Trade and Employment on the periodic review and development of company law. The first review of the group in 2001 made substantial recommendations for changes to company law, which may become law in the future. Some of the Companies (Auditing and Accounting) Act 2003 (C(AA)A 2003 is a result of recommendations made by the Company Law Review Group.

D. The Stock Exchange

The Irish Stock Exchange began in Ireland in the late eighteenth century. It provides a market for the buying and selling of securities. The stock exchange is a company limited by guarantee, with its member firms as guarantors. It is bound by legislation, including the Stock Exchange Act 1995. The stock exchange has responsibility for reporting suspected insider dealing under the Companies Act 1990.

Insider Dealing

Previously, insider dealing was only unethical. It has been a criminal offence in Ireland since the Companies Act 1990. Insider dealing (or insider trading) occurs when people with confidential, price-sensitive information acquired by an inside connection to a company use that information to make profits for themselves or others by dealing in securities with people who are not privy to the information.

An 'insider' is a person connected with the company within the previous six months who is in possession of 'relevant information'. (The prohibition also extends to persons who receive information from such insiders.)

A 'person connected with a company' has been widely defined and would include officers, shareholders and people in business relations with a company, such as solicitors or auditors.

'Dealing' is defined in section 107, CA 1990 and covers acquiring, disposing, underwriting, offering, making agreements in relation to shares and attempting to or inducing another person to do so.

'Securities' are defined as shares or debentures proposed/issued in Ireland or elsewhere and quoted on a recognised stock exchange.

Section 108(1), CA 1990 states that it is unlawful for a person to deal with company securities if he or she was connected to the company within the past six months and is in possession of *information likely to affect the share price if it was generally available*. This is 'relevant information'. Section 108(2) makes it unlawful for a person to deal with company securities connected to another company and to use confidential, price-sensitive information in relation to an actual, contemplated or cancelled transaction of one or both companies. Section 108(3) makes it unlawful for a person to deal with company securities based on information from an 'insider' prohibited under section 108(1) or 108(2). Sections 108 (4) and (5) make it unlawful for an insider prohibited under sections 108 (1) or (2) to cause another to deal in securities.

The civil sanction for breach under section 109, CA 1990 requires any other party to the transaction who was not in possession of relevant information to be compensated for any loss, i.e. the difference in price between what the securities' dealt price was and the price at which they would have been dealt if the other party had known of the information. Also, the insider dealer must account to the company for any profit accruing from dealing in securities. The amount of compensation is the actual profit or loss minus any amount already paid by the 'insider' to the other as a result of the same transaction. An action under section 109 must be brought within two years of completion of the transaction.

The criminal sanction is in section 111. On a summary conviction, the punishment is twelve months in prison and/or a fine of €1,270. On an indictment, the punishment is ten years in prison and/or a fine of €253,948 plus a twelve-month ban on dealing in both cases.

Under section 115 the stock exchange has a duty to report suspected or actual insider dealing to the Director of Public Prosecutions. This duty extends to directors and other managers of the stock exchange and its members. (Members of the exchange should report suspected insider dealing to the exchange.) Alternatively, a person interested in the proceeding may apply to the High Court to direct the relevant authority to make a report.

Stock Exchange Investigations: To enable the stock exchange to report to the Director of Public Prosecutions, section 117 provides that the manager of the exchange may investigate suspected insider dealing and require a person to give information relevant to the investigation.

The stock exchange must also present an annual report to the Minister for Enterprise, Trade and Employment, giving details of complaints and reports as well as investigations that did not lead to reports. This report is also laid before the Oireachtas.

As a result of the EU origins of this part of the 1990 Act, section 116 imposes a duty of co-operation on stock exchanges within the European Union. Before answering a request for information or aid from another exchange, the Irish Stock Exchange must advise the Minister for Enterprise and Employment, who may disallow a reply if:

(1) a criminal or civil proceeding has already commenced in Ireland;

(2) a person has been convicted in Ireland in relation to this case;

(3) the case would adversely affect the security, sovereignty or public policy of the State.

Exempt Transactions: Section 110 makes certain transactions exempt from the prohibition on dealing in securities:

- inherited securities;
- employee profit-sharing schemes;
- *bona fide* transactions by personal representatives of parties;
- *bona fide* transactions from mortgages/charges on shares;
- *bona fide* acquisitions of share by a director.

Private Companies: The 1990 Act applies only to public companies listed on the stock exchange, i.e. approximately eighty-two companies. Other companies are regulated by directors' fiduciary duties and also the disclosure provisions in the 1990 Companies Act: section 30 prohibits directors dealing in companies' shares and debentures, and section 59 requires a company to keep a register of directors' and secretaries' shares and interests.

APPENDIX
Table A, Companies Act 1963

[1963.]   *Companies Act,* 1963   [*No.* **33.**]

SCHEDULES

Sections, 2, 13, 16, 395.

FIRST SCHEDULE.

TABLE A, TÁBLA A, AND TABLES B, C, D AND E.

TABLE A.

PART I.

REGULATIONS FOR MANAGEMENT OF A COMPANY LIMITED BY
SHARES NOT BEING A PRIVATE COMPANY.

Interpretation.

1. In these regulations:

"the Act" means the Companies Act, 1963 (No. 33 of 1963);

"the directors" means the directors for the time being of the
company or the directors present at a meeting of the board of
director and includes any person occupying the position of
director by whatever name called;

"the register" means the register of members to be kept as
required by section 116 of the Act;

"secretary" means any person appointed to perform the duties of
the secretary of the company;

"the office" means the registered office for the time being of the
company;

"the seal" means the common seal of the company.

Expressions referring to writing shall, unless the contrary
intention appears, be construed as including references to
printing, lithography, photography, and any other modes of
representing or reproducing words in a visible form.

Unless the contrary intention appears, words or expressions
contained in these regulations shall bear the same meaning as in
the Act or in any statutory modification thereof in force at the
date at which these regulations become binding on the company.

295

Share Capital and Variation of Rights.

2. Without prejudice to any special rights previously conferred on the holders of any existing shares or class of shares, any share in the company may be issued with such preferred, deferred or other special rights or such restrictions, whether in regard to dividend, voting, return of capital or otherwise, as the company may from time to time by ordinary resolution determine.

3. If at any time the share capital is divided into different classes of shares, the rights attached to any class may, whether or not the company is being wound up, be varied or abrogated with the consent in writing of the holders of three-fourths of the issued shares of that class, or with the sanction of a special resolution passed at a separate general meeting of the holders of the shares of the class.

4. The rights conferred upon the holders of the shares of any class issued with preferred or other right shall not, unless otherwise expressly provided by the terms of issue of the shares of that class, be deemed to be varied by the creation or issue of further shares ranking *pari passu* therewith.

5. Subject to the provisions of these regulations relating to new shares, the shares shall be at the disposal of the directors, and they may (subject to the provisions of the Companies Acts, 1963 to 1983) allot, grant options over or otherwise dispose of them to such persons, on such terms and conditions and at such times as they may consider to be in the best interests of the company and its shareholders, but so that no share shall be issued at a discount and so that in the case of shares offered to the public for subscription by a public limited company, the amount payable on application on each share shall not be less than one-quarter of the nominal amount of the share and the whole of any premium thereon.

6. The company may exercise the powers of paying commissions conferred by section 59 of the Act, provided that the rate per cent and the amount of the commission paid or agreed to be paid shall be disclosed in the manner required by that section, and the rate of the commission shall not exceed the rate of 10 per cent. of the price at which the shares in respect whereof the same is paid are issued or an amount equal to 10 per cent. of such price (as the case may be). Such commission may be satisfied by the payment of cash or the allotment of fully or

partly paid shares or partly in one way and partly in the other. The company may also, on any issue of shares, pay such brokerage as may be lawful.

7. Except as required by law, no person shall be recognised by the company as holding any share upon any trust, and the company shall not be bound by or be compelled in any way to recognise (even when having notice thereof) any equitable, contingent, future or partial interest in any share or any interest in any fractional part of a share or (except only as by these regulations or by law otherwise provided) any other rights in respect of any share except an absolute right to the entirety thereof in the registered holder: this shall not preclude the company from requiring the members or a transferee of shares to furnish the company with information as to the beneficial ownership of any share when such information is reasonably required by the company.

8. Every person whose name is entered as a member in the register shall be entitled without payment to receive within 2 months after allotment or lodgement of a transfer (or within such other period as the conditions of issue shall provide) one certificate for all his shares or several certificates each for one or more of his shares upon payment of 12½ new pence for every certificate after the first or such less sum as the directors shall from time to time determine, so, however, that in respect of a share or shares held jointly by several persons the company shall not be bound to issue more than one certificate, and delivery of a certificate for a share to one of several joint holders shall be sufficient delivery to all such holders. Every certificate shall be under the seal or under the official seal kept by the company by virtue of section 3 of the Companies (Amendment) Act, 1977, and shall specify the shares to which it relates and the amount paid up thereon.

9. If a share certificate be defaced, lost or destroyed, it may be renewed on payment of 2s. 6d. or such less sum and on such terms (if any) as to evidence and indemnity and the payment of out-of-pocket expenses of the company of investigating evidence as the directors think fit.

10. The company shall not give, whether directly or indirectly, and whether by means of a loan, guarantee, the provision of security or otherwise, any financial assistance for the purpose of or in connection with a purchase or subscription made or to be

made by any person of or for any shares in the company or in its holding company, but this regulation shall not prohibit any transaction permitted by section 60 of the Act.

Lien.

11. The company shall have a first and paramount lien on every share (not being a fully paid share) for all moneys (whether immediately payable or not) called or payable at a fixed time in respect of that share; but the directors may at any time declare any share to be wholly or in part exempt from the provisions of this regulation. The company's lien on a share shall extend to all dividends payable thereon.

12. The company may sell, in such manner as the directors think fit, any shares on which the company has a lien, but no sale shall be made unless a sum in respect of which the lien exists is immediately payable, nor until the expiration of 14 days after a notice in writing, stating and demanding payment of such part of the amount in respect of which the lien exists as is immediately payable, has been given to the registered holder for the time being of the share, or the person entitled thereto by reason of his death or bankruptcy.

13. To give effect to any such sale, the directors may authorise some person to transfer the shares sold to the purchaser thereof. The purchaser shall be registered as the holder of the shares comprised in any such transfer, and he shall not be bound to see to the application of the purchase money, nor shall his title to the shares be affected by any irregularity or invalidity in the proceedings in reference to the sale.

14. The proceeds of the sale shall be received by the company and applied in payment of such part of the amount in respect of which the lien exists as is immediately payable, and the residue, if any, shall (subject to a like lien for sums not immediately payable as existed upon the shares before the sale) be paid to the person entitled to the shares at the date of the sale.

Calls on Shares.

15. The directors may from time to time make calls upon the members in respect of any moneys unpaid on their shares (whether on account of the nominal value of the shares or by way of premium) and not by the conditions of allotment thereof made

payable at fixed times, provided that no call shall exceed one-fourth of the nominal value of the share or be payable at less than one month from the date fixed for the payment of the last preceding call, and each member shall (subject to receiving at least 14 days' notice specifying the time or times and place of payment) pay to the company at the time or times and place so specified the amount called on his shares. A call may be revoked or postponed as the directors may determine.

16. A call shall be deemed to have been made at the time when the resolution of the directors authorising the call was passed and may be required to be paid by instalments.

17. The joint holders of a share shall be jointly and severally liable to pay all calls in respect thereof.

18. If a sum called in respect of a share is not paid before or on the day appointed for payment thereof, the person from whom the sum is due shall pay interest on the sum from the day appointed for payment thereof to the time of actual payment at such rate, not exceeding 5 per cent. per annum, as the directors may determine, but the directors shall be at liberty to waive payment of such interest wholly or in part.

19. Any sum which by the terms of issue of a share becomes payable on allotment or at any fixed date, whether on account of the nominal value of the share or by way of premium, shall, for the purpose of these regulations, be deemed to be a call duly made and payable on the date on which, by the terms of issue, the same becomes payable, and in case of non-payment all the relevant provisions of these regulations as to payment of interest and expenses, forfeiture or otherwise, shall apply as if such sum had become payable by virtue of a call duly made and notified.

20. The directors may, on the issue of shares, differentiate between the holders as to the amount of calls to be paid and the times of payment.

21. The directors may, if they think fit, receive from any member willing to advance the same, all or any part of the moneys uncalled and unpaid upon any shares held by him, and upon all or any of the moneys so advanced may (until the same would, but for such advance, become payable) pay interest at such rate not exceeding (unless the company in general meeting otherwise directs) 5 per cent. per annum, as may be agreed upon

between the directors and the member paying such sum in advance.

Transfer of Shares.

22. The instrument of transfer of any share shall be executed by or on behalf of the transferor and transferee, and the transferor shall be deemed to remain the holder of the share until the name of the transferee is entered in the register in respect thereof.

23. Subject to such of the restrictions of these regulations as may be applicable, any member may transfer all or any of his shares by instrument in writing in any usual or common form or any other form which the directors may approve.

24. The directors may decline to register the transfer of a share (not being a fully paid share) to a person of whom they do not approve, and they may also decline to register the transfer of a share on which the company has a lien. The directors may also decline to register any transfer of a share which, in their opinion, may imperil or prejudicially affect the status of the company in the State or which may imperil any tax concession or rebate to which the members of the company are entitled or which may involve the company in the payment of any additional stamp or other duties on any conveyance of any property made or to be made to the company.

25. The directors may also decline to recognise any instrument of transfer unless—

> *(a)* a fee of 2s. 6d. or such lesser sum as the directors may from time to time require, is paid to the company in respect thereof; and

> *(b)* the instrument of transfer is accompanied by the certificate of the shares to which it relates, and such other evidence as the directors may reasonably require to show the right of the transferor to make the transfer; and

> *(c)* the instrument of transfer is in respect of one class of share only.

26. If the directors refuse to register a transfer they shall, within 2 months after the date on which the transfer was lodged

with the company, send to the transferee notice of the refusal.

27. The registration of transfer may be suspended at such times and for such periods, not exceeding in the whole 30 days in each year, as the directors may from time to time determine.

28. The company shall be entitled to charge a fee not exceeding 2s 6d. on the registration of every probate, letters of administration, certificate of death or marriage, power of attorney, notice as to stock or other instrument.

Transmission of Shares.

29. In the case of the death of a member, the survivor or survivors where the deceased was a joint holder, and the personal representatives of the deceased where he was a sole holder, shall be the only persons recognised by the company as having any title to his interest in the shares; but nothing herein contained shall release the estate of a deceased joint holder from any liability in respect of any share which had been jointly held by him with other persons.

30. Any person becoming entitled to a share in consequence of the death or bankruptcy of a member may, upon such evidence being produced as may from time to time properly be required by the directors and subject as hereinafter provided, elect either to be registered himself as holder of the share or to have some person nominated by him registered as the transferee thereof, but the directors shall, in either case, have the same right to decline or suspend registration as they would have had in the case of a transfer of the share by that member before his death or bankruptcy, as the case may be.

31. If the person so becoming entitled elects to be registered himself, he shall deliver or send to the company a notice in writing signed by him stating that he so elects. If he elects to have another person registered, he shall testify his election by executing to that person a transfer of the share. All the limitations, restrictions and provisions of these regulations relating to the right to transfer and the registration of transfers of shares shall be applicable to any such notice or transfer as aforesaid as if the death or bankruptcy of the member had not occurred and the notice or transfer were a transfer signed by that member.

32. A person becoming entitled to a share by reason of the death or bankruptcy of the holder shall be entitled to the same dividends and other advantages to which he would be entitled if he were the registered holder of the share, except that he shall not, before being registered as a member in respect of the share, be entitled in respect of it to exercise any right conferred by membership in relation to meetings of the company, so, however, that the directors may at any time give notice requiring any such person to elect either to be registered himself or to transfer the share, and if the notice is not complied with within 90 days, the directors may thereupon withhold payment of all dividends, bonuses or other moneys payable in respect of the share until the requirements of the notice have been complied with.

Forfeiture of Shares.

33. If a member fails to pay any call or instalment of a call on the day appointed for payment thereof, the directors may, at any time thereafter during such time as any part of the call or instalment remains unpaid, serve a notice on him requiring payment of so much of the call or instalment as is unpaid together with any interest which may have accrued.

34. The notice shall name a further day (not earlier than the expiration of 14 days from the date of service of the notice) on or before which the payment required by the notice is to be made, and shall state that in the event of non-payment at or before the time appointed the shares in respect of which the call was made will be liable to be forfeited.

35. If the requirements of any such notice as aforesaid are not complied with, any share in respect of which the notice has been given may at any time thereafter, before the payment required by the notice has been made, be forfeited by a resolution of the directors to that effect.

36. A forfeited share may be sold or otherwise disposed of on such terms and in such manner as the directors think fit, and at any time before a sale or disposition the forfeiture may be cancelled on such terms as the directors think fit.

37. A person whose shares have been forfeited shall cease to be a member in respect of the forfeited shares, but shall, notwithstanding, remain liable to pay to the company all moneys which, at the date of forfeiture, were payable by him to the

company in respect of the shares, but his liability shall cease if and when the company shall have received payment in full of all such moneys in respect of the shares.

38. A statutory declaration that the declarant is a director or the secretary of the company, and that a share in the company has been duly forfeited on a date stated in the declaration, shall be conclusive evidence of the facts therein stated as against all persons claiming to be entitled to the share. The company may receive the consideration, if any, given for the share on any sale or disposition thereof and may execute a transfer of the share in favour of the person to whom the share is sold or disposed of and he shall thereupon be registered as the holder of the share, and shall not be bound to see to the application of the purchase money, if any, nor shall his title to the share be affected by any irregularity or invalidity in the proceedings in reference to the forfeiture, sale or disposal of the share.

39. The provisions of these regulations as to forfeiture shall apply in the case of nonpayment of any sum which, by the terms of issue of a share, becomes payable at a fixed time, whether on account of the nominal value of the share or by way of premium, as if the same had been payable by virtue of a call duly made and notified.

Conversion of Shares into Stock.

40. The company may by ordinary resolution convert any paid up shares into stock, and reconvert any stock into paid up shares of any denomination.

41. The holders of stock may transfer the same, or any part thereof, in the same manner, and subject to the same regulations, as and subject to which the shares from which the stock arose might previously to conversion have been transferred, or as near thereto as circumstances admit; and the directors may from time to time fix the minimum amount of stock transferable but so that such minimum shall not exceed the nominal amount of each share from which the stock arose.

42. The holders of stock shall, according to the amount of stock held by them, have the same rights, privileges and advantages in relation to dividends, voting at meetings of the company and other matters as if they held the shares from which the stock arose, but no such right, privilege or advantage (except

participation in the dividends and profits of the company and in the assets on winding up) shall be conferred by an amount of stock which would not, if existing in shares, have conferred that right, privilege or advantage.

43. Such of the regulations of the company as are applicable to paid up shares shall apply to stock, and the words "share" and "shareholder" therein shall include "stock" and "stockholder".

Alteration of Capital.

44. The company may from time to time by ordinary resolution increase the share capital by such sum, to be divided into shares of such amount, as the resolution shall prescribe.

45. The company may by ordinary resolution—

(*a*) consolidate and divide all or any of its share capital into shares of larger amount than its existing shares;

(*b*) subdivide its existing shares, or any of them, into shares of smaller amount than is fixed by the memorandum of association subject, nevertheless, to section 68 (1) (*d*) of the Act;

(*c*) cancel any shares which, at the date of the passing of the resolution, have not been taken or agreed to be taken by any person.

46. The company may by special resolution reduce its share capital, any capital redemption reserve fund or any share premium account in any manner and with and subject to any incident authorised, and consent required, by law.

General Meetings.

47. All general meetings of the company shall be held in the State.

48. (1) Subject to paragraph (2) of this regulation, the company shall in each year hold a general meeting as its annual general meeting in addition to any other meeting in that year, and shall specify the meeting as such in the notice calling it; and not more than 15 months shall elapse between the date of one annual general meeting of the company and that of the next.

(2) So long as the company holds its first annual general meeting within 18 months of its incorporation, it need not hold it in the year of its incorporation or in the year following. Subject to regulation 47, the annual general meeting shall be held at such time and place as the directors shall appoint.

49. All general meetings other than annual general meetings shall be called extraordinary general meetings.

50. The directors may, whenever they think fit, convene an extraordinary general meeting, and extraordinary general meetings shall also be convened on such requisition, or in default, may be convened by such requisitionists, as provided by section 132 of the Act. If at any time there are not within the State sufficient directors capable of acting to form a quorum, any director or any 2 members of the company may convene an extraordinary general meeting in the same manner as nearly as possible as that in which meetings may be convened by the directors.

Notice of General Meetings.

51. Subject to sections 133 and 141 of the Act, an annual general meeting and a meeting called for the passing of a special resolution shall be called by 21 days' notice in writing at the least, and a meeting of the company (other than an annual general meeting or a meeting for the passing of a special resolution) shall be called by 14 days' notice in writing at the least. The notice shall be exclusive of the day on which it is served or deemed to be served and of the day for which it is given, and shall specify the place, the day and the hour of the meeting, and in the case of special business, the general nature of that business, and shall be given, in manner hereinafter mentioned, to such persons as are, under the regulations of the company, entitled to receive such notices from the company.

52. The accidental omission to give notice of a meeting to, or the non-receipt of notice of a meeting by, any person entitled to receive notice shall not invalidate the proceedings at the meeting.

Proceedings at General Meetings.

53. All business shall be deemed special that is transacted at an extraordinary general meeting, and also all that is transacted at an annual general meeting, with the exception of declaring a

dividend, the consideration of the accounts, balance sheets and the reports of the directors and auditors, the election of directors in the place of those retiring, the re-appointment of the retiring auditors and the fixing of the remuneration of the auditors.

54. No business shall be transacted at any general meeting unless a quorum of members is present at the time when the meeting proceeds to business; save as herein otherwise provided, three members present in person shall be a quorum.

55. If within half an hour from the time appointed for the meeting a quorum is not present, the meeting, if convened upon the requisition of members, shall be dissolved; in any other case it shall stand adjourned to the same day in the next week, at the same time and place or to such other day and at such other time and place as the directors may determine, and if at the adjourned meeting a quorum is not present within half an hour from the time appointed for the meeting, the members present shall be a quorum.

56. The chairman, if any, of the board of directors shall preside as chairman at every general meeting of the company, or if there is no such chairman, or if he is not present within 15 minutes after the time appointed for the holding of the meeting or is unwilling to act, the directors present shall elect one of their number to be chairman of the meeting.

57. If at any meeting no director is willing to act as chairman or if no director is present within 15 minutes after the time appointed for holding the meeting, the members present shall choose one of their number to be chairman of the meeting.

58. The chairman may, with the consent of any meeting at which a quorum is present, and shall if so directed by the meeting, adjourn the meeting from time to time and from place to place, but no business shall be transacted at any adjourned meeting other than the business left unfinished at the meeting from which the adjournment took place. When a meeting is adjourned for 30 days or more, notice of the adjourned meeting shall be given as in the case of an original meeting. Save as aforesaid it shall not be necessary to give any notice of an adjournment or of the business to be transacted at an adjourned meeting.

59. At any general meeting a resolution put to the vote of the

meeting shall be decided on a show of hands unless a poll is (before or on the declaration of the result of the show of hands) demanded—

    (a) by the chairman; or

    (b) by at least three members present in person or by proxy; or

    (c) by any member or members present in person or by proxy and representing not less than one-tenth of the total voting rights of all the members having the right to vote at the meeting; or

    (d) by a member or members holding shares in the company conferring the right to vote at the meeting being shares on which an aggregate sum has been paid up equal to not less than one-tenth of the total sum paid up on all the shares conferring that right.

Unless a poll is so demanded, a declaration by the chairman that a resolution has, on a show of hands, been carried or carried unanimously, or by a particular majority, or lost, and an entry to that effect in the book containing the minutes of the proceedings of the company shall be conclusive evidence of the fact without proof of the number or proportion of the votes recorded in favour of or against such resolution.

The demand for a poll may be withdrawn.

60. Except as provided in regulation 62, if a poll is duly demanded it shall be taken in such manner as the chairman directs, and the result of the poll shall be deemed to be the resolution of the meeting at which the poll was demanded.

61. Where there is an equality of votes, whether on a show of hands or on a poll, the chairman of the meeting at which the show of hands takes place or at which the poll is demanded, shall be entitled to a second or casting vote.

62. A poll demanded on the election of a chairman or on a question of adjournment shall be taken forthwith. A poll demanded on any other question shall be taken at such time as the chairman of the meeting directs, and any business other than that on which a poll is demanded may be proceeded with pending the

taking of the poll.

Votes of Members.

63. Subject to any rights or restrictions for the time being attached to any class or classes of shares, on a show of hands every member present in person and ever proxy shall have one vote, so, however, that no individual shall have more than one vote, and on a poll every member shall have one vote for each share of which he is the holder.

64. Where there are joint holders, the vote of the senior who tenders a vote, whether in person or by proxy, shall be accepted to the exclusion of the votes of the other joint holders; and for this purpose, seniority shall be determined by the order in which the names stand in the register.

65. A member of unsound mind, or in respect of whom an order has been made by any court having jurisdiction in lunacy, may vote, whether on a show of hands or on a poll, by his committee, receiver, guardian or other person appointed by that court, and any such committee, receiver, guardian or other person may vote by proxy on a how of hands or on a poll.

66. No member shall be entitled to vote at any general meeting unless all calls or other sums immediately payable by him in respect of share in the company have been paid.

67. No objection shall be raised to the qualification of any voter except at the meeting or adjourned meeting at which the vote objected to is given or tendered, and every vote not disallowed at such meeting shall be valid for all purposes. Any such objection made in due time shall be referred to the chairman of the meeting, whose decision shall be final and conclusive.

68. Votes may be given either personally or by proxy.

69. The instrument appointing a proxy shall be in writing under the hand of the appointer or of his attorney duly authorised in writing, or, if the appointer is a body corporate either under seal or under the hand of an officer or attorney duly authorised. A proxy need not be a member of the company.

70. The instrument appointing a proxy and the power of attorney or other authority, if any, under which it is signed, or a

notarially certified copy of that power or authority shall be deposited at the office or at such other place within the State as is specified for that purpose in the notice convening the meeting, not less than 48 hours before the time for holding the meeting or adjourned meeting at which the person named in the instrument proposes to vote, or, in the case of a poll, not less than 48 hours before the time appointed for the taking of the poll, and, in default, the instrument of proxy shall not be treated as valid.

71. An instrument appointing a proxy shall be in the following form or a form as near thereto as circumstances permit—

"

Limited.

I/We of ....

in the County of ....,being a

member/members of the above-named company hereby appoint ....

....

of ....

or failing him ....

of ....

as my/our proxy to vote for me/us on my/our behalf at the (annual or extra-ordinary, as the case may be) general meeting of the company to be held on the .... day of ...., 19 ...... and at any adjournment thereof.

Signed this ....day of ...., 19............

This form is to be used *in favour of/against, the resolution.

Unless otherwise instructed the proxy will vote as he thinks fit.

*Strike out whichever is not desired."

72. The instrument appointing a proxy shall be deemed to confer authority to demand or join in demanding a poll.

73. A vote given in accordance with the terms of an instrument of proxy shall be valid notwithstanding the previous death or insanity of the principal or revocation of the proxy or of the authority under which the proxy was executed or the transfer of the share in respect of which the proxy is given, if no intimation in writing of such death, insanity, revocation or transfer as aforesaid is received by the company at the office before the commencement of the meeting or adjourned meeting at which the proxy is used.

Bodies Corporate acting by Representatives at Meetings.

74. Any body corporate which is a member of the company may, by resolution of its directors or other governing body, authorise such person as it thinks fit to act as its representative at any meeting of the company or of any class of members of the company, and the person so authorised shall be entitled to exercise the same powers on behalf of the body corporate which he represents as that body corporate could exercise if it were an individual member of the company.

Directors.

75. The number of the directors and the names of the first directors shall be determined in writing by the subscribers of the memorandum of association or a majority of them.

76. The remuneration of the directors shall from time to time be determined by the company in general meeting. Such remuneration shall be deemed to accrue from day to day. The directors may also be paid all travelling, hotel and other expenses properly incurred by them in attending and returning from meetings of the directors or any committee of the directors or general meetings of the company or in connection with the business of the company.

77. The shareholding qualification for directors may be fixed by the company in general meeting and unless and until so fixed no qualification shall be required.

78. A director of the company may be or become a director or other officer of, or otherwise interested in, any company promoted by the company or in which the company may be interested as shareholder or otherwise, and no such director shall be accountable to the company for any remuneration or other benefits received by him as a director or officer of, or from his interest in, such other company unless the company otherwise directs.

Borrowing Powers.

79. The directors may exercise all the powers of the company to borrow money, and to mortgage or charge its undertaking, property and uncalled capital, or any part thereof, and subject to section 20 of the Companies (Amendment) Act, 1983 to issue

debentures, debenture stock and other securities, whether outright or as security for any debt, liability or obligation of the company or of any third party, so, however, that the amount for the time being remaining undischarged of moneys borrowed or secured by the directors, as aforesaid (apart from temporary loans obtained from the company's bankers in the ordinary course of business) shall not at any time, without the previous sanction of the company in general meeting, exceed the nominal amount of the share capital of the company for the time being issued, but nevertheless no lender or other person dealing with the company shall be concerned to see or inquire whether this limit is observed. No debt incurred or security given in excess of such limit shall be invalid or ineffectual except in the case of express notice to the lender or the recipient of the security at the time when the debt was incurred or security given that the limit hereby imposed had been or was thereby exceeded.

Powers and Duties of Directors.

80. The business of the company shall be managed by the directors, who may pay all expenses incurred in promoting and registering the company and may exercise all such powers of the company as are not, by the Companies Act 1963 to 1983 or by these regulations, required to be exercised by the company in general meeting, subject, nevertheless, to any of these regulations, to the provisions of the Act and to such directions, being not inconsistent with the aforesaid regulations or provisions, as may be given by the company in general meeting; but no direction given by the company in general meeting shall invalidate any prior act of the directors which would have been valid if that direction had not been given.

81. The directors may from time to time and at any time by power of attorney appoint any company, firm or person or body of persons, whether nominated directly or indirectly by the directors, to be the attorney or attorneys of the company for such purposes and with such powers, authorities and discretions (not exceeding those vested in or exercisable by the directors under these regulations) and for such period and subject to such conditions as they may think fit, and any such power of attorney may contain such provisions for the protection of persons dealing with any such attorney as the directors may think fit, and may also authorise any such attorney to delegate all or any of the powers, authorities and discretions vested in him.

82. The company may exercise the powers conferred by section 41 of the Act with regard to having an official seal for use abroad, and such powers shall be vested in the directors.

83. A director who is in any way, whether directly or indirectly, interested in a contract or proposed contract with the company shall declare the nature of his interest at a meeting of the directors in accordance with section 194 of the Act.

84. A director shall not vote in respect of any contract or arrangement in which he is so interested, and if he shall so vote, his vote shall not be counted, nor shall he be counted in the quorum present at the meeting but neither of these prohibitions shall apply to—

    (a) any arrangement for giving any director any security or indemnity in respect of money lent by him to or obligations undertaken by him for the benefit of the company; or

    (b) any arrangement for the giving by the company of any security to a third party in respect of a debt or obligation of the company for which the director himself has assumed responsibility in whole or in part under a guarantee or indemnity or by the deposit of a security; or

    (c) any contract by a director to subscribe for or underwrite shares or debentures of the company; or

    (d) any contract or arrangement with any other company in which he is interested only as an officer of such other company or as a holder of shares or other securities in such other company;

and these prohibitions may at any time be suspended or relaxed to any extent and either generally or in respect of any particular contract, arrangement or transaction by the company in general meeting.

85. A director may hold any other office or place of profit under the company (other than the office of auditor) in conjunction with his office of director for such period and on such terms as to remuneration and otherwise as the directors may determine, and no director or intending director shall be

disqualified by his office from contracting with the company either with regard to his tenure of any such other office or place of profit or as vendor, purchaser or otherwise, nor shall any such contract or any contract or arrangement entered into by or on behalf of the company in which any director is in any way interested, be liable to be avoided, nor shall any director so contracting or being so interested be liable to account to the company for any profit realised by any such contract or arrangement by reason of such director holding that office or of the fiduciary relation thereby established.

86. A director, notwithstanding his interest, may be counted in the quorum present at any meeting whereat he or any other director is appointed to hold any such office or place of profit under the company or whereat the terms of any such appointment are arranged, and he may vote on any such appointment or arrangement other than his own appointment or the arrangement of the terms thereof.

87. Any director may act by himself or his firm in a professional capacity for the company, and he or his firm shall be entitled to remuneration for professional services as if he were not a director; but nothing herein contained shall authorise a director or his firm to act as auditor to the company.

88. All cheques, promissory notes, drafts, bills of exchange and other negotiable instruments and all receipts for moneys paid to the company shall be signed, drawn, accepted, endorsed or otherwise executed, as the case may be, by such person or persons and in such manner as the directors shall from time to time by resolution determine.

89. The directors shall cause minutes to be made in books provided for the purpose—

   (a) of all appointments of officers made by the directors;

   (b) of the names of the directors present at each meeting of the directors and of any committee of the directors;

   (c) of all resolutions and proceedings at all meetings of the company and of the directors and of committees of directors.

90. The directors on behalf of the company may pay a gratuity

or pension or allowance on retirement to any director who has held any other salaried office or place of profit with the company or to his widow or dependants, and may make contributions to any fund and pay premiums for the purchase or provision of any such gratuity, pension or allowance.

Disqualification of Directors.

91. The office of director shall be vacated if the director—

(*a*) ceases to be a director by virtue of section 180 of the Act; or

(*b*) is adjudged bankrupt in the State or in Northern Ireland or Great Britain or makes any arrangement or composition with his creditors generally; or

(*c*) becomes prohibited from being a director by reason of any order made under section 184 of the Act; or

(*d*) becomes of unsound mind; or

(*e*) resigns his office by notice in writing to the company; or

(*f*) is convicted of an indictable offence unless the directors otherwise determine; or

(*g*) is for more than 6 months absent without permission of the directors from meetings of the directors held during that period.

Rotation of Directors.

92. At the first annual general meeting of the company all the directors shall retire from office, and at the annual general meeting in every subsequent year, one-third of the directors for the time being, or, if their number is not three or a multiple of three, then the number nearest one-third shall retire from office.

93. The directors to retire in every year shall be those who have been longest in office since their last election but as between persons who became directors on the same day, those to retire shall (unless they otherwise agree among themselves) be determined by lot.

94. A retiring director shall be eligible for re-election.

95. The company, at the meeting at which a director retires in manner aforesaid, may fill the vacated office by electing a person thereto, and in default the retiring director shall, if offering himself for re-election, be deemed to have been re-elected, unless at such meeting it is expressly resolved not to fill such vacated office, or unless a resolution for the re-election of such director has been put to the meeting and lost.

96. No person other than a director retiring at the meeting shall, unless recommended by the directors, be eligible for election to the office of director at any general meeting unless not less than 3 nor more than 21 days before the day appointed for the meeting there shall have been left at the office notice in writing signed by a member duly qualified to attend and vote at the meeting for which such notice is given, of his intention to propose such person for election and also notice in writing signed by that person of his willingness to be elected.

97. The company may from time to time by ordinary resolution increase or reduce the number of directors and may also determine in what rotation the increased or reduced number is to go out of office.

98. The directors shall have power at any time and from time to time to appoint any person to be a director, either to fill a casual vacancy or as an addition to the existing directors, but so that the total number of directors shall not at any time exceed the number fixed in accordance with these regulations. Any director so appointed shall hold office only until the next following annual general meeting, and shall then be eligible for re-election but shall not be taken into account in determining the directors who are to retire by rotation at such meeting.

99. The company may, by ordinary resolution, of which extended notice has been given in accordance with section 142 of the Act, remove any director before the expiration of his period of office notwithstanding anything in these regulations or in any agreement between the company and such director. Such removal shall be without prejudice to any claim such director may have for damages for breach of any contract of service between him and the company.

100. The company may, by ordinary resolution, appoint

another person in place of a director removed from office under regulation 99 and without prejudice to the powers of the directors under regulation 98 the company in general meeting may appoint any person to be a director either to fill a casual vacancy or as an additional director. A person appointed in place of a director so removed or to fill such a vacancy shall be subject to retirement at the same time as if he had become a director on the day on which the director in whose place he is appointed was last elected a director.

Proceedings of Directors.

101. The directors may meet together for the despatch of business, adjourn and otherwise regulate their meetings as they think fit. Questions arising at any meeting shall be decided by a majority of votes. Where there is an equality of votes, the chairman shall have a second or casting vote. A director may, and the secretary on the requisition of a director shall, at any time summon a meeting of the directors. If the directors so resolve, it shall not be necessary to give notice of a meeting of director to any director who, being resident in the State, is for the time being absent from the State.

102. The quorum necessary for the transaction of the business of the directors may be fixed by the directors, and unless so fixed shall be two.

103. The continuing directors may act notwithstanding any vacancy in their number but, if and so long as their number is reduced below the number fixed by or pursuant to the regulations of the company as the necessary quorum of directors, the continuing directors or director may act for the purpose of increasing the number of directors to that number or of summoning a general meeting of the company but for no other purpose.

104. The directors may elect a chairman of their meetings and determine the period for which he is to hold office, but if no such chairman is elected, or, if at any meeting the chairman is not present within 5 minutes after the time appointed for holding the same, the directors present may choose one of their number to be chairman of the meeting.

105. The directors may delegate any of their powers to committees consisting of such member or members of the board

as they think fit; any committee so formed shall, in the exercise of the powers so delegated, conform to any regulations that may be imposed on it by the directors.

106. A committee may elect a chairman of its meetings; if no such chairman is elected, or if at any meeting the chairman is not present within 5 minutes after the time appointed for holding the same, the members present may choose one of their number to be chairman of the meeting.

107. A committee may meet and adjourn as it thinks proper. Questions arising at any meeting shall be determined by a majority of votes of the members present, and where there is an equality of votes, the chairman shall have a second or casting vote.

108. All acts done by any meeting of the directors or of a committee of directors or by any person acting as a director shall, notwithstanding that it be afterwards discovered that there was some defect in the appointment of any such director or person acting as aforesaid, or that they or any of them were disqualified, be as valid as if every such person had been duly appointed and was qualified to be a director.

109. A resolution in writing signed by all the directors for the time being entitled to receive notice of a meeting of the directors shall be as valid as if it had been passed at a meeting of the directors duly convened and held.

Managing Director.

110. The directors may from time to time appoint one or more of themselves to the office of managing director for such period and on such terms as to remuneration and otherwise as they think fit, and, subject to the terms of any agreement entered into in any particular case, may revoke such appointment. A director so appointed shall not, whilst holding that office, be subject to retirement by rotation or be taken into account in determining the rotation of retirement of directors but (without prejudice to any claim he may have for damages for breach of any contract of service between him and the company), his appointment shall be automatically determined if he ceases from any cause to be a director.

111. A managing director shall receive such remuneration

whether by way of salary, commission or participation in the profits, or partly in one way and partly in another, as the directors may determine.

112. The directors may entrust to and confer upon a managing director any of the powers exercisable by them upon such terms and conditions and with such restrictions as they may think fit, and either collaterally with or to the exclusion of their own powers, and may from time to time revoke, withdraw, alter or vary all or any of such powers.

Secretary.

113. Subject to section 3 of the Companies (Amendment) Act, 1982, the secretary shall be appointed by the directors for such term, at such remuneration and upon such conditions as they may think fit; and any secretary so appointed may be removed by them.

114. A provision of the Act or these regulations requiring or authorising a thing to be done by or to a director and the secretary shall not be satisfied by its being done by or to the same person acting both as director and as, or in place of, the secretary.

The Seal.

115. The seal shall be used only by the authority of the directors or of a committee of directors authorised by the directors in that behalf, and every instrument to which the seal shall be affixed shall be signed by a director and shall be countersigned by the secretary or by a second director or by some other person appointed by the directors for the purpose.

Dividends and Reserves.

116. The company in general meeting may declare dividends, but no dividend shall exceed the amount recommended by the directors.

117. The directors may from time to time pay to the members such interim dividends as appear to the directors to be justified by the profits of the company.

118. No dividend or interim dividend shall be paid otherwise than in accordance with the provisions of Part IV of the

Companies (Amendment) Act, 1983 which apply to the company.

119. The directors may, before recommending any dividend, set aside out of the profits of the company such sums as they think proper as a reserve or reserves which shall, at the discretion of the directors, be applicable for any purpose to which the profits of the company may be properly applied, and pending such application may, at the like discretion, either be employed in the business of the company or be invested in such investments as the directors may lawfully determine. The directors may also, without placing the same to reserve, carry forward any profits which they may think it prudent not to divide.

120. Subject to the rights of persons, if any, entitled to shares with special rights as to dividend, all dividends shall be declared and paid according to the amounts paid or credited as paid on the shares in respect whereof the dividend is paid, but no amount paid or credited as paid on a share in advance of calls shall be treated for the purposes of this regulation as paid on the share. All dividends shall be apportioned and paid proportionately to the amounts paid or credited as paid on the shares during any portion or portions of the period in respect of which the dividend is paid; but if any share is issued on terms providing that it shall rank for dividend as from a particular date, such share shall rank for dividend accordingly.

121. The directors may deduct from any dividend payable to any member all sums of money (if any) immediately payable by him to the company on account of calls or otherwise in relation to the shares of the company.

122. Any general meeting declaring a dividend or bonus may direct payment of such dividend or bonus wholly or partly by the distribution of specific assets and in particular of paid up shares, debentures or debenture stock of any other company or in any one or more of such ways, and the directors shall give effect to such resolution, and where any difficulty arise in regard to such distribution, the directors may settle the same as they think expedient, and in particular may issue fractional certificates and fix the value for distribution of such specific assets or any part thereof and may determine that cash payments shall be made to any members upon the footing of the value so fixed, in order to adjust the rights of all the parties, and may vest any such specific assets in trustees as may seem expedient to the directors.

123. Any dividend, interest or other money payable in cash in respect of any shares may be paid by cheque or warrant sent through the post directed to the registered address of the holder, or, where there are joint holders, to the registered address of that one of the joint holders who is first named on the register or to such person and to such address as the holder or joint holders may in writing direct. Every such cheque or warrant shall be made payable to the order of the person to whom it is sent. Any one of two or more joint holders may give effectual receipts for any dividends, bonuses or other moneys payable in respect of the shares held by them as joint holder.

124. No dividend shall bear interest against the company.

Accounts.

125. The directors shall cause proper books of account to be kept relating to—

     (*a*) all sums of money received and expended by the company and the matters in respect of which the receipt and expenditure takes place; and

     (*b*) all sale and purchases of goods by the company; and

     (*c*) the assets and liabilities of the company.

Proper books shall not be deemed to be kept if there are not kept such books of account as are necessary to give a true and fair view of the state of the company's affairs and to explain its transactions.

126. The books of account shall be kept at the office or, subject to section 147 of the Act, at such other place as the directors think fit, and shall at all reasonable times be open to the inspection of the directors.

127. The directors shall from time to time determine whether and to what extent and at what times and places and under what conditions or regulations the accounts and books of the company or any of them shall be open to the inspection of members, not being directors, and no member (not being a director) shall have any right of inspecting any account or book or document of the company except as conferred by statute or authorised by the directors or by the company in general meeting.

128. The directors shall from time to time, in accordance with sections 148, 150, 157 and 158 of the Act cause to be prepared and to be laid before the annual general meeting of the company such profit and loss accounts, balance sheets, group accounts and reports as are required by those sections to be prepared and laid before the annual general meeting of the company.

129. A copy of every balance sheet (including every document required by law to be annexed thereto) which is to be laid before the annual general meeting of the company together with a copy of the directors' report and auditors' report shall, not less than 21 days before the date of the annual general meeting be sent to every person entitled under the provisions of the Act to receive them.

Capitalisation of Profits.

130. The company in general meeting may upon the recommendation of the directors resolve that any sum for the time being standing to the credit of any of the company's reserves (including any capital redemption reserve fund or share premium account) or to the credit of profit and loss account be capitalised and applied on behalf of the members who would have been entitled to receive the same if the same had been distributed by way of dividend and in the same proportions either in or towards paying up amounts for the time being unpaid on any shares held by them respectively or in paying up in full unissued shares or debentures of the company of a nominal amount equal to the sum capitalised (such shares or debentures to be allotted and distributed credited as fully paid up to and amongst such holders in the proportions aforesaid) or partly in one way and partly in another, so however, that the only purpose for which sums standing to the credit of the capital redemption reserve fund or the share premium account shall be applied shall be those permitted by sections 62 and 64 of the Act.

130A. The company in general meeting may on the recommendation of the directors resolve that it is desirable to capitalise any part of the amount for the time being standing to the credit of any of the company's reserve accounts or to the credit of the profit and loss account which is not available for distribution by applying such sum in paying up in full unissued shares to be allotted as fully paid bonus shares to those members of the company who would have been entitled to that sum if it were distributed by way of dividend (and in the same proportions), and the directors shall give effect to such resolution.

131. Whenever such a resolution is passed in pursuance of regulation 130 or 130A, the directors shall make all appropriations and applications of the undivided profits resolved to be capitalised thereby and all allotments and issues of fully paid shares or debentures, if any, and generally shall do all acts and things required to give effect thereto with full power to the directors to make such provision as they shall think fit for the case of shares or debentures becoming distributable in fractions (and, in particular, without prejudice to the generality of the foregoing, to sell the shares or debentures represented by such fractions and distribute the net proceeds of such sale amongst the members otherwise entitled to such fractions in due proportions) and also to authorise any person to enter on behalf of all the members concerned into an agreement with the company providing for the allotment to them respectively credited as fully paid up of any further shares or debentures to which they may become entitled on such capitalisation or, as the case may require, for the payment up by the application thereto of their respective proportions of the profits resolved to be capitalised of the amounts remaining unpaid on their existing shares and any agreement made under such authority shall be effective and binding on all such members.

Audit.

132. Auditors shall be appointed and their duties regulated in accordance with sections 160 to 163 of the Act.

Notices.

133. A notice may be given by the company to any member either personally or by sending it by post to him to his registered address. Where a notice is sent by post, service of the notice shall be deemed to be effected by properly addressing, prepaying and posting a letter containing the notice, and to have been effected in the case of the notice of a meeting at the expiration of 24 hours after the letter containing the same is posted, and in any other case at the time at which the letter would be delivered in the ordinary course of post.

134. A notice may be given by the company to the joint holders of a share by giving the notice to the joint holder first named in the register in respect of the share.

135. A notice may be given by the company to the persons entitled to a share in consequence of the death or bankruptcy of a member by sending it through the post in a prepaid letter addressed to them by name or by the title of representatives of the deceased or Official Assignee in bankruptcy or by any like description at the address supplied for the purpose by the persons claiming to be so entitled, or (until such an address has been so supplied) by giving the notice in any manner in which the same might have been given if the death or bankruptcy had not occurred.

136. Notice of every general meeting shall be given in any manner hereinbefore authorised to—

(a) every member; and

(b) every person upon whom the ownership of a share devolves by reason of his being a personal representative or the Official Assignee in bankruptcy of a member, where the member but for his death or bankruptcy would be entitled to receive notice of the meeting; and

(c) the auditor for the time being of the company.

No other person shall be entitled to receive notices of general meetings.

Winding Up.

137. If the company is wound up, the liquidator may, with the sanction of a special resolution of the company and any other sanction required by the Act, divide among the members in specie or kind the whole or any part of the assets of the company (whether they shall consist of property of the same kind or not) and may, for such purpose, set such value as he deems fair upon any property to be divided as aforesaid and may determine how such division shall be carried out as between the members or different classes of members. The liquidator may, with the like sanction, vest the whole or any part of such assets in trustees upon such trusts for the benefit of the contributories as the liquidator, with the like sanction, shall think fit, but so that no member shall be compelled to accept any shares or other

securities whereon there is any liability.

Indemnity

138. Every director, managing director, agent, auditor, secretary and other officer for the time being of the company shall be indemnified out of the assets of the company against any liability incurred by him in defending any proceedings, whether civil or criminal, in relation to his acts while acting in such office, in which judgment is given in his favour or in which he is acquitted or in connection with any application under section 391 of the Act in which relief is granted to him by the court.

PART II.

REGULATIONS FOR THE MANAGEMENT OF A PRIVATE COMPANY LIMITED BY SHARES.

1. The regulations contained in Part I of Table A (with the exception of regulations 8, 24, 51, 54, 84 and 86) shall apply. *As amended by 1977 S5 (4).*

2. The company is a private company and accordingly—

 (a) the right to transfer shares is restricted in the manner hereinafter prescribed;

 (b) the number of members of the company (exclusive of persons who are in the employment of the company and of persons who, having been formerly in the employment of the company, were while in such employment, and have continued after the determination of such employment to be, members of the company) is limited to fifty, so, however, that where two or more persons hold one or more shares in the company jointly, they shall, for the purpose of this regulation, be treated as a single member;

 (c) any invitation to the public to subscribe for any shares or debentures of the company is prohibited;

 (d) the company shall not have power to issue share warrants to bearer.

3. The directors may, in their absolute discretion, and without assigning any reason therefor, decline to register any transfer of any share, whether or not it is a fully paid share.

4. Subject to sections 133 and 141 of the Act, an annual general meeting and a meeting called for the passing of a special resolution shall be called by 21 days' notice in writing at the least and a meeting of the company (other than an annual general meeting or a meeting for the passing of a special resolution) shall be called by 7 days' notice in writing at the least. The notice shall be exclusive of the day on which it is served or deemed to be served and of the day for which it is given and shall specify the day, the place and the hour of the meeting and, in the case of special business, the general nature of that business and shall be given in manner authorised by these regulations to such persons as are under the regulations of the company entitled to receive such notices from the company.

5. No business shall be transacted at any general meeting unless a quorum of members is present at the time when the meeting proceeds to business; save as herein otherwise provided, two members present in person or by proxy shall be a quorum.

6. Subject to section 141 of the Act, a resolution in writing signed by all the members for the time being entitled to attend and vote on such resolution at a general meeting (or being bodies corporate by their duly authorised representatives) shall be as valid and effective for all purposes as if the resolution had been passed at a general meeting of the company duly convened and held, and if described as a special resolution shall be deemed to be a special resolution within the meaning of the Act.

7. A director may vote in respect of any contract, appointment or arrangement in which he is interested, and he shall be counted in the quorum present at the meeting.

8. The directors may exercise the voting powers conferred by the shares of any other company held or owned by the company in such manner in all respects as they think fit and in particular they may exercise the voting powers in favour of any resolution appointing the directors or any of them as directors or officers of such other company or providing for the payment of remuneration or pensions to the directors or officers of such other company. Any director of the company may vote in favour of the exercise of such voting rights, notwithstanding that he may be or may be about to become a director or officer of such other company, and as such or in any other manner is or may be interested in the exercise of such voting rights in manner aforesaid.

9. Any director may from time to time appoint any person who is approved by the majority of the directors to be an alternate or substitute director. The appointee, while he holds office as an alternate director, shall be entitled to notice of meetings of the directors and to attend and vote thereat as a director and shall not be entitled to be remunerated otherwise than out of the remuneration of the director appointing him. Any appointment under this regulation shall be effected by notice in writing given by the appointer to the secretary. Any appointment so made may be revoked at any time by the appointer or by a majority of the other directors or by the company in general meeting. Revocation by an appointer shall be effected by notice in writing given by the appointer to the secretary.

10. Every person whose name is entered as a member in the register shall be entitled without payment to receive within 2 months after allotment or lodgment of a transfer (or within such other period as the conditions of issue shall provide) one certificate for all his shares or several certificates each for one or more of his shares upon payment of 12½ new pence for every certificate after the first or such less sum as the directors shall from time to time determine, so, however, that in respect of a share or shares held jointly by several persons the company shall not be bound to issue more than one certificate, and delivery of a certificate for a share to one of several joint holders shall be sufficient delivery to all such holders. Every certificate shall be under the seal and shall specify the shares to which it relates and the amount paid up thereon. *Inserted by 1977 S5 (5).*

Note:—Regulations 3, 4, 5 and 10 of this Part are alternative to regulations 24, 51, 54 and 8 respectively of Part I. Regulations 7 and 8 of this Part are alternative to regulations 84 and 86 of Part I. *As amended by 1977 S5 (6).*

Tábla A, Cuid I and Cuid II have not been included here. They are the Irish language version of Table A, Part I and Part II.

INDEX